LOBSTER SHACKS

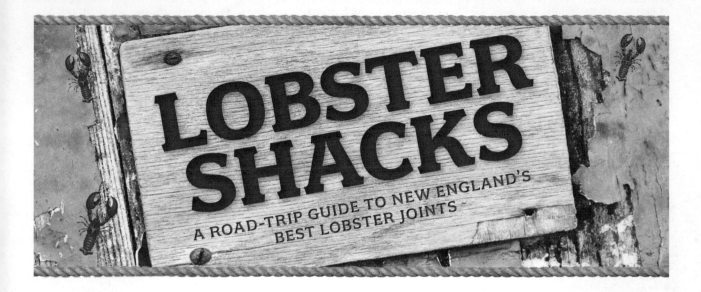

LOBSTER SHACKS

A ROAD-TRIP GUIDE TO NEW ENGLAND'S BEST LOBSTER JOINTS

MIKE URBAN

The Countryman Press
Woodstock, Vermont

Book design and composition by Ponderosa Pine Design, Vicky Vaughn Shea

Published by The Countryman Press, P.O. Box 748, Woodstock, VT 05091
Distributed by W. W. Norton & Company, Inc., 500 Fifth Avenue, New York, NY 10110
Printed in the United States of America

10 9 8 7 6 5 4 3 2 1

Lobster Shacks
978-0-88150-999-1

Photo and Illustration Credits

Front Cover
All photos taken by and copyright ©Mike Urban, except: upper right-hand corner, photo courtesy of Cobie's Clam Shack, Kelly Slezak, photographer; upper row, second from left, courtesy of the Lobster Pot, East Wareham, Massachusetts; rope, ©iStockphoto.com/Dirk Rietschel; lobster illustration, ©iStockphoto.com/derrrek; background sign, ©iStockphoto.com/xyno

Back Cover
All photos taken by and copyright © Mike Urban

Text
All photos are taken by and copyright ©Mike Urban, except: Page 15, background image used in boxes, ©iStockphoto.com/iatsun; Page 25, courtesy of Lenny and Joe's Fish Tale; Page 40, background image used in boxes, ©iStockphoto.com/fatmayilmaz; Page 45, photography by Rachael Blount Girard; Pages 52, 53, 54, 55, courtesy of the Lobster Pot, East Wareham, Massachusetts; Page 58, ©iStockphoto.com/LauriPatterson; Page 62, courtesy of Cobie's Clam Shack, Kelly Slezak, photographer; Page 63, courtesy of Arnold's Lobster and Clam Bar; Page 92, courtesy of Woodman's of Essex; Pages 108, 138, courtesy of Portland Lobster Company

Maps created by: Ponderosa Pine Design

Front cover locations: lower left, Lobster Landing, Clinton, Connecticut; lower right, The Lobster Dock, Boothbay Harbor, Maine; upper photos, left to right: the Clam Shack, Kennebunkport, Maine; the Lobster Pot, East Wareham, Massachusetts; (next two) Stewman's Lobster Pound, Bar Harbor, Maine; Cobie's, Brewster, Massachusetts.

Back cover locations: top, left to right: Boothbay Lobster Wharf, Boothbay Harbor, Maine; Ken's Place, Scarborough, Maine; Captain Scott's Lobster Dock, New London, Connecticut; The Lobster Shack, Branford, Connecticut; Red's Eats, Wiscasset, Maine. Middle of cover: Boothbay Lobster Wharf, Boothbay Harbor, Maine.

To my mother and father

Lobster Shack Two Lights,
Cape Elizabeth, Maine.

Contents

Five Islands Lobster Company, Georgetown, Maine

Introduction

Few things characterize New England and its cuisine better than a fresh lobster, served with steamed clams, corn on the cob, chowder, coleslaw, red potatoes, and any of a number of other tasty side dishes. And the best place to enjoy such seaside feasts is at a dine-in-the-rough lobster shack. There are dozens of such shacks up and down the coast, and they come in a variety of sizes, shapes, vintages, and architectural styles. But they all have one thing in common: a passionate commitment to serving up those bi-clawed, meaty-tailed red crustaceans that diners so passionately crave on summertime outings in coastal New England.

This book contains detailed descriptions and color photos of more than 60 of New England's finest lobster shacks, including directions on finding them (many are squirreled away on the docks of remote fishing towns and villages); colorful histories of the shacks; biographies of their iconoclastic owners (often lobstermen and their families); unique and interesting dishes to sample (everything from lobster pie to lobster gazpacho); and lots of recipes from the shacks themselves for you to try at home.

So pack up your car, switch on your GPS, tie on your lobster bib, and get ready for some fine eating and some great road-time adventures, as this guide takes you deep into the heart of coastal New England's fabled lobster country.

Happy travels—oh, and bring an appetite!

PORTLAND Maine Lobster Co. U.S.A.

DANGER MEN COOKING

"Hard Shell" Jumbo Lobsters 2 Pounds and over $11.95 per Pound

LOBSTER

PICK YOUR OWN LOBSTERS

ABEL'S LOBSTER POUND SHORE DINNERS SERVED INSIDE OR OUT ON THE SHORE

RESTAURANT 12 NOON 9 PM there is a difference!

CODEND FISH LOBSTER CLAMS

THURSTON FOR LOBSTER

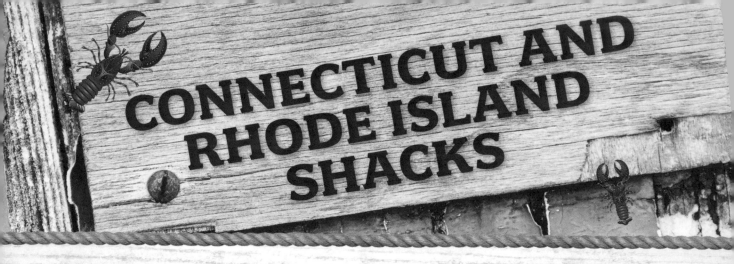

CONNECTICUT AND RHODE ISLAND SHACKS

The Connecticut and Rhode Island shorelines are dotted with small cities, scenic towns, and dozens of beaches and harbors where sun seekers and pleasure boaters flock in the summertime to go for a swim or take to the water in everything from kayaks and skiffs to cabin cruisers to multi-masted sailboats.

There is also a small yet scrappy lobster-fishing industry scattered in pockets all along the southern New England coast—and where there are lobsters being trapped, there are lobster shacks! Though not as ubiquitous as in places like coastal Maine, there are a number of fine, casual, dine-in-the-rough places where you may order up freshly boiled or steamed lobsters, or enjoy lobster rolls and lobster bisque with family and friends while taking in the placid beauty of Long Island Sound or the miles of scenic shoreline along Narragansett Bay in Rhode Island.

One of the unique features in this part of the lobster world is the hot, buttered lobster roll. This tasty treat is said to have been invented in the Connecticut town of Milford. It spread throughout the state and has begun showing up in lobster shacks as far north as Acadia in Maine. Unlike the traditional lobster roll, with chilled lobster meat tossed with mayonnaise, the hot roll features warm lobster meat slathered in melted butter and served in a toasted, buttered, split-top bun.

Regardless of whether you prefer your lobster roll hot and buttered or cold and mayo'ed, you're going to find plenty of good lobster in this balmiest part of New England.

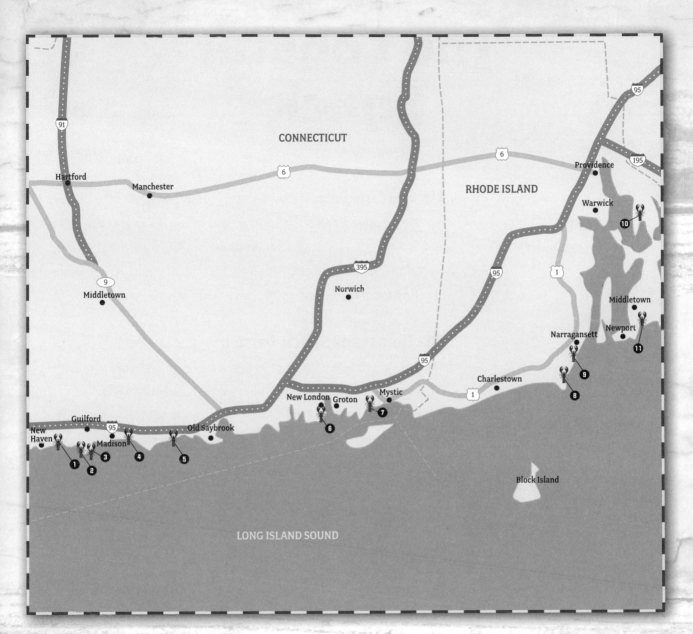

The Lobster Shack

50 Maple Street, Branford, CT

☎ 203-483-8414

Open mid-May to mid-October

It's only fitting that we begin our journey at a place that goes by the name Lobster Shack. This little gem is housed in a cheerful, shiny, maroon-colored trailer situated at the far end of a graveled parking lot in Birbarie Marina on the Branford River, just a few blocks from the Branford town center and several miles east of New Haven, Connecticut.

The Reluctant Shack Owner

The Lobster Shack is the brainchild of Arlene and Nick Crismale—it originated out of Nick's many years in the lobster- and clam-harvesting businesses, but it took some convincing to get Arlene on board. Nick was working as a lobsterman out of Branford, and with Arlene's occasional assistance, he ran a wholesale and retail lobster pound for eight years in a marina right across from their current location.

About 10 years ago, Nick came across a small, white trailer for sale in New London, Connecticut, and he suggested to Arlene that they buy it and set up a lobster stand next to the pound. Arlene, who had recently retired from full-time work at the local phone company, wasn't keen on the idea; Nick went ahead and purchased the trailer anyway, and it sat idle for the next several years while the Crismales went about their lives.

In 2006 Arlene was working part-time at a gallery in Orange, Connecticut. As the gallery grew, her hours there increased to the point that she started losing interest in the job. She was finally persuaded by her husband to look into setting up and running the modest food stand that he had been dreaming about. The more Arlene researched the idea, the more excited she got about it. By the time the Lobster Shack debuted

Lobster Shack owner Arlene Crismale.

in the spring of 2007, she couldn't wait to open her order window and start selling hot, buttery lobster rolls to the boaters in the marina and anyone else who could find them in their tucked-away location.

What's in a Name?

From the moment the white trailer opened that spring, the place took off, and word spread quickly through Branford and neighboring communities about the great new food stand down in the marina. Arlene was so busy getting the place up and running that she hadn't really given any thought to what the proper name for the eatery should be. While working the order window one day in that first year, she overheard a customer saying into his cell phone, "I'm at the shack. You know, the shack in the marina." Arlene asked him about what he'd said and he responded, "That's what everybody calls this place." Arlene thus christened her nascent business the Lobster Shack, since that's what her growing clientele were already calling the place.

Right around the time Arlene got the shack up and running, Nick abandoned the lobster business, which had been suffering for a number of years as a result of a mysterious lobster die-off in Long Island Sound. He switched over to clamming, and bought a custom-made, 65-foot boat he had manufactured in Canada. Since that time, the Lobster Shack has been buying its fresh-picked lobster meat from Garbo Lobster in Groton, Connecticut, and from another supplier in Portland, Maine. The Crismalis know their

What Is Dining in the Rough?

To dine in the rough means to eat without all the frills of a typical full-service restaurant. It's a particularly popular way to enjoy seafood (especially lobster) in coastal New England.

You order your food at a window or counter, settle up your tab with the cashier, and receive an order number. When your order is ready, your number is called out, and you fetch your food from the pickup counter.

Seating at dine-in-the-rough establishments is up to you. You find a place to sit, more often than not at a picnic table outdoors. Tableware consists of plastic utensils and throwaway plates, cups, and bowls. When you're done with your meal, you toss your tableware and lobster shells into the nearest trash receptacle.

When you dine in the rough, your kids can run around, conversations may be loud, and fun is most definitely the order of the day. Plus, you can typically wear just about anything you want, including a bathing suit, and not feel out of place.

lobster, and they accept only the freshest, firmest, tastiest meat from their suppliers.

The Signature Lobster Roll and More

The menu at the Lobster Shack is simple and spare, which seems to be fine with the steady stream of customers who frequent the stand. That's the way Arlene wants it, and she's reluctant to add much to the menu, preferring to keep things focused on what she can do best.

The lobster roll leads the parade from the small kitchen inside the trailer. It consists of 4 ounces of warm lobster meat (claw and tail portions only), bathed in real melted butter and spritzed with juice from fresh-squeezed lemons wrapped in cheesecloth. The bun is a toasted sub roll, which nicely accommodates the serving of lobster meat. Your sandwich comes wrapped in a piece of light aluminum foil on a small plastic tray, a classic dine-in-the-rough presentation.

The other staple sandwich is Italian sausage, peppers, and onions, also served on a grilled sub roll. This is particularly popular with the large community of Italian Americans who live in

Waiting in the shade for one of the Lobster Shack's fine lobster rolls.

Branford and all along the Connecticut shore. Longhini Sausage Company of New Haven supplies the sausages. Hummel Hot Dogs, also of New Haven, supplies the foot-long franks that are grilled and served in split-top buns, another choice at the Lobster Shack.

Homemade lobster bisque is popular, as are the two types of chowder—traditional creamy New England style and the broth-only Rhode Island style, which is made by Nick from his daily clam catches. Speaking of Nick's clams, you can also get raw clams on the half shell in half-dozen and dozen quantities at the Lobster Shack.

One item that was added to the menu recently, and to great success, is the hot shrimp roll. It features 4 ounces of cooked Maine shrimp (the little, sweet variety, something of a rarity outside the state of Maine), spritzed with lemon and melted butter and served on a grilled sub roll.

And aside from the bags of chips, assorted sodas, bottled water, and some very refreshing gelato for dessert, that's about it for the Lobster Shack's menu. All in all, it's small but very satisfying.

You may bring your own libations and side dishes, and many people do so, especially in the early evening. (The Lobster Shack closes down at 5:30 PM, except for weekend evenings in the summer, when it stays open until 7 PM.) There's frequently live music from 4 to 7 PM on Sundays, and people linger past the closing of the trailer, which is fine with Arlene, as long as they tie down the umbrellas and clean up after themselves.

After four full seasons in operation (the shack's fifth anniversary is in 2012), Arlene says she wishes they'd started the business 10 years ago. She loves talking with her customers, giving them a satisfying meal or snack and providing them with a place where they can relax next to the water and forget their cares for a little while. Judging from the perpetual smile on her face, it's somewhat surprising that she had to be convinced to open the Lobster Shack in the first place. But shack lovers in Branford and beyond are glad that she did.

Guilford Lobster Pound

The **Guilford Lobster Pound** is located on the docks in picturesque Guilford Harbor, about a mile from Guilford's bucolic town green and a world away from the hustle and bustle of I-95 and Route 1, which cut through just north of the town's center. This little lobster operation is a microcosm of many larger lobster outfits farther north, especially those in Maine: a cedar-shingled shack with cold-water tanks and lobster-fishing gear inside; a lengthy dock stacked with wire lobster traps that extends along the edge of the harbor; a lobsterman's boat tied to the dock right next to the shed; a bunch of picnic tables scattered about the dock for diners; and a small, canopied tour boat that takes sightseers out into Long Island Sound for a shoreline cruise to view the local flora and fauna. There's also some fine lobster to be had at the pound, either bought live and taken home to cook, or tucked into sweet, buttery lobster rolls to be enjoyed right there on the dock.

505A Whitfield Street, Guilford, CT

203-453-6122

www.guilfordlobsterpound.com

Open mid-May to mid-October

The Lobstering Life in Guilford

Owner Bart Mansi has run this small-scale lobster pound since 1991, when the restaurant next door subdivided its property and put the pound and its then minuscule dock up for sale. Mansi, who had been lobstering in the New Haven area to the west since the mid-1970s, jumped at the chance to have his own dock and pound. He lobsters nearly every day in-season, going out at around 4 AM to check, empty, and bait his traps, and coming back to load his catch into the waiting tanks at the pound.

Barrel-chested and tastefully inked on his forearms, Bart has the look of a seasoned lobsterman. He has seen the ups and downs of the

The lobster roll at Guilford Lobster Pound is chock-full of fresh lobster meat.

lobster business on Long Island Sound over the years, and he's now one of maybe 10 licensed lobstermen still fishing the waters between New Haven and Old Saybrook. (A lot of lobstermen got out of the business during a lobster die-off caused by pesticides in the late 1990s.)

His 46-foot boat, the *Erica Paige*, named after his daughter, is moored alongside the dock in back of the pound, and he goes out to check his traps, whether or not the pound is open. (They're closed Monday and Tuesday in the summertime and only open Friday, Saturday, and Sunday in the shoulder seasons when local schools are in session.)

Guilford Lobster Pound's welcome sign.

You can get a good look at the lobstering life at the Guilford Lobster Pound, because it's got everything right there on a small scale and out in the open—from the boat and traps to the cold-water tanks to the boiler inside the shed. If Bart's around, he'll be happy to explain how he traps and sells his lobsters and show you around the place.

Good Things Take Time

After 10 years or so of lobstering and selling live lobsters to local restaurants and seafood markets and to locals who motored down to the pound, Bart and his wife, Janice, decided it would be nice to build a new, expansive deck on back of the pound and serve lobster rolls, chowder, and a few other items in a dine-in-the-rough setup. They applied for permits to expand their dock, and it took several years to jump through all the hoops in order to get started.

In the meantime, the lobster die-off began, and the Mansis struggled to stay in business as they wrangled over their dock permits and waited hopefully for the lobsters to return in good numbers. Though the lobster fishery hasn't returned to its previous levels, Bart still traps and sells enough to get by, and in the spring of 2007, the Mansis were finally able to realize their dream of having an on-the-water eatery right on their newly christened dock.

Lobster Rolls, Chowder, and Stuffies

The menu at Guilford Lobster Pound is as simple as the metal food stand that sits on the deck by the shack—it's a little pushcart that serves as Janice's base of operations for food preparation. The number one item on the menu is the hot buttered lobster roll, done in classic Connecticut style and brimming with fresh-picked lobster meat, which comes directly from the lobsters cooked in the pound. The roll consists of about 4 ounces of lobster meat, warmed in melted butter and stacked in a split-top hot dog bun.

Nearly as popular as the lobster roll is the clam chowder, which is done in the clear-broth Rhode Island style, with plenty of diced clams and chunks of red potato in each serving. A lobster roll and a cup of chowder are usually enough to satisfy any hungry customer. For those who wish to avoid the seafood side of things, steamed hot dogs are available, as are bags of potato chips, which go great with any of the "main courses."

Bart and Janice recently added stuffed clams to the menu, fare that's more often found in Rhode Island shacks and a welcome addition to the offerings at Guilford Lobster Pound. The "stuffies," as they're called, consist of breaded stuffing filled with minced clams and spicy sausage, all packed into a good-sized quahog clamshell. The Mansis get their stuffies from a friend in New Haven, who makes them in his home and delivers them to the pound regularly throughout the summer. They make a great appetizer or midafternoon snack.

Guilford Lobster Pound is a BYO establishment, and many people bring beer, wine, side dishes, and table settings to supplement their meals. The atmosphere is relaxed and festive, and the view of surrounding marsh grasses and Long Island Sound just outside the harbor is spectacular. Boaters are welcome to tie up to the dock and come ashore for some good eats, and everything from kayaks to cabin cruisers take advantage of the Mansis' hospitality.

So why drive all the way to Maine to get the lobster pound experience when you can get a good taste of it right on the shores of Guilford harbor? Bart and Janice Mansi are warm and welcoming hosts, and if you decide to check out their modest eatery on the docks, you're in for a treat.

CHEF BOB'S RHODE ISLAND CLAM CHOWDER

The clear-broth chowder that's served up at Guilford Lobster Pound is anything but clear. There are lots of wonderful herbs and spices swimming in the super-tasty broth, along with generous portions of clams, red potatoes, and chopped celery. It's an excellent way to begin any meal—seafood or otherwise—and can even be a meal in itself with a loaf of crispy bread and maybe a salad on the side.

INGREDIENTS

1	head celery
3	Vidalia onions
5	pounds red potatoes
1	cup olive oil
4	tablespoons chopped fresh garlic
2½	pounds chopped quahog clams, undrained
1	tablespoon dry basil
1	tablespoon black pepper
1½	teaspoons dry dill
1½	teaspoons sifted sage
1	tablespoon chopped parsley
6	cups clam juice

Chop the celery and onions in ¼-inch dice. Cube the red potatoes in ½-inch dice. In a large saucepan, heat the olive oil and add the celery, onions, and garlic. Cook approximately 5 minutes, stirring occasionally. Add the clams and simmer, approximately 5 minutes. Add the red potatoes and spices and mix thoroughly. Add the clam juice, bring to a boil, then let simmer until the potatoes are soft, about 20 minutes. Serve. Makes 8–12 servings.

The Place

901 Boston Post Road, Guilford, CT

☎ 203-453-9276

theplaceguilford.com

Open late April to late October

Some shacks boil their lobsters; others steam them. Debates rage over which is the better method for cooking the perfect lobster. At The Place in Guilford, the preferred (nay, the only) way lobster is cooked is over an open-flame fire pit that slowly roasts the big, red crustaceans to tender, smoky, flavorful perfection.

The Place is definitely one of the most unique eateries on the Connecticut shoreline (the entire New England shoreline, for that matter). If you happen to stumble upon this roadside oddity, it looks almost tribal, with customers seated on tree stumps at brightly painted, red-topped tables and a light scent of wood smoke wafting above the completely alfresco dining area. When it rains, and on hot and sunny days, a large, red-and-white, circus-like tarp is hoisted on a cable over the dining area, lending an even more exotic look and feel to the place.

But the food here, though prepared in what some may consider a primitive manner, is anything but. The fire-roasted seafood is unique and delectable, especially the shellfish, which are cooked over the open flames and served with such treats as fire-roasted corn on the cob, veggie kabobs, barbecued chicken, rib-eye steaks, and various types of fish fillets.

An Unusual Restaurant

The small red sign stuck in the lawn in front of The Place on US Route 1 says it all, and quite succinctly: AN UNUSUAL RESTAURANT. This one-of-a-kind place got its start back in the 1940s when a local sea captain named Whitey set up a clambake stand on Route 1 and started selling steamed

Put your rump on a stump in The Place's picnic area.

Two lobsters over the flames at The Place.

and fire-roasted clams to passing motorists. You just pulled in, sat down on a tree stump, placed your order, and waited for your fresh steamed or roasted seafood to appear.

From the beginning, one of the hallmarks of The Place has been its 18-foot-long, 3-foot-wide, 4-foot-high cinderblock wood-fed fire pit. It's the centerpiece of the outdoor dining area, and to this day, it's still where virtually all of The Place's food gets cooked. It's quite a sight to behold, especially at night, when embers dance in the darkened night above the pit, and college-age workers shuffle screens, metal baskets, and foil packets of food from one metal rack to another over the open flames.

The wood that feeds the pit is purchased from a mill about 10 miles north of The Place in North Guilford. It comes in the form of long planks sheered off the outer edges of hardwood trees before the cores of the trunks are milled into lumber. So, though the fire pit does release some smoke into the air, the wood that it's coming from is actually being recycled very

thoughtfully. And it's most enjoyable, on a summer evening, to sit outside on a tree stump in a campfire-type setting with the faint scent of wood smoke in the air.

The Brothers Knowles

Back in the 1960s a local teenager named Vaughn Knowles started working summers at The Place as part of the cook/waitstaff. A few years later, Whitey decided to cash out and put the eatery up for sale. Vaughn jumped at the chance to own The Place, and he and Whitey worked out a deal. In 1971 The Place opened with Vaughn at the helm, and shortly thereafter his brother Gary joined him. Initially they stuck with the same five-item menu established by Whitey: lobsters, roasted clams, corn on the cob, shrimp, and steamers.

The two brothers have been at The Place ever since, and you may see them nearly every evening, dressed in their THE PLACE-emblazoned T-shirts and caps and wearing appropriately casual shorts and using flame-retardant gloves when tending the food over the flames. They've expanded the menu somewhat over the years, but not so much that it can't all fit on a red-and-white wooden sign that looms over one corner of the dining area and and can be read from nearly every seat in the house.

BYO Everything (Almost)

The Place is definitely a BYO establishment, and many parties bring coolers full of beer, bottles of wine, and

The roasted clams are not to be missed at The Place.

slowly decompose, and Gary and Vaughn have to replace fifty or so stumps each year. So you need to keep coming back to retain your stump-worthiness.)

In keeping with the fresh and earthy spirit of this unusual eatery, Vaughn's wife, Judy, places fresh flowers from the Knowleses' yard in empty glass sherry bottles on each table every night. The tables, by the way, are tree stumps themselves, topped with bright-red, shellacked, round pieces of heavy plywood, adding yet more color to the dining area and making tablecloths somewhat superfluous.

occasionally more exotic libations. In addition, you're welcome to bring all your own side dishes, such as salads, breads, cheeses, fruits, desserts, whatever you think best to trick out your meal. The Knowleses will supply the seafood and other grilled entrées and all the nonalcoholic beverages. Many regulars bring their own tablecloths, silverware, candles, and other accoutrements, making the dining area even more festive than it already is.

"Put Your Rump on a Stump" has become the unofficial slogan for The Place, and it's emblazoned across the back of their official T-shirt. Stumps-as-chairs remains a time-honored tradition here, and many regular customers have stumps named after them. Once the Knowles brothers deem you "stump-worthy," your name is painted on the side of a stump, and it becomes your place of honor each time you come in for a meal. (Keep in mind that stumps do

Let's Eat, Already!

We haven't even gotten to the best part: what to order for dinner. There are a few must-haves at The Place that date back to its origins and that have remained among the most popular items on the menu. First, there are the fire-roasted clams. Good-sized little-necks are placed on a heavy metal screen over the open flames until they pop open. Then you have the option of going for the Clam Special, which calls for a spicy cocktail sauce to be brushed over the open clams for the last couple of minutes of cooking, or taking them plain with a bit of butter. The roasting littlenecks are delivered to your table, hot screen and all, so you have to wait a bit before indulging.

Once they've cooled to a reasonable temperature (it just takes a couple of minutes), you may either spear them with the small wooden forks provided or, in the grand Place tradition, slurp them straight from the warm shells, which you then toss on the ground where they will eventually get crushed underfoot and become part of the ground cover.

Then there's the roasted corn on the cob. The Place buys native corn by the burlap bagful, and they load a bunch of ears still in their husks into a metal

◑ A Lobster Lexicon ◐

Here are some useful, sometimes colorful, terms relating to lobsters. Feel free to use them when patronizing lobster shacks or checking out lobster-fishing operations on the New England coastline. Who knows? Maybe you'll get a choice "bug" (or at least an appreciative smile from the staff) for your efforts.

bug: Slang for a lobster.

chicken: A small lobster, usually weighing between 1 and 1¼ pounds.

hard-shell: A lobster whose shell has fully formed and hardened. Such lobsters typically contain more meat. Most connoisseurs prefer hard shells, believing the meat in a hard-shell lobster to be more substantial, richer in protein, and more fully developed. Hard-shell lobster is the priciest kind.

soft-shell: A lobster that has recently molted and whose new shell is still soft and easily cracked. A soft-shell lobster has less meat in it, since it's just starting to grow into its new, larger shell. So you're paying for more shell and less meat, and the price of soft-shell lobster is less. Many lobstermen and others, however, like soft shells best, claiming the meat in a soft shell, though less plentiful, is sweeter and more tender than hard-shell meat.

shedder: A lobster in the molting, or soft-shell, stage. Sometimes used in a derogatory way.

cull: A lobster that is missing one claw. Culls are often used in bisques, stews, and lobster rolls, as they lack the visual appeal necessary when served whole.

pistol, or bullet: A lobster with no claws, usually the result of fighting or defending itself against other lobsters or predators. (Don't despair. Lobsters usually regenerate their claws.)

tomalley: The lobster's liver. It's greenish in color and highly valued by lobster connoisseurs for its rich flavor.

coral: The eggs, or roe, found in a female lobster, so named because of the coral color the roe takes on when it's cooked. Some people consider the coral a delicacy.

sleeper: A lobster that is lethargic and sluggish and that doesn't show much, if any, life when plucked from the cold-water tank. Such lobsters are often near death and, though safe to eat, should be declined in favor of a livelier, healthier one.

basket and place it over the flames. The husks send up sparks into the night, and after a short while, the basket is removed and the husks stripped off by cooks wearing heavy-duty gloves. Each ear of corn is then dipped into a vat of melted butter and delivered hot to your table on a paper plate. It's a taste treat you won't forget any time soon. (The butter for the corn and lobsters, by the way, is melted in a couple of old campfire-style coffee percolators set next to the edge of the fire pit, with one-pound chunks of butter dropped in periodically to meet demand.)

The Place's Famous Flame-Roasted Lobster

Finally, you're ready for the flame-roasted lobster. Few, if any, other shacks cook their lobsters over an open flame, and it's a sight to behold. The bugs start out in a boiling pot next to the fire pit, where they're more or less cooked through to a bright orangish-red. Then they're placed on their arched backs, with their tail flippers pinned down under one edge of a wire basket. After a minute or two of roasting in this fashion, the lobsters are flipped over for a good roasting on the belly side. The tail is split by the cook staff, and the claws are given a swift crack to make the eating easier. The end result is lobster meat that is moist, tender, and smoky in flavor—a truly unique taste treat for lobster aficionados who think they've tried it all.

The Place closes for the season in October, but the festive atmosphere starts up again about a month later when an outfit leases the land from the Knowleses for a couple of months and fills it with Christmas trees for sale. It's as if this little patch of land on Route 1 in Guilford is enchanted, with nothing but warm and wonderful things happening there nearly year-round. Come spring, the fire pit is stoked, the seafood brought in, and the fun starts all over again.

The Place's famous menu board says it all.

Lenny and Joe's Fish Tale

Known for decades as the go-to place for deep-fried seafood after a day of sun and sand at nearby Hammonasset Beach State Park, Lenny and Joe's Fish Tale in Madison, Connecticut, has always done a nice side-business with steamed lobsters. Originally relegated to seasonal status outside the shack, Lenny and Joe's recently expanded their kitchen and brought their lobster cooking indoors to make lobsters and steamers a year-round option on the menu.

✖ 1301 Boston Post Road, Madison, CT

☎ 203-245-7289

🦞 www.ljfishtale.com

Open year-round

It Started in a Lean-To

Lenny and Joe's was founded in 1978 as a small roadside shack in Madison with a couple of deep fryers, an order counter, and four picnic tables inside a screened porch. Within a couple of years, brother/partners Lenny and Joe Goldberg decided to try adding lobsters to their menu. They set up a freestanding, propane-fired burner with a big pot on it next to the shack and started steaming lobsters out in the open.

After a couple of years, they built a lean-to on one side of the shack and put a few burners and pots and a separate order counter outside for their burgeoning lobster, steamers, and chowder trades. As Lenny and Joe's grew in popularity, so did their lobster sales, primarily because they priced their lobsters lower than others on the Connecticut shore at that time and because they cooked them up quickly, which made the customers happy, especially when they also ordered deep-fried items and didn't want to wait extra long for the lobsters to catch up.

Lenny and Joe's Drive-In, circa 1980, with the lobster stand on the right.

When they built their much larger current building back in 1989, the lobster-cooking operation moved to a sheltered side porch and retained its Memorial-Day-to-Labor-Day seasonality. As Lenny and Joe's continued to grow in size and popularity, the lobster pots remained a steady little side-business.

Lobsters from Popeye

The Goldbergs have always believed in sourcing their seafood locally whenever possible, for reasons of freshness and to support the local fisheries. For a number of years, they bought their lobsters from a local salt named Wally Heck, an old-school lobsterman and wholesaler in nearby Westbrook. Wally would trap his lobsters in Long Island Sound and store them in his makeshift pound in the tidal Menunketesuck River in Westbrook.

Heck was the quintessential lobsterman, trapping in the morning on his dilapidated boat, then delivering to customers in the afternoon or whenever they ran out—sometimes in the middle of the dinner hour. He had massive forearms from hauling up lobster traps for many years, and the Goldbergs nicknamed him Popeye. Heck supplied Lenny and Joe's with lobsters for years until he retired. With the lobster die-off in Long Island Sound a dozen years ago, the Goldbergs now work with wholesalers who bring them lobsters from Rhode Island, Massachusetts, Maine, and even Nova Scotia.

Steamed lobster and clams with all the fixings.

The New Lobster Stand

In 2010 the Goldbergs decided it was time to ratchet up their lobster sales, so they built an expansion on one side of the kitchen area and installed a high-end stainless steel steamer for lobsters and steamed clams and a state-of-the-art broiler for other seafood. They call this new area the Lobster Stand, where you can get lobster, steamers, Alaskan king crab legs, corn on the cob, chowder, and healthy, broiled seafood dishes that have steered clear of the deep fryers.

The most popular item from the stand is the Lobster Dinner Special, which consists of a one-pound steamed lobster, salt potatoes, corn on the cob or other seasonal steamed vegetable, and a generous cup of melted butter. You can double your fun with the twin lobster special, which features two one-pound bugs with all the trimmings. Then there's the Fish Tale Lobster Feast—Lenny and Joe's equivalent of the shore dinner (a dinner assembled around the daily catch)—which has lobster, a cup of chowder, a quart of steamers, potatoes, veg, and butter. Lenny and Joe's steamers come from Mike's Seafood in Maine and are delivered fresh several times a week by Mike himself.

If a 1-pounder won't do, there's a 1½-pound lobster special dinner with a larger lobster, potatoes, vegetable, and butter. Lenny and Joe's serves hard-shell lobsters only, when they can get them, resorting to soft shells when they're the only kind available.

One of the Finest Lobster Rolls on the Shore

Lenny and Joe's has always prided itself on one of its best-selling items: the hot lobster roll with melted butter on top and a toasted bun underneath. They sell tens of thousands of these tasty sandwiches every year, and with good reason. Kids in particular love the taste of lobster meat dipped in butter, but they don't always have the patience or the fortitude (or strength, for that matter) to crack and pick and eat an entire lobster. So the lobster rolls fly out of the kitchen into the eager and expectant hands of many of Lenny and Joe's younger customers.

Take It Outside

Lenny and Joe's has ample seating indoors for year-round dining, but when weather permits (roughly

> ## LENNY AND JOE'S WORLD-FAMOUS COLESLAW
>
> This coleslaw makes a great side dish with any seafood, including lobster. Whip up a batch and amaze your family and friends.
>
> ### INGREDIENTS
>
> | | |
> |---|---|
> | ⅔ | cup mayonnaise |
> | 2 | tablespoons white vinegar |
> | ¼ | cup sugar |
> | 1 | teaspoon salt |
> | | pinch white pepper |
> | 1 | teaspoon celery seed |
> | 1 | head white cabbage, shredded |
> | 1 | carrot, shredded |
> | 1 | cup red cabbage, shredded |
>
> In a large mixing bowl, blend the mayonnaise and white vinegar. Add the sugar, salt, pepper, and celery seed to the mayonnaise/vinegar mix and whisk thoroughly. Add the white cabbage, carrots, and red cabbage, and mix well. Chill and serve. Yields 6–8 servings.

early May through September), you should really go out to the sea of picnic tables in the tree-shaded, gravel-floored grove just outside the back door. There you'll find a variety of places to sit and enjoy your meal, and there's plenty to look at while you dine. A number of years ago, the Goldbergs had a carousel installed in the outdoor dining area, and kids love to go round and round on the brightly painted ponies and dolphins (and lobsters!) that spin endlessly. It costs a dollar for each ride on the carousel, and Lenny and Joe's donates all the proceeds to local charities.

So far, they've raised over $700,000.

There's also an ice-cream stand and a souvenir kiosk that sells L and J's famous T-shirts and hats. The shack sells more than 30,000 shirts per year, between their Madison drive-in and their full-service restaurant in Westbrook.

Lenny and Joe's has upped its commitment to fresh, steamed lobster and to healthy, broiled seafood, and they continue to offer high quality and amazing value. Oh, and they still have plenty of amazing deep-fried seafood (and that excellent hot, buttered lobster roll). So this place should be high on your list of lobster must-try's next time you're cruising the Connecticut shoreline or motoring your way up I-95.

Lenny and Joe's carousel has raised over $700,000 for local charities.

Lobster Landing

Welcome to Lobster Landing, down by Clinton harbor.

✕ 152 Commerce Street, Clinton, CT

☎ 860-669-2005

Open mid-April to late December

WHEN YOU VEER OFF ROUTE 1 in downtown Clinton and drive toward the town's small yet busy marina, you eventually come face-to-face with a delightfully dilapidated little shack right on the water with its hand-painted sign overhead declaring in lopsided lettering that you're standing on the threshold of Lobster Landing.

Owners Enea and Cathie Bacci (Enea goes by his last name, Bacci) have lovingly developed this little seaside shack into a culinary and cultural magnet for their adopted seaside hometown. They get their lobster from nineteen local lobster boats that offload around the harbor and on Lobster Landing's small dock, giving the place some pretty solid street cred in the lobster world.

The menu is spare and direct and is posted on a simple whiteboard in front of the small, open-air food counter just outside the shack: lobster rolls; sausage, pepper, and onion sandwiches; hot dogs; chips; soda; some ice cream; and little else. But the real (nay, the only) reason to come to Lobster Landing is for the meaty, buttery hot lobster roll for which it is best known.

The roll distinguishes itself in a couple of ways. First, it's chock-full of buttery, fresh-picked meat (you can see them picking meat in the shack throughout the day); they certainly don't skimp, loading up the oversize bun until the lobster crowns out of the top.

The second thing is the bun itself. It's an Italian grinder roll, long and narrow, soft and fluffy; and it's toasted on a conventional, patio-type propane barbecue grill, adding an extra crunch to the sandwich. One lobster roll should be enough, but don't be surprised if you find yourself craving a second.

Feel free to bring your own beer or wine to enjoy on Lobster Landing's harborside deck and picnic tables out front. Given the Italian flavor of the place, a chilled pinot grigio or a bottle or two of Moretti beer might be in order for your light repast by the sea.

Captain Scott's Lobster Dock

80 Hamilton Street, New London, CT

☎ 860-439-1741

🦞 www.captscotts.com

Open early April to mid-October

The dining scene in New London, Connecticut, is diverse and intriguing and sometimes a bit contradictory. Captain Scott's Lobster reflects all of these traits in one form or another.

Take its location: You drive through downtown New London, then head down a stretch of road in an industrial area until you see a sign on the side of a building beckoning you to Captain Scott's down a side street to the left. You hang a left and proceed a block or so between old factory buildings and toward what appears to be a dead end. Then a driveway of sorts suddenly appears to the left at the dead end, runs uphill a bit, then parallels the electrified Amtrak Acela train tracks.

Another 50 yards or so down the driveway brings you to the parking lot for Captain Scott's Lobster Dock, a long, narrow shingled shack that's bordered on one side by the tracks and on the other by a marina. You're sort of in a limbo between boats and rails, but it's a fine limbo to be in, especially once you've partaken of the fine food from Captain Scott's kitchen.

An Offshoot of New London Lobstering

Captain Scott's is owned and run by Sue Tierney, an energetic restaurateur and busy mom who splits her time between Captain Scott's and her young children at home. How did she find her way to this remote slice of New London's water/train front?

It all started with her brother, Scott (no, not *the* Captain Scott—more on the captain later). For years, brother Scott was a lobsterman out of New London, docking his boat beneath the I-95 Gold Star Memorial

Sue Tierney, owner of Captain Scott's Lobster Dock.

Bridge, which spans the Thames River between New London and Groton. Sue used to help him on the boat in the summer when she was in high school. Scott decided he wanted to expand his lobstering business and get into wholesaling, which meant he would need a place for lobstermen to offload their catch.

Searching the New London waterfront, he found a sliver of land on Shaw's Cove between the marina and train tracks, and he bought it. At the time, there was a forlorn, dilapidated shack on the property, piles of junk, and not much else. He cleaned up the grounds, fixed up the shack, and retrofitted it for his wholesaling business.

In the mid-1990s a small food stand opened on one end of the shack and started serving up lobsters and eventually chowders and deep-fried seafood. Over the next several years, the restaurant started taking off while Scott's lobster wholesaling struggled during the lobster die-off in Long Island Sound in the late 1990s. He eventually got out of lobstering and wholesaling, and a small, well-stocked fresh-seafood market took over some of the vacant space in the back portion of the shack.

Never a Dull Moment

Situated between boats and trains as it is, there's always a lot of activity to check out while dining at Captain Scott's. Commercial, pleasure, and charter fishing boats are constantly coming and going, and Acela trains glide by at least once every hour or two. And several times a year, you may enjoy live music at

Who Is Captain Scott?

The sea captain for whom the shack is named is owner Sue Tierney's grandmother's great-great-grandfather. Captain Thomas A. Scott (1830–1907) came to New London in 1871, when his marine construction company was commissioned to help build the famous Race Rock Lighthouse in Long Island Sound. He became a beloved citizen of New London and lived much of the rest of his life there.

What Captain Scott may be best known for, however, is an act of bravery that made its way into the pages of *Ripley's Believe It or Not*, where he is referred to as the "Human Cork." Here's how the story goes:

While navigating his tugboat in New York's North River in January 1870, Captain Scott came alongside a sinking ferryboat with hundreds of passengers on board. Acting quickly, the captain managed to plug the hole in the ferry by using his body as a stopper at the listing boat's waterline. Though he suffered severe injuries to his arm while acting as the human plug, he survived, and everyone on the boat was saved.

How's that for derring-do? No wonder he went into lighthouse construction the following year. Captain Scott clearly had a taste for lifesaving and danger!

Captain Scott's. There's even an annual BisqueFest, when four different types of bisque are served and four separate bands perform throughout the day.

The layout of the place is linear, in keeping with the long, narrow shape of the property. First there's

LANDLUBBERS			
Hamburger	2.95	w/cheese	3.25
Long Hot Dog	2.75	w/cheese 3.00	w/kraut 3.25
Grilled Chicken Sandwich			5.95
Chicken Tenders w/fries		5.95	7.95

LOBSTER DINNERS
served with corn on the cob, red potatoes or fries, and coleslaw

1 1/4 lb. shore	mkt.
Twin Cull-2 one claw lobsters	mkt.
larger sized lobsters also available	

The good captain and his lobster dinners menu.

the shack, with its awning-shaded order and pickup windows facing downtown New London. In front of that are 14 open-air picnic tables, followed by an open-air shingled pavilion with another 18 sheltered picnic tables, followed by 10 or so additional open-air tables on the other side of the pavilion—all lined up in shotgun fashion. If she were so inclined, Sue could host quite an Oktoberfest with this setup. (Captain Scott's is BYO, by the way.)

Lotsa Lobster

Lobster leads the list with dinners that feature a steamed lobster (choose your size), accompanied by corn on the cob, red potatoes or french fries, and coleslaw. Their lobsters come from Garbo Lobster, a major distributor based in Maine with a branch in nearby Groton. Steamers are also available, if you want to have a true shore dinner. There's also a tasty lobster

bisque, with big chunks of lobster meat in a creamy, sherry-infused broth.

The lobster rolls come in both hot and cold styles and in two sizes. The hot version, which is the most popular, features fresh chunks of lobster meat bathed in melted butter and served on a toasted bun. The cold roll has lobster meat tossed in mayonnaise, a small amount of finely diced celery, and a dash of pepper. It's also served on a toasted bun with a crispy piece of lettuce between bun and meat. The large roll (hot and cold) has 4 ounces of meat in a foot-long bun, and the smaller version has about an ounce less of meat and comes on a standard hot dog roll.

Sue says the fish-and-chips dinner is one of the most popular items from the deep fryers, but she's partial to the sea scallops that brother Mark harvests for Captain Scott's when they're in season. All the deep-fried seafood dinners, which come with red potatoes or fries and coleslaw, are more than reasonably priced, which makes this place popular with seafood-hungry families.

Before you go, be sure to check out the small ice-cream stand next to the food windows. It serves Gifford's ice cream, a real treat from central Maine that's quite hard to find in southern New England. As you drive back out to civilization, with ice-cream cone in hand, you'll still probably marvel that such a charming place exists in the tangled, contradictory heart of New London, Connecticut.

Abbott's Lobster in the Rough

Each year in the spring, **Abbott's Lobster** in the Rough holds a contest to see who will be the first in line to order a lobster when Abbott's opens up on the first Friday in May. In 2011 the Lynch family of Bridgewater, Connecticut, took top honors when they arrived on Wednesday, May 4, spent two nights sleeping in their SUV (their dog, Max, with them), and were queued up at the head of the line when the order window opened precisely at noon on Friday, May 6. Sitting by the waterside a short while later, enjoying their long-anticipated meal, the entire Lynch clan agreed it was well worth the wait.

Such is the fanaticism that Abbott's engenders among its large and loyal fan base. This place is the King Kong of lobster shacks in southern New England, known far and wide as an absolutely great place to spend a summer afternoon or evening, enjoying fresh lobsters and clams on the beautiful banks of Noank Harbor.

117 Pearl Street, Noank, CT

860-536-7719

www.abbotts-lobster.com

Open early May to mid-October

A Long and Colorful History

Abbott's was founded more than 50 years ago by Ernie Abbott, who bought an old chowder and bisque cannery on Noank harbor and converted it into a large, airy lobster shack with lots of picnic tables scattered around the grounds. Regular customers Jerry and Ruth Mears used to sit at the tables by the water during their frequent visits in the 1970s, enjoying their lobster feasts and gazing out on the beautiful harbor and the islands beyond.

At the time, Jerry was a research scientist at Pfizer Inc.'s massive research facility in nearby Groton, and Ruth worked in the nascent cable

Dining on Abbott's dock is the way to go.

television industry. Nearing retirement at Pfizer, Jerry wondered what it would be like to run a fun place like Abbott's, with its crazy/busy summers tempered by long breaks much of the rest of the year.

Abbott passed away in the mid-1970s, and his daughter ran the shack for several years. When she decided to sell it in the early 1980s, Jerry and Ruth bought Abbott's, said goodbye to their previous careers, and became the wide-eyed, eager new owners. Both quickly found that the learning curve was much steeper than it appeared to be when they dreamed about the business from their perches on the picnic tables as customers. But they persevered, and Abbott's kept rolling along into the 1980s.

The Mears's daughter Deirdre helped out with the business when she wasn't in school or traveling during her college years. She watched her parents initially struggle to keep Abbott's on an even keel, and

she played an increasingly important part in the management of the place as the years went by. She eventually became the owner.

Deirdre recalls that Abbott's got its big break in the mid-1980s when *Roadfood* authors Jane and Michael Stern wrote a glowing review of the place for the *Hartford Courant* newspaper. Up to that point, most of Abbott's customers were loyal locals; now people started coming to the shack from all over southern New England and beyond. A few years later, *Gourmet* magazine named Abbott's one of the ten top lobster shacks in the country, and the place has been hopping ever since.

Low-Steaming the Lobsters

From the beginning, Abbott's has used a method of low-steaming their lobsters in drawer-sized cast-iron vaults that were built in the 1960s. Each of the 15 steamer vaults in Abbott's kitchen seals shut with a hand-cranked wheel; the setup resembles something you might see in the engine room of a World War II–vintage ship. The kitchen crew loads the lobsters into a vault, seals it shut with a spin of the wheel, and activates the steam, which comes from Abbott's massive gas-fired boiler. It's an old-fashioned-cooking method that takes a little more time than modern steaming

Owner Dierdre Mears demonstrates the vintage low-steam cookers in Abbott's kitchen.

methods, but it produces a perfectly cooked lobster with firm meat and all of its natural flavor intact.

The lobsters at Abbott's have traditionally been of local origin, but in the past 10 years or so, most now come from Canada and Maine. Abbott's sells tens of thousands of lobsters every summer, and their 15 low-steam vaults are taxed to the max between Memorial Day and Labor Day. Lobster dinners feature a steamed lobster weighing 1¼ pounds and up (your choice), coleslaw, potato chips (Wachusett chips from Fitchburg, Massachusetts), and of course, a generous cup of melted butter.

The (Hot) Lobster Roll Rocks

As is the case with many lobster shacks these days, lobster-roll sales are, well, on a roll. It seems that many people love eating lobster but don't want to do battle by cracking the shells and wrestling the sweet lobster meat out of its former owner. So a nice, neat sandwich laden with fresh-picked lobster meat is the preferred route for an increasing number of customers.

Abbott's hot lobster roll is famous throughout southern New England and with good reason. You get about 4 ounces of meat that's been packed into a souf-flé cup for warming, then upended on a toasted, buttered hamburger bun with a final drizzling of warm butter over the meat.

There's also a traditional cold lobster roll served on a toasted, split-top hot dog bun. The lobster is mixed with a bit of celery and Abbott's house dressing. Both styles of lobster roll are served with a bag of Wachusett potato chips and dill pickle chips.

Because the fresh steamed lobsters usually take

ABBOTT'S HOT LOBSTER ROLL

It's said that Helen of Troy had a face that launched a thousand ships. It may also be said that Abbott's hot lobster roll has launched a thousand SUVs—and that's just in any given summer month! You can get your lobster roll at Abbott's either hot or cold, but hot is definitely the way to go. It's the traditional method of preparing a lobster roll along Connecticut's shoreline, and the hot, buttered style is spreading to other parts of New England.

Like many lobster-roll recipes, Abbott's is quite simple, but it has a couple of twists that make it a standout among others throughout New England—namely the shaping of the lobster meat in a soufflé cup and the type of bun on which it's served.

INGREDIENTS

1	cup (4 ounces) coarsely chopped cooked lobster meat
2	tablespoons melted top quality butter
1	hamburger roll
	dill pickle slices

Pack the lobster meat into a 4-ounce soufflé cup or other small microwaveable container. Warm the meat through in a micro-wave (20 to 40 seconds) while toasting the hamburger bun in a toaster or on a griddle. Place the heated lobster meat on the toasted bun by carefully turning over the soufflé cup. Pour the melted butter over the lobster meat. Serve with a couple of sliced dill pickle chips as garnish. Serves 1. Increase ingredient amounts proportionately for additional servings, making rolls one at a time for best flavor.

a while to prepare, Abbott's has an excellent "Abbot-tizer's Special" to keep your stomach from rumbling until your steamed bug is ready. This tasty, tasteful appetizer plate features fresh uncooked vegetables, fresh fruit, cheese, crackers, and Abbott's own dipping sauce. You may upsize this snack into a meal if you're a vegetarian or if lobster isn't your thing.

Abbott's sits on the banks of scenic Noank Harbor.

There are also some tempting boiled jumbo shrimp, served with Abbott's flavorful cocktail sauce, that come half a dozen to a serving. Other appetizers and side dishes include clear-broth Rhode Island–style clam chowder, lobster bisque, crab cakes, steamed clams and mussels, and on weekends a raw bar that features oysters and clams on the half shell. Also, consider trying a stuffed clam—a mixture of finely minced clam meat and herbs in a bread stuffing that's packed into a good-sized quahog clamshell.

Two more dinners of note: If you really want to experience Abbott's to the fullest, order the New England Seafood Feast. It starts with clam chowder and chilled, boiled shrimp, followed by a large bowl of steamed clams and mussels, and finishes with a steamed lobster, butter, pickles, and chips. And for those disinclined toward seafood, there's a crispy, tender, oven-roasted half chicken.

The Abbott's Dining Experience

In addition to the amazingly fresh seafood, Abbott's offers a wonderful setting for a meal outdoors, with great harbor views, lots of activity, and a good vibe all around. Abbott's does get very crowded in the summertime, especially at lunch and dinner and even more so on weekends. So, for a more low-pressure experience, try midweek, midafternoon, when the crowds have abated and the wait isn't as long.

First things first: finding Abbott's is a bit of a challenge. If you've got GPS, you should be fine; if you don't, just take your time and follow the signs to Noank, a pleasant seaside village just west of the more famous town of Mystic. Once you're in town, you'll see a sign or two pointing you in the right direction, and you'll know you're almost there when you encounter six speed bumps over a quarter-mile stretch of Pearl Street as it runs alongside Noank Harbor to your left.

Once you've found Abbott's and parked, take a walk toward the cheerful red-and-white awning that covers Abbott's large front porch and order window. You may encounter a long line at the busiest times, but it moves quickly. The menu is posted on the wall and on a freestanding board next to the window, so be ready to order when it's your turn. Once your order is in, step around or through the building and scope out a place to sit at any of the dozens of open-air picnic tables.

While you're waiting for your order number to be called over the loudspeaker, soak in the magnificent views of Noank Harbor, which is home to all sorts of watercraft—from dinghies to old-fashioned schooners to luxurious motorized yachts and tall-masted sailboats. Some Abbott's customers come by boat and tie up to Abbott's dock. You can see three states from Abbott's: Connecticut; Fisher's Island, which is off to the right and is part of New York; and Watch Hill, Rhode Island, straight offshore in the distance, about 10 miles away.

Abbott's Anti-Aircraft

Also, gaze skyward and take note of the series of thin, parallel wires strung above the outdoor dining area. They resemble an array of small clotheslines, but they're there to discourage ravenous seagulls from making off with your food. The wires are spaced about a foot apart, which is enough to discourage any avian incursions.

For your further entertainment, go out on the white-and-red-painted dock and gaze over the edge, where you'll see good-sized striped bass waiting for oyster crackers to be thrown to them by Abbott's patrons. The crackers are fine for the fish to snack on, but Abbott's warns against feeding them anything else.

When your order number's called, go back inside to the Big Red Counter (not back to the order window), and your food will be waiting there for you. Abbott's is a BYO establishment for beer and wine, but you must purchase all nonalcoholic beverages on the premises. Be sure to check out the desserts while at the order window because there are some great cakes, sundaes, and shortcake as well as a small ice-cream stand next to the main shack. Count on spending at least a couple of hours at Abbott's, because once you settle down by the water and gaze out at the boats, you're not going to want to leave any time soon.

No Deep-Fried? No Problem!

Abbott's doesn't have any deep fryers on the premises to cook up breaded shellfish or fries or onion rings. What they do have is a companion restaurant a couple hundred yards or so to the south. At Costello's Clam Shack, you can get any sort of deep-fried goodies you want.

If your group is split between steamed lobsters and deep-fried food, Abbott's will gladly phone your order over to Costello's, and you can walk over, pick it up, walk back, and enjoy it in Abbott's dining area. Keep in mind that Costello's has a killer second-floor, open-air deck with commanding views of the same harbor that Abbott's gazes upon. So you may want to walk your lobsters over there and enjoy them with your fried clams and scallops. (Or you can order lobsters cooked on the premises at Costello's.) Either way, you're going to like what you see *and* what you eat! (Call 860-572-2779; or visit www.costellosclamshack.com.)

Champlin's Seafood Restaurant

256 Great Island Road, Galilee, RI

401-783-3152

www.champlins.com

Open year-round

If you happen to be in the Galilee section of Narragansett, perhaps hanging out at one of the nearby state beaches or coming to or from Block Island on the ferry, Champlin's is your one-stop source for whole steamed lobsters and other seafood, and for dining in-the-rough on a deck outdoors or in the comfort of one of Champlin's indoor, enclosed dining rooms.

Co-owner Brian Handrigan says that Champlin's can accommodate almost 400 diners at a time between all their various indoor and outdoor seating areas; and in the middle of summer, they frequently reach that capacity. Don't let that deter you; Champlin's knows how to handle a crowd of hungry seafood seekers, and they'll treat you well from the time you arrive until you walk out the door in search of more seaside fun.

A Seafood Fun Palace

Champlin's is housed in a sprawling, two-story building situated along the docks in Galilee, next to other commercial fishing operations and restaurants, and a couple hundred yards or so up the road from the Block Island ferry terminal. It's the perfect spot for Champlin's wholesale and retail seafood businesses and for their renowned dine-in-the-rough eatery.

There's a lot going on in this place. For starters, the excellent retail market is front and center on the first floor. Walk through the front door, and you're immediately greeted with the smell of fresh fish and

The Stairway to Champlin's upstairs seafood deck.

other seafood, much of which is on display in glass cases right across from the door. They also ice down fish fillets and several different types of clams and put them out on tables around the concrete-floored room for your perusal and selection.

On one side of the market are a couple of aquamarine cold-water lobster tanks where you can pick your own lobster and have it sent upstairs to be cooked. (There's a two-dollar service charge for the cooking and butter, but you save money over what you'd pay if you ordered upstairs.) There are always plenty of bugs to choose from at Champlin's because they've got 18 inshore boats and one or two deepwater boats regularly delivering their catches to Champlin's commercial dock out back. The best lobsters come into the seafood market or are taken straight upstairs to the kitchen.

Once you're done checking out the market, go back outside and seek out one of the outdoor staircases that lead to the second-floor restaurant. On busy summer days, they won't be hard to find because there's often a line trailing down the stairs and along the street. Grab a paper menu and begin studying it so you're ready to place your order when you make it to the order window.

A Waterfront Fixture for Decades

Champlin's got its start in 1932 as a small seafood market, buying its wares from the local fishing boats and selling to locals and tourists who were in search of fresh fish and shellfish. Retailing led to

Lobster dinner at Champlin's.

wholesaling (it's usually the other way around), and Champlin's presence on the Galilee docks (home to Rhode Island's largest commercial fishing fleet) grew steadily. Soon, seafood from Champlin's was being trucked to such faraway places as the Fulton Fish Market in New York City and the Fish Pier in Boston. Lobsters have always been a big part of their wholesale business and their identity as a large regional wholesaler.

With all the locals and tourists coming and going between the nearby state beaches, Block Island, and the other local attractions, it seemed inevitable that an eatery would become part of the mix. Champlin's restaurant opened its doors in the early 1960s.

It started as an in-the-rough operation, with an order and pickup counter and a bunch of picnic tables outside around the seafood market and by the docks. A second-floor seafood deck was built next to the order/pickup counter, and a couple of pine-paneled indoor dining rooms were added over the years. Now there are about half a dozen different places to sit and eat on the premises, perhaps the most attractive being the outdoor deck overlooking Galilee's commercial harbor. You can watch the fishing boats and the Block Island ferry come and go all day long.

Some Lobster Facts

Champlin's catches and sells tens of thousands of pounds of lobsters every year, and they've become experts on the subject of *Homarus americanus*. Here are some lobster facts, as gleaned from Champlin's entertaining and informative carryout menu, which you'll probably have time to study while you wait in line to order your lobster.

- ▶ Lobsters take 18 to 24 months to develop from the time of impregnation to the hatching of the egg.
- ▶ An infant lobster is the size of a mosquito when it leaves its mother's body.
- ▶ As a lobster grows, it sheds its shell, increasing in weight by 25 percent each time.
- ▶ A lobster will shed its shell 24 times in its first year of life.
- ▶ A mature lobster molts once every year or so, sometimes longer.
- ▶ A lobster is approximately seven years old before it's legal to harvest. It will weigh approximately 1 pound at that point.
- ▶ A lobster's age in years may be determined by taking its weight in pounds, multiplying that by four, then adding three. (Who figured *that* out?)

Watch Out for the Clam Bake!

On the lobster side of the menu, there's a thick, creamy, flavorful lobster bisque for openers that's chock-full of freshly picked lobster meat. The Lobster Dinner features a 1¼-pound bug trimmed out with coleslaw and a choice of red potatoes or french fries. A couple of add-ons that will make for a true shore dinner are a quart of steamers and perhaps an ear of native corn on the cob. The Twin Lobster Dinner consists of lobsters only; anything else (if you have room) is à la carte.

The real belt-buster at Champlin's is what they call the Clam Bake. It's not baked, but it does have clams, along with a whole bunch of other stuff, including lobster, mussels, corn on the cob, fried flounder, and Italian sausage. Sounds like a good dish to share with a loved one, doesn't it?

Champlin's lobster roll, a very popular choice in the summertime, is a cold roll with a bit of mayo and diced celery, served on a piece of lettuce and wedged into a toasted, split-top bun. There's also a ton of deep-fried seafood offerings of every sort, and the portions are enormous, so order prudently in terms of quantity.

Before You Depart . . .

A couple more fun things to do at Champlin's before going forth to walk off that meal: First, check out the gallery of historical photos lining the walls in the pine-paneled dining rooms next to the order window. There are shots of Champlin's when it first started

From Champlin's deck, you can almost reach out and touch the Block Island ferry.

out as a modest seafood market; a bunch of photos showing the often-extensive damage that Champlin's has sustained from a number of hurricanes; and even some whimsical shots of two feet and more of snow piled on top of the seafood deck tables in winter. Photos of many of the boats that have serviced Champlin's over the years also grace the walls.

Speaking of Champlin's ambassadors on the sea, go outside and take a look at all the lifesaving ring buoys around the perimeter of the building's facade. Each has the name of a boat that has at one time or another sailed and fished as part of Champlin's dedicated fleet.

And finally, don't forget to duck into the first-floor Champlin's ice-cream stand, which is located between the seafood market and the docks. Grab a cone or a sundae as a digestif, then start walking off those calories. A great place for a stroll is down the street toward the Block Island Ferry docks. There are a couple of kitschy, souvenir-type shops and a couple of bar-type establishments that are always hopping in the summertime. For a quieter constitutional, try heading the other way out of Champlin's and take a short walk to check out the nearby Salty Brine State Beach or the more distant Point Judith Lighthouse. Champlin's is a great place to begin or end any day of fun and exploration in southwestern Rhode Island. Have a great time, and try not to overdo it!

Aunt Carrie's

✕ 1240 Ocean Road, Narragansett, RI

☎ 401-783-7930

🦞 www.auntcarriesri.com

Open early April to late September

Aunt Carrie's has been around for nearly a hundred years, and it is perhaps best known as the place where the clam cake is said to have been invented. And, though clams in all their forms (fried, stripped, caked, chowdered) may be enjoyed here on any warm summer day or night, those in the know come to Aunt Carrie's for the magnificent lobster and the amazing variety of shore dinners trimmed out with whole lobsters, steamed clams, corn, chowder, and more.

The Aunt Carrie's Story

In the early 1900s a woman named Carrie Cooper, her husband, and their children used to make regular trips from their home in Connecticut to the beaches in southwestern Rhode Island to camp out and enjoy short holidays by the sea. Narragansett was their usual destination, and to make their sojourns more affordable, they started selling fresh-squeezed lemonade to the local fishermen and fellow tourists. Lemonade led to clam chowder, which eventually led to the aforementioned clam cakes, which Carrie concocted by dicing up some freshly dug-up clams from the beach and mixing them into her corn fritters, then frying them up in the family skillet.

The clam cakes and chowder developed a devoted following, and the Coopers decided to open a seasonal snack stand near the current location of Point Judith lighthouse. They eventually bought a small piece of land a mile or so north of the lighthouse, where they built the Aunt Carrie's that we know today. It's been updated and added on to over the years, but the building still retains all the cedar-shingled,

The hardworking counter crew at Aunt Carrie's.

storm-shuttered charm of the original shack.

The Cooper family is currently in the third and fourth generations of Aunt Carrie's ownership, and they're gearing up for the big 100th anniversary, which will occur in 2020. (You can never start planning centennial celebrations too soon.) Elsie Cooper is currently the matriarchal head of the clan and business, and she takes great pride in all that her family has accomplished over the years.

Shore Dinners, Rhode Island Style

Though Aunt Carrie's started as a shack and continues with the grand tradition of ordering at a takeout window and dining in the rough, one of the building expansions created a full-service dining room that wraps around one side and the back of the original building. It's become very popular for beachgoers to come down from Scarborough State Beach to the north and the Block Island ferry dock area to the south, grab a table in the dining room, and tuck into an old-fashioned Rhode Island shore dinner.

You'd better be hungry when you order the Shore Dinner at Aunt Carrie's, because the food just keeps on coming. You begin with a bowl of clam chowder. There are three kinds to choose from: milk, which is similar in color to classic New England clam chowder, though not as thick in consistency; tomato, a red-hued chowder made with fresh tomatoes and not to be confused with Manhattan clam chowder; and plain chowder—the classic Rhode Island version, which consists of clams, potatoes, and flavorful broth.

How to Eat a Lobster

There are several schools of thought on the best way to eat a lobster, each with its merits. Here is one of the more generally accepted methods. You'll see some version of it imprinted on plates, platters, and place mats at lobster joints throughout New England.

1. Twist off the claws.
2. Crack each claw with a nutcracker, remove the broken pieces of shell, and carefully extract the claw meat in one piece, if possible.
3. Use the nutcracker to break open the knuckles at the base of the claw, and use a small fork or your pinkie finger to push out the tender knuckle meat.
4. Separate the tailpiece from the main body by arching the back until it cracks. (An alternative is to twist the tailpiece until it separates from the body. This often causes less "collateral damage" from water and bits of lobster flying loose, which can occur during the arching method.)
5. Grasp the flippers on the tailpiece, bend them back, and break them off, one by one. Insert a fork or your finger where the flippers were removed and carefully push the tail meat out of the larger end of the tail shell.
6. Unhinge the back and remove the outer shell. The green mass inside is the liver—a delicacy to many lobster connoisseurs.
7. Open the body by cracking it sideways. Poke around carefully in this section to find more meat near where the small legs meet the body.
8. Take each of the small legs, break them open at the joints, and suck the meat out (or squeeze it out using your teeth).
9. Dispose of your lobster shells thoughtfully.
10. If you're still hungry, order up another bug and repeat the entire process!

Next up is a full quart of steamed clams, served with melted butter. Then it's on to the main course, a one-two punch of a fish-and-chips plate—which includes fries or mashed potatoes, salad or coleslaw, and a slice of homemade bread—and a 1¼-pound lobster. Carrie's gets its lobster from the nearby port of Galilee a mile or so to the south, and there are fresh shipments every day. They boil them up to a nice crimson color in their gas-fired cooker in the kitchen.

Still not full? The Shore Dinner also includes one of Aunt Carrie's famous homemade desserts. You may choose from a half-dozen different pies, or there's Indian pudding, ice cream, and strawberry shortcake (when strawberries are in season). Elsie's daughter, Laura, does a lot of the baking in the kitchen, and there are always lots of fresh pies, loaves of bread, and other goodies coming out of the ovens to enjoy with your meal or to take with you on the road.

If all this seems too much to handle, you may opt to leave the lobster off the list, but why bother? If anything, that freshly cooked lobster meat will simply serve as a palate cleanser between the main course and dessert. There's also a mini Shore Dinner option with less of everything on it but quite a feast nonetheless.

Hot *and* Cold Lobster Rolls

The lobster roll at Aunt Carrie's won a Best of Rhode Island 2009 award from *Rhode Island Monthly* magazine, indicative of the high quality that Aunt Carrie's puts into its lobster offerings.

You may get your roll either cold and mixed with mayonnaise or hot and served with a side of freshly drawn butter. Both are chock-full of succulent lobster meat picked fresh that day, and you have your choice between a grilled and buttered roll or Aunt Carrie's fresh homemade bread. Carrie's has also come up with its own version of the BLT: a bacon, *lobster*, and tomato sandwich. It's served on lightly toasted homemade bread, and it's a tasty variation on an American classic.

There's More across the Street

A few years back, Elsie Cooper decided to open a shingled ice-cream stand and gift shop across the street from the restaurant. Aunt Carrie's Ice Cream Shoppe features over 40 different flavors from the Ice Cream Machine, a confectionary company in Cumberland, Rhode Island. You may also get the same fine pie offerings as those across the street at the shack—only here, they're offered in the form of frappes (aka milk shakes). And for those with a hankering for something thirst quenching, try a cool, slushy Del's frozen lemonade.

Aunt Carrie's has become a time-honored summertime tradition among Rhode Islanders and those who travel back and forth between nearby Block Island and the mainland. All the wooden-shingled charm of the building and the solid, delectable offerings on the menu make this place a classic that's destined to be around for another hundred years, maybe more.

Blount Clam Shack

Blount's Giant
Lobster Roll.

🍴 335 Water Street, Warren, Rhode Island

☎ 401-245-3210

🦞 www.blountseafood.com

Open May to early September

IF YOU SEEK THE BIG KAHUNA OF LOBSTER ROLLS in eastern Rhode Island, you should pay a visit to the twin blue trailers of Blount Clam Shack. This quaint operation is perched on the edge of Warren, Rhode Island's busy and colorful waterfront on the upper reaches of Narragansett Bay, several miles southeast of Providence.

The shack is best known for its deep-fried seafood and for its out-of-this-world chowders. Its parent company, Blount Seafood, is one of the premier purveyors of gourmet chowders to restaurants and gourmet food shops around the country. But when you're sizing up the clam shack's menu board in front of the trailers, it's hard to ignore the banner-like announcement that claims Blount to be "Home of the Giant Lobster Roll."

For $19.99 you can get an oversized 5 ounces of fresh-picked chunks of lobster meat (claw, tail, and knuckle), served on a nine-inch-long toasted bun and garnished with a tangy dill/mayo sauce that's spread on the bun and drizzled on top of the lobster meat. Blount uses select claw and knuckle meat and no shredded meat from the legs or tail. French fries and coleslaw are included as part of the package.

The big roll and trimmings go great with a cup of Blount's famous chowder and perhaps a cold draft beer from their Express Trailer, which serves only chowder, clam cakes, and beer or wine.

There are two other Blount Clam Shack locations—one in Crescent Park in East Providence and another, newer one in Fall River, Massachusetts. Each serves a standard cold lobster roll mixed with mayo. But you can only get the Giant Lobster Roll at the Warren location, and they close right after Labor Day every year. So what are you waiting for?

Anthony's Seafood

963 Aquidneck Avenue,
Middletown, RI

☎ 401-846-9620

🦞 www.anthonysseafood.com

Open year-round

Not far from the madding crowds of downtown Newport, yet far enough to allow for a spacious, airy dining room and hassle-free parking, you'll find one of the area's best places to get lobster and all sorts of other seafood—and to enjoy it in a relaxed, casual, dine-in-the-rough atmosphere to boot. And, by Newport's standards, it's also quite easy on the pocketbook!

Anthony's Seafood has deep roots in the Newport community, and it's the seafood place of choice for more locals than any other restaurant around. Co-owner Steve Bucolo is thankful for the legions of loyal patrons who frequent Anthony's—and they do so throughout the year, without being scared off by the hordes of tourists that invade Newport each summer. That's because Anthony's is a 10-minute drive north of downtown Newport on Aquidneck Avenue in the town of Middletown, only several miles away by car but worlds away in terms of sanity.

Roots on the Newport Docks

Anthony's founder, Anthony T. Bucolo, opened a wholesale lobster company on Spring Wharf in downtown Newport in 1956. Over the next 30 years, he expanded into the wholesale fish business and seafood production while continuing his lobster wholesaling. Many local restaurants depended on regular, daily shipments from Anthony's for the freshest lobsters and seafood around.

In the early 1970s Anthony decided to open a retail seafood market on the wharf, and it was a hit. By 1980, the modern Anthony's began to take shape when Bucolo and his eldest son, Steve, opened the

Anthony's owners Steve (left) and Mike Bucolo.

SS Newport, a floating dockside restaurant in downtown Newport.

After suffering a heart attack in 1986, Anthony retired and sold the business to an outsider; Steve and his brother, Michael, stayed on. Things didn't go well under the new ownership, and Anthony felt compelled to buy back the business in 1989 and put his sons in charge. Steve and Michael have been running Anthony's Seafood ever since.

The amazing seafood counter at Anthony's.

In the late 1990s, things were getting awfully expensive in downtown Newport, and Anthony's was serving a bigger and bigger crowd of regular customers from the cities of Middletown and Portsmouth to the north. So they decided to move the business to a less expensive, more centrally located (for locals, anyway) spot on the main thoroughfare running right up the middle of Aquidneck Island. For the past 14 years, Anthony's has thrived in its Middletown location, where it still operates as a seafood wholesaler, a fish market, and a wonderful, casual restaurant.

Outstanding Food in a Nondescript Setting

Anthony's is located along a commercial stretch of Aquidneck Avenue, mixed in with all sorts of suburban-looking businesses. The building is set back from the street about a hundred feet, allowing for ample free parking (a blessing in the Newport area) in its asphalted front yard. The building's facade looks more like a seafood wholesale operation, with its boxy, warehouse-like appearance. The only thing that tips you off to the good things inside are the half dozen or so picnic tables with umbrellas out front. (Anthony's is in the process of spiffing up the outdoor eating area with a new canopy over the tables and a refurbished facade.)

Step inside and you are face-to-face with a gorgeous, 28-foot-long glass case filled with the freshest seafood on shaved ice that you're likely to see anywhere. From local clams, oysters, scallops, fish fillets, and prepared seafood dishes to super-fresh wild Alaskan salmon, Anthony's market has everything in the way of fresh seafood.

Down at the right-hand end of the seafood display case is an order counter for those wishing to dine at Anthony's. There are lots of copies of the menu to pick up and peruse before placing your order. Once you do, you'll be given a foot-tall metal pole with a rounded base for setting on your table and a plastic card displaying a numeral on the top to identify your order number. Go grab a seat in either of the two spacious indoor dining areas or at one of the tables outside; place your order number stick on your table; and a server will bring your made-to-order meal right to your table when it's ready.

To alleviate any confusion in the ordering and

seating processes, especially during busy summer evenings, Steve and his sister, Lisa, act as constantly vigilant hosts, helping guide people to open tables and giving them some idea how long they may be waiting in line or waiting for their food. Michael Bucolo runs the seafood market and pitches in on the restaurant side as needed. And Steve's son Logan is starting to learn the ropes at Anthony's. It's truly a family operation.

A Time-Tested Menu

Over 50 years in the seafood business has given the Bucolos plenty of time and valuable experience in shaping their menu into something that is outstanding and worth the short drive from downtown Newport. There's a wide variety of seafood dishes—fried, baked, boiled, grilled, you name it. They've taken their time with recipes and dishes, trying a few new things on the menu each year, sticking with those that work, and jettisoning those that don't.

Lobster has always been an important part of the mix at Anthony's, and it shows in the current offerings. First, there's the boiled lobster dinners, which typically come with 1¼- and 1¾-pound lobsters and include locally grown corn on the cob and boiled potatoes. There's a big lobster-boiling pot in Anthony's large, busy kitchen that doubles as a chowder maker at the beginning of the day, so it's always filled with plenty of good seafood flavor.

Then there's the Shore Dinner, which consists of steamers, mussels, Portuguese chourico (pronounced shor-EESE) sausage, corn, potatoes, onions, broth, and butter—quite a seafood feast that's served in a large bowl, almost like a bouillabaisse. Lobster and shore dinners come together in the colossal New England Mega Meal, where you add a lobster (either size) to your Shore Dinner for a belt-busting bowl of seafood fun.

Anthony's lobster-salad roll distinguishes itself first and foremost by its size. You get a full 6 ounces of fresh-picked lobster meat that's tossed with mayonnaise, a small amount of finely chopped celery, and a dash of white pepper. It's served on a foot-long, New England–style hot dog bun, which makes for one of the biggest lobster rolls you may ever see. The roll comes with french fries and coleslaw and is priced in the vicinity of $18.50.

There's also a worthy baked, stuffed lobster that's only served during the winter season, in an attempt to lure in locals on a year-round basis. Give it a try if you happen to be at Anthony's when it appears on the specials menu.

Other Items of Note at Anthony's

One of the standouts at Anthony's is the Portuguese Fish Chowder. This spicy, flavorful dish contains fresh cod, shrimp, scallops, and chourico. Served by the cup or bowl, it's not to be missed.

Stuffed quahog clams, aka stuffies, are another popular opener here. Anthony's stuffs theirs with minced clams, chourico, onions, peppers, and spices. You can get them seasoned mild or hot.

The deep fryers remain constantly busy here, cooking up whole-belly clams, fish-and-chips (cod or flounder—your choice), shrimp, scallops, calamari, french fries, and onion rings. For those wishing to avoid deep-fried and boiled dinners, there's a very nice baked stuffed sole topped with a creamy lobster sauce at a more than reasonable price. (It helps to be in the seafood-wholesaling business—you get a constant supply of the freshest stuff with which to stock your restaurant, at very reasonable prices.)

There are also a few tasty, grilled fish fillets: swordfish with pesto or garlic herb butter; tuna steak with apricot ginger teriyaki; and salmon with pesto marinara. Seafood not your thing? There are several possibilities, including a half-pound burger, chicken tenders, a buffalo chicken sandwich, and a very good baked eggplant Parmesan.

What with all the chourico sausage in many of these dishes, you may be led to think that the Bucolos are Portuguese. No, they're Sicilian. However, as Steve says, "In this part of Rhode Island, the Italian, Portuguese, and Greek cultures have come together, the foods have blended, and the outcome is some very good eating." You can say that again!

ANTHONY'S PORTUGUESE FISH CHOWDER

There are fish chowders, and then there are *fish chowders*, concoctions that just hit it out of the park. Anthony's Portuguese Fish Chowder is one of those four-baggers. Creamy, spicy, flavorful, and full of fresh seafood and spicy sausage, it's a meal unto itself and a crowd-pleasing comfort food.

INGREDIENTS

1	tablespoon lightly salted butter	⅓	cup flour
2	tablespoons diced celery	2	cups clam juice
3	tablespoons diced onion	½	pound medium raw shrimp (peeled and deveined)
1¼	cup diced chourico (smoked Portuguese sausage)	½	pound sliced sea scallops
½	cup white wine	1	pound chunked codfish (or other medium-firm white fish)
	pinch of red chili pepper flakes		
	pinch black pepper	2½	cups diced potatoes, cooked firm
½	tablespoon paprika	3	teaspoons fresh parsley
1	tablespoon Tabasco sauce	3 to 4	cups half-and-half

Heat a heavy skillet to medium high and melt the butter slowly. Sauté the celery, onion, and chourico until vegetables are translucent and chourico is lightly cooked. Add white wine, red chili pepper flakes, pepper, paprika, Tabasco, and mix together. Slowly add flour, stirring constantly over medium-high heat, to make a roux that's dark and paste-like in consistency. Add the clam juice and whisk vigorously until smooth. Add the shrimp, scallops, and codfish. Bring to a simmer, then add the cooked potatoes and parsley. Before serving, slowly add the half-and-half and heat until steaming, not boiling, stirring constantly. Serves 10–12.

CAPE COD SHACKS

When you venture onto Cape Cod, you're starting to enter the land of the lobster. Virtually all restaurants on the Cape serve lobster in one form or another—from whole lobsters to lobster rolls to lobster bisques and stews. Lobster is more plentiful in this region's coastal waters than in places farther south, and Cape Cod shack owners take advantage of the local bounty.

There are dozens of dine-in-the-rough places to enjoy lobster each night during summer on the Cape, and among those are 10 places that really do it right. Some serve only lobster rolls and lobster bisque; others go all the way, with whole lobsters, rolls, bisque, stew, salad, and many more unusual and exotic dishes.

The inner Cape, from Buzzards Bay, Bourne, and Sandwich east to Chatham and Orleans, is a bustling tourist zone, particularly in the southern reaches. The inner Cape's northern realms, along the southern shore of Cape Cod Bay, features some lovely towns, like Dennis and Brewster, where the shacks tend to be a bit more elegant.

Heading farther north into the outer Cape, between Orleans and Provincetown, you'll find some excellent places to enjoy lobsters that were most likely trapped somewhere nearby that same day in places like Eastham, Wellfleet, and Provincetown.

Regardless of where you set up camp on the Cape and where you seek out your lobster feast, you're in for a treat in this one-of-a-kind lobster-lover's vacationland.

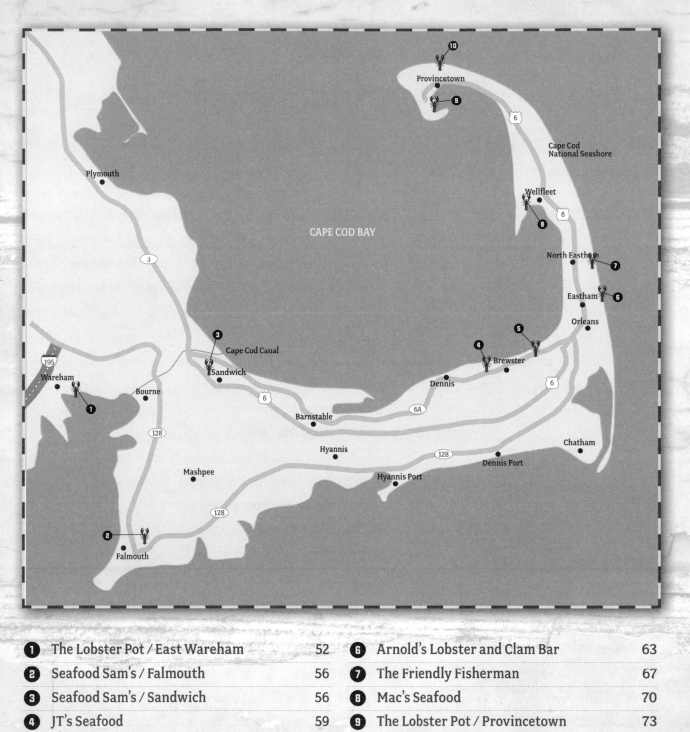

The Lobster Pot

3155 Cranberry Highway, East Wareham, MA

☎ 508-759-3876

🦞 www.lobsterpotrestaurant.biz

Open early March to late November

Deep in the heart of **Cranberry Country** and just a couple of miles west of the Cape Cod Canal on the Buzzard's Bay/Wareham border sits a good-sized dine-in-the-rough lobster place on a busy highway. It has the look and feel of a middle-American roadside sandwich shop, yet in actuality, it's a lobster lover's dream come true. For more than 35 years, the Lobster Pot of East Wareham, Massachusetts, has been serving up steamed bugs to the multitudes of locals and vacationers who have been lucky enough to discover this place and make it a regular stop-off for a big lobster dinner and more.

Roots on the Boston Docks

Not to be confused with the restaurant of the same name in Provincetown, this Lobster Pot restaurant has roots going back to the early twentieth century, when Italian immigrant Gaetano Tringali bought a surplus wooden boat from the Navy in 1908 and retrofitted it into a commercial fishing vessel. With the T-Wharf in Boston Harbor as his home port, Tringali fished the local waters for decades with his two sons before selling the boat in the early 1960s. It was then shipped off to Gloucester, where it remained part of that town's active fishing fleet until just a few years ago.

Gaetano's daughter Mary opened a snack bar on the wharf in Boston, serving longshoremen while her father and brothers fished. She married Joseph Marino, and their two sons, Guy and Joe, started helping out at the snack stand before their ages hit double digits. After Gaetano sold his boat, the young Marino boys left the snack stand on the docks and began working with their father in his produce business

The Lobster Pot's order counter, with the cold-water lobster tanks off to the left.

in Boston. Eventually, they moved to East Wareham, about 50 miles south of Boston, and opened the Lobster Pot restaurant in 1975.

Initially a smallish shack by the roadside on the Cranberry Highway, a couple of expansions in the 1980s more than tripled the size of the place. With an expansive, glassed-in dining area in front and a bunch of open-air tables by the street underneath a protective awning, the stage was set for seafood fun on a large scale.

The Lobster Pot's Shore Dinner.

Guy and Joe have worked tirelessly to build their lobster shack into a premier Cape Cod seafood destination. The Lobster Pot draws heavily from the Boston and Worcester areas as well as Providence, Rhode Island. There are numerous marinas in the Wareham area where pleasure craft are docked, and the Lobster Pot is well known among the sunbathers who frequent nearby Onset Beach. This mainland part of the Cape is less well known, probably because it's west of the canal, but from the crowds that come to the Lobster Pot throughout the summer, you'd never know it.

Simple, Tasty Fare

Guy claims that simplicity is the key to their delectable seafood offerings, but there's a little more to it than that. Take their lobsters, for instance. Unlike most shacks, which buy theirs from local inshore fishermen, the Pot gets theirs from large offshore boats, which set their traps anywhere from 12 to 50 miles off the Cape Cod coast. These "megatraps" snare prime, often large, cold-water lobsters, the type preferred by many who eat lobster on a regular basis.

In addition, lobsters at the Pot are steamed in a convection steamer—a large, stainless steel contraption that can cook up to 50 lobsters at a time in a controlled environment. The end result is succulent, flavorful lobster meat that hasn't been relegated to a tank of scalding seawater. It's almost scientific the way the Marinos prepare their lobsters, and the result is consistently tasty bugs, from little 1-pounders to 10-pound behemoths. Also, the Martinos believe strongly that the customer should crack his or her own lobster, guaranteeing the freshest possible flavor, and they'll supply the tools needed to crack even the biggest of bugs served from their cold-water tanks.

A Couple of TV Awards

The Lobster Pot recently won regional TV station NECN's Best Lobster Roll in New England award for their meaty sandwich. It's a simple, well-stocked roll, consisting of 5 ounces of lobster meat mixed with just a bit of mayonnaise, and that's it. The lobster is served on a lettuce leaf tucked inside a toasted, split-top hot dog bun, and the meat dwarfs the bun beneath it. You'll definitely need the plastic fork that comes on the side to spear all those pieces of succulent lobster that cascade down the sides. The Marinos use claw and tail meat in their rolls, believing them to be best suited for their brand of lobster roll.

Chowder is another specialty here. Again, the Lobster Pot took top honors in NECN's clam chowder contest a couple of years ago, beating out such venerable institutions as Legal Sea Foods and the Union Oyster House, both in Boston. The chowder is chock-full of clams, perfectly seasoned, and thickened with real cream, not half-and-half. The Marinos say it took them 20 years to perfect their recipe and to figure out how to make it in large and consistent batches every day. People come from all over Massachusetts for just a cup or a bowl, even during the off-season times of late fall and early spring. Again, simplicity in ingredients and method of preparation are key to the chowder's well-earned reputation.

A couple of meaty lobster rolls from the Lobster Pot.

Seafood Dinners at the Pot

These come in three varieties: baked, broiled, and deep-fried. Haddock and scallop dinners are the best choices on the baked and broiled dinner selections, which include homemade coleslaw, made fresh daily, and a choice of french fries or rice pilaf.

The deep-fried dinners are far more popular, and they feature a wide variety of seafood treats, including haddock, whole-belly clams, clam strips, calamari, shrimp, scallops, and oysters. The Marinos shuck their own locally sourced clams, so they're as fresh as can be. The dinners come in plate and platter (regular and large) sizes that include french fries, coleslaw, and plenty of tartar sauce.

Getting back to the lobsters, there are a variety of dinners that feature the red crustacean. First, you can order lobsters à la carte as singles or as twins from 1⅛ pound and up. (There are some truly big ones—8 pounds and up—regularly appearing in their cold-water tanks.) Then there's the Shore Dinner, which features a lobster, steamed clams, corn on the cob, clam broth, and melted butter. Want to take it up a notch? Try the Captain's Dinner with its 1½-pound bug and all the same trimmings as the Shore Dinner. Steamed clams can be ordered à la carte as an appetizer or a meal, and there are cherrystone clams and oysters on the half shell from the Pot's raw bar.

Kids love eating at the Lobster Pot, with its open,

Hard-Shell versus Soft-Shell Lobster

In the world of lobsters, there are hard-shell ones, soft-shell ones, and some that are somewhere in between. Here's what it all means.

A hard-shell lobster is one whose outer shell is fully formed and hard to the pinch or touch. The lobster inside the shell has fully grown to fill out the shell, and the meat within is rich, dense, and tightly packed. Those who prefer to eat hard-shell lobsters claim that the meat tastes better, is more nutritious and substantial, and they're not as messy to eat.

A soft-shell lobster has recently molted out of its hard shell. Mature lobsters do this approximately once per year. A soft-shell lobster's exterior is soft to the touch and may often be cracked after cooking without having to use metal crackers or other devices. A soft-shell lobster hasn't yet grown to fill its new shell, so there's more water and less meat in it. Some people (including lots of lobstermen) prefer soft-shell lobsters for eating because they believe the meat is sweeter and more flavorful.

Hard-shell lobsters tend to be more prevalent in the spring through July or so, when molting begins. From the latter part of summer through the fall, soft-shells dominate lobstermen's catches. The soft-shells gradually transform into hard-shells, so many autumn lobsters may fall between the two classifications.

Because of the difference in meat density between the two types, hard-shells tend to cost more per pound, but you get more meat, pound for pound, in such lobsters. As far as flavor goes, it's really a matter of personal preference. So in your own lobster ramblings, try both and decide which you prefer.

informal indoor and outdoor seating. There's a children's menu that features a fish & chips boat with haddock, a clam strips boat, and a chicken finger boat. All boats come with a lightweight portion of seafood or chicken, french fries, and tartar sauce on the side.

Keep this place in mind as a great spot to kick off or wrap up a visit to the Cape. Though it's tucked away in a quiet corner of southeastern Massachusetts, it's oh-so-worth checking out for its outstanding lobster and the good value that it serves up nearly year-round.

It's hard to miss the Lobster Pot on the Cranberry Highway in East Wareham, Massachusetts.

Seafood Sam's

🍴 356 Palmer Avenue, Falmouth, MA

☎ 508-540-7877

and

🍴 6 Coast Guard Road, Sandwich, MA

☎ 508-888-4629

🦞 www.seafoodsams.com

Open early March to mid-November

One of the first shacks you'll want to check out once you've crossed either of the two bridges onto the Cape proper is Seafood Sam's. There are two Seafood Sam's locations to consider, each one strategically located not very far from the Bourne and Sagamore bridges—the only two ways to cross the Cape Cod Canal by car. These two shacks are owned and run by brothers Mike and Jeff Lewis, who have been in the seafood business for more than 30 years and who each bought a Seafood Sam's eatery from founder Sam Vecchione back in the early 1990s. (Sam, by the way, is in his late 80s and still stops in regularly for something to eat.)

It Started in a Laundromat

Back in 1974, Sam Vecchione came down to the Cape from Plymouth, Massachusetts, where he had been working at a seafood place called the Lobster Hut. Starting with only the most basic of kitchen equipment, he opened his first Seafood Sam's in East Yarmouth in an old Laundromat. Things went well, and over the next 35 years, there were as many as five Seafood Sam's locations on the Cape.

After weathering various economic ups and downs, Seafood Sam's settled down into three locations, two of which were purchased by Mike and Jeff Lewis in the early 1990s, when Sam decided to retire and sell the businesses. Mike owns the Falmouth location, and Jeff is the owner of Seafood Sam's flagship restaurant right next to the Cape Cod Canal in Sandwich.

Both locations are handsome, upscale-looking restaurants, with

Three generations of Seafood Sam's, Falmouth: owner Michael, seated, right; manager Shaun, standing; and grandson Jaelon.

meticulously kept buildings and grounds and brightly painted in Seafood Sam's trademark green and blue colors. From the outside, you'd expect to be entering a fine-dining seafood eatery, but in both instances, when you walk through the front door, you're greeted by a shining, stainless steel order counter manned by a cheerful staff of order takers. Each location has a variety of dining areas to settle into, all brightly decorated and some that feature outdoor seating. So despite the fancy look of the place inside and out, you're dining in the rough, and the atmosphere is casual and very family-friendly.

Eight Ways to Enjoy Lobster

Seafood Sam's has developed a reputation over the years for serving solid, consistent, high-quality, sometimes innovative seafood, most of it taken from local waters just off the Cape. Though Sam's is a full-blown shack with lots of deep-fried seafood, we're going to focus on the lobster portion of the menu.

Most shacks offer lobster in just a couple of ways, mostly whole and/or as a lobster roll or perhaps in a bisque. At Seafood Sam's, there are eight—count 'em—eight fine lobster entrées to enjoy, along with the chowders and deep-fried seafood platters, and other items on Sam's menu. Here they are:

1. Lobster Bisque. With a splash of sherry and lots of small chunks of lobster meat, Seafood Sam's creamy lobster bisque is great as a meal served in a bowl or as a starter or side dish in a cup.
2. Lobster Roll. The lobster meat in this sandwich

Seafood Sam's colorful menu offers a lot more in addition to lobster.

is tender and sweet. It's a cold roll, the meat mixed with mayonnaise and a bit of white pepper and served on a grilled hot dog bun.

3. Lobster Salad. A great choice for the health-conscious, this dinner-size salad features lettuce, fresh tomato, cucumber, olives, any of a number of local vegetables in-season, and, of course, a generous helping of tender, sweet lobster meat on top, with your choice of dressing.
4. Deep-Fried Lobster Meat and Gulf Shrimp Platter. This enticing one-two punch comes with fries and coleslaw and drawn lemon and butter.
5. Lobster Ravioli Platter. Another popular item, especially with the locals, this dish features lobster-stuffed ravioli topped with a rich, creamy lobster Newburg sauce.

6. Fried Lobster Meat Platter. Sweet, tender lobster-claw meat only, gently sautéed in a pan with butter.

7. Baked Lazy Man's Lobster Casserole Platter. For those who like others to do all the work for them, this oven-baked delight contains

lobster-claw meat poached in butter, dredged in breadcrumbs, and baked to a golden brown crunch.

8. Lobster Dinner Platter. It doesn't get any more straightforward than this, especially for the lobster purist. A fresh, locally caught, whole steamed 1¼-pound lobster, served with lemon and drawn butter.

There it is: a little bit of something for lobster lovers of all persuasions. If you can't find something in this array of lobster dishes, then you probably aren't a lobster fan!

Which Sam's to Choose?

Depending on where you're staying on the Cape or what you're planning to do while you're there, each of the two Lewis-owned Seafood Sam's can make your Cape Cod vacation that much better. If you plan to visit the Cape Cod Bay towns of Barnstable, Dennis, and Brewster, and perhaps head up to the Outer Cape, then the Sandwich location is your best bet, with its proximity to Routes 6 and 6A. If your travels will take you to the Cape's busy southern shore between Falmouth and Chatham on Route 28, then head to Sam's Falmouth location, which is also next to one of the large satellite parking lots for people heading by ferry over to Martha's Vineyard.

Either way, you can't go wrong, as the Lewis brothers have put lots of hard work and love into these places. The food is great, the atmosphere convivial, and the prices very wallet-friendly.

SEAFOOD SAM'S LOBSTER BISQUE

Owner Mike Lewis likes to keep a good mix of lobster dishes on his menu, and the lobster bisque at Seafood Sam's is one of the shack's most popular lobster offerings.

INGREDIENTS

4	quarts half-and-half
1	pound lobster meat (leg and body)
2	cups lobster juice or lobster base
¾	cups butter (1½ sticks)
2	tablespoons paprika
2	shots Tabasco
1	cup all-purpose flour
¾	cup dry sherry

In medium saucepan, heat the half-and-half until scalding. In a separate pan, heat the lobster meat and lobster juice to boiling, then turn down to a simmer. In a separate large pot, add the butter, paprika, and Tabasco, and melt butter over low heat.

Add the flour, stirring it in over low heat until mixture is frothy. Add the half-and-half to the flour mixture and bring to a boil. Remove from heat and add the lobster meat and juice and the dry sherry. Stir thoroughly and serve warm. Makes 12–16 servings.

JT's Seafood

Brewster may be one of the toniest towns on all of Cape Cod, and the elegant look and feel of JT's Seafood on Route 6A would seem to back up this impression. But don't be put off by JT's fancy exterior or its gold-lettered sign by the road. JT's is a bona fide shack, lobster and otherwise, and it serves some fine fresh seafood, including fresh lobster in various forms, to even the most casually dressed, road-weary diners who walk through its front door.

2689 Main Street, Brewster, MA

508-896-3355

www.jt-seafood.com

A Neat-Freak Owner and His Caribbean Chefs

JT's is owned by the husband-and-wife team of Bud and Cary Noyes, who took possession of the place in 2004 and transformed it from an Italian restaurant into the fine seafood eatery that it is today. Bud is the gung ho force behind the operation, arriving at work at 5 AM in-season and often staying well into the evening. He calls himself a neat freak, and it shows in the meticulously kept dining areas and grounds of the restaurant. The sage-colored clapboard exterior, with its white trim and black-and-gold awnings, makes the place seem far more elegant and formal than it really is.

Bud claims that one of the main reasons for his success is his reliable cook staff, who hail mostly from the Caribbean islands. JT's head chef, Ledor August, comes from Haiti each year to run JT's kitchen, and he has brought along many interesting and innovative recipes and dishes. Be sure to take a peek into the bustling kitchen, which is situated behind the counter, when you place your order.

JT's sign beckons with the lure of lobster dinners and lobster rolls.

Customers Come from Around the World

While you're waiting to order your food, check out the maps on the wall across from the counter. One map is of New England, another shows the United States, and a third is a map of the world. Each map contains dozens, nay, hundreds of pushpins showing the origins of JT's diners. Be sure to ask for a pushpin to mark your spot on one of the maps, and be sure to play fair—some pins are stuck in such unlikely places as the North Pole, Greenland, and Antarctica.

There's an informative menu over the order counter and paper versions of the same on a shelf next to the counter. When your number is called and you snag your meal, you may choose from a variety of dining spots. For starters, there are a few round, umbrellaed tables in front of JT's that provide a view of Route 6A and the foot traffic passing by the shack.

Ledor Auguste, JT's head chef.

This is where many of JT's ice-cream customers settle down to enjoy their frozen treats. (There's a separate ice-cream-ordering window at the front of the building.)

Inside, there's a tastefully appointed dining room with approximately 20 wooden booths and tables on two levels. Nautical artwork covers the walls, in keeping with Brewster's understated tone of elegance. Finally, out back is a covered wooden deck with a number of picnic tables overlooking the rear parking area and the woods beyond. This is perhaps the best spot for families with youngsters who like to get up and move about. (There are also some books and toys for tikes just inside the door between the deck and the rear of the restaurant.)

Lobster, Lobster Rolls, and Then Some

Though lobster constitutes a relatively small part of JT's business, Bud believes that his establishment is just about the only place you can dine on bugs in a casual atmosphere in Brewster. One eye-catching item on the sign out front announces the Lobster Dinner for the competitive price of $19.99. For 20 clams (read dollars), you get a 1¼-pound steamed lobster, drawn butter, a lemon wedge, corn on the cob, and a biscuit. Bud gets his lobsters from Cape Tip Seafood in Provincetown, where some of the best lobsters on the Cape come from.

Lobster rolls have been an increasingly popular item on JT's menu, and with good reason: they're served in both cold and hot varieties—a rarity on the

Cape, where cold rolls have reigned for decades. The cold roll consists of a generous 5 ounces of freshly picked lobster claw and knuckle meat, blended with Hellmann's mayonnaise, a bit of diced celery, and some light seasonings for extra zing. The bun is a traditional New England split-top hot dog bun lightly grilled.

A friend of Bud's from Connecticut suggested several years ago that he try selling hot lobster rolls like they have along the northern shore of Long Island Sound. August and the rest of the kitchen staff gave it a try, and in short order, lobster roll sales doubled. The hot roll also consists of 5 ounces of claw and knuckle meat sautéed in butter, then served on a split-top bun with butter on the side. Take your pick between hot and cold at JT's. You really can't go wrong.

A Bit on the Upscale Side

While dining at JT's, don't lose sight of the fact that you are in Brewster, and the locals have come to expect something above the usual shack fare from time to time. Rising to the occasion, JT's has a couple of interesting and unusual lobster dishes in addition to their steamed and rolled varieties for you to consider.

First, there's a grilled whole lobster with a leblanc sauce that's offered as a dinner special from time to time. Then there's a salmon Newburg dish with lobster meat in a thick and rich Newburg sauce. And in a more traditional mode, try JT's Shore Dinner, which features a steamed lobster, drawn butter, and lemon wedge along with one pound of steamed local clams with broth, all trimmed out with corn on the cob and a biscuit.

There's also a fine lobster bisque on the menu that's characterized by large chunks of lobster meat. Try a cup or a bowl as an appetizer or a meal.

So worry not while passing through Brewster in search of lobster among all the sophisticated and spiffed-up colonial structures along 6A. Just pull into JT's and let the Noyeses and their capable staff take care of all your lobster needs.

JT'S LOBSTER NEWBURG SAUCE

At JT's Seafood, they go upscale with some of their specials, which are featured on a regular basis throughout the summer. Head chef Ledor Auguste developed this Lobster Newburg sauce, which is great served over grilled salmon or any other firm-fleshed fish fillet.

INGREDIENTS

½	cup (1 stick) butter
1½	cups flour
2	cups chopped celery
8	cups lobster stock
1	cup sherry
¼	teaspoon white pepper
½	cup lobster meat

To make the roux, melt the butter in a heavy pot or large skillet. Slowly add the flour, stirring constantly over low heat until the roux becomes thick and dark brown and is reduced to approximately ¼ cup in volume. Add the other ingredients, stirring constantly, with the lobster meat going in last. Continue to stir under low heat until desired temperature and consistency is achieved. Yields approximately 6–10 servings.

Cobie's

✕ 3260 Main Street, Brewster, MA

☎ 508-896-7021

🦞 www.cobies.com

Open May through mid-September

CERTAIN CLAM SHACKS SHY AWAY FROM serving whole boiled or steamed lobsters yet offer excellent lobster rolls, full of succulent meat tucked into a toasted bun. Cobie's is one such shack, focusing on its deep fryers and ice-cream stand for most of its offerings while simultaneously serving up one of the best lobster rolls on the Cape.

Owner Rob Slavin claims that, though the lobster roll is just about the only offering in the lobster category at Cobie's, it's one of the shack's most popular items. And Slavin thinks he has hit on a secret ingredient that makes his roll stand out among all the many good ones to be found on the Cape: he uses only knuckle meat in his lobster rolls—no claw or tail or body meat, just the tender chunks found in the twisted, knotty pieces of shell between the claws and the body.

Growing up in Connecticut, Slavin was schooled in the philosophy that knuckle meat is the best meat in a lobster. Unlike the sometimes stringy tail meat or densely packed claw meat, knuckle meat, by virtue of its extra tough outer shell, is perhaps the tenderest, sweetest portion of the lobster's edible parts.

In order to get enough such meat without jettisoning all the other parts of the lobster, Slavin gets his knuckle meat from St. Ours & Company, a seafood specialty supplier in East Weymouth, Massachusetts, that handles custom orders for seafood restaurants and markets.

Cobie's lobster roll has that 100 percent knuckle meat mixed with just a bit of mayonnaise and nothing else. It's a cold roll that is served on a thin piece of lettuce and tucked into a toasted, buttered New England–style roll.

If you haven't tried an all-knuckle-meat lobster-roll sandwich, roll over to Cobie's, order one up, and see what you think. Rob Slavin thinks you'll be pleasantly surprised.

Arnold's Lobster and Clam Bar

If there's one place on the Cape to go for consistently great lobster and other seafood, Arnold's in Eastham, Massachusetts, would be it. Owner Nate Nickerson has built his in-the-rough operation from a modest shingled shack named after the malt shop on the 1970s TV show *Happy Days* into a highly efficient, clean, and constantly busy establishment that has something for everybody in the way of food and fun.

Consider this: You can begin your meal at Arnold's with some fine, freshly shucked oysters on the half shell from nearby Wellfleet at Arnold's small yet cozy raw bar, followed by a perfectly steamed lobster, then capped off with an ice-cream treat from the stand outside along the side of the building. Feeling full? Work off those calories (or at least pretend that you're working them off) at Arnold's world-class, 18-hole miniature golf course right next to the restaurant; or bike or hike the Cape Cod Rail Trail, which runs in back of Arnold's, along the eastern edge of the shack's parking lot.

Arnold's is no well-kept secret, especially in the middle of summer, when hundreds of diners may be swarming over the place at any given time. But Nickerson is a savvy businessman, and he has developed his kitchen and ice-cream setups into finely tuned machines that keep lines moving at a rapid pace. Don't be put off by the crowds; prepare to be amazed at how quickly you're served and how well you're taken care of.

Shack Roots That Run Deep

Arnold's got its start as a hot dog stand named Whitey's back in the early 1950s before morphing into Gertrude's Beach Box, a fried-seafood

3580 Route 6, Eastham, MA

508-255-2575

www.arnoldsrestaurant.com

Open mid-May to mid-October

Arnold's distinctive roof sign is easily seen from Route 6.

stand best known for proprietress Gertrude's clam cakes. Gertrude carried on for 20-some-odd years when Cape Cod native Nate Nickerson came along and bought the place from her.

Being a fan of *Happy Days*, and knowing that much of his clientele most likely watched the show, Nickerson chose the name "Arnold's" for his shack, and he mimicked the malt shop on the show by installing drive-in order boxes in the parking places and putting his waitresses on roller skates. The main difference was that Nickerson's joint served up deep-fried seafood—and lots of it—in addition to burgers and hot dogs and fries and malts.

It was only a matter of time before everyone grew weary of the drive-in motif, so Nate went to a more conventional shack setup with an order counter and

Arnold's lobster rolls brim with fresh-picked lobster meat.

a bunch of tables for dining nearby. Somewhere along the line, lobsters became part of the extensive menu. In 1993 Arnold's burned to the ground. This gave Nickerson a chance to rethink his operation and to build with the future in mind.

Build he did. Arnold's new shack was significantly larger than the one that burned down, and he added a sizable ice-cream stand onto one side of it. The dining areas grew in size and number. The 18-hole mini-golf course followed, then Nate's son created a shingled raw bar within the enclosed dining room. There's a lot going on in this place, so plan on sticking around for a while.

High-Tech Steaming Does the Trick

Thousands upon thousands of lobsters are served at Arnold's every summer, both whole and in Arnold's famous lobster rolls. How do they stay on top of all those lobster orders and deliver consistently tasty fare day after day?

The secret's in the steamer. Nate is a big believer in steaming lobsters instead of boiling them. For years, Arnold's used a standard convection steamer to cook their bugs, but customer demand called for another solution to keep pace with the rapid increase in business. Nickerson purchased a couple of combi-steamers from the German manufacturer Rational for some $50,000, and the new steamers have revolutionized food preparation at Arnold's. Here's how it works:

Large batches of lobsters (up to a hundred at a

time) are loaded into a combi-steamer and brought to 155°F, as measured by a probe in a lobster's tail. The lobsters are taken out and placed in a blast chiller for a short time, then transferred to the walk-in cooler for temporary storage. As orders are taken at the counter for lobsters, they're put back in the Rational and steamed for three or four minutes. They come out perfectly firm and flavorful, and the kitchen staff can handle virtually any flood of lobster orders that may come in.

Variety Is the Spice of (Lobster) Life

Lobster dinners come in three varieties. For the purist, there's the Lobster à la Carte, which is a lobster weighing between 1¼ and 3 pounds (larger ones are also available), served on its own, with drawn butter and a slice of lemon. The next step up is the Lobster Special, which features a 1⅛-pound bug that comes with corn on the cob and a cup of clam chowder.

At the top of the food chain is the New England Lobster Shore Dinner, which comes with a pound of steamers and corn on the cob. All lobster meals are competitively priced on a daily basis. Arnold's gets its lobsters, by the way, from large offshore boats that ply the waters many miles distant off Cape Cod's outer shore, where cold-water lobsters are found in abundance.

The same steaming technique is used for the lobsters that are handpicked for the other goodies on the menu. For openers, try Arnold's creamy Maine lobster bisque, lightly spiced and with a dash of sherry. Any of the salads on Arnold's menu (Caesar, bleu cheese, Greek, Nantucket strawberry spinach, and more) can be topped with a generous helping of fresh-picked lobster meat for an additional $15 dollars or so, pushing

---

ARNOLD'S SEAFOOD CASSEROLE

Arnold's chef, Susie Buckley, came up with this rich, tasty seafood dish that's great for any special occasion.

INGREDIENTS

½	pound fresh scallops
1	pound lobster meat
1	pound cooked shrimp, peeled and deveined
3	cups fresh sliced mushrooms
3	tablespoons butter
1	tablespoon flour
1	cup sour cream
4	tablespoons softened butter
2	teaspoons Worcestershire sauce
2	teaspoons cooking sherry
	salt and pepper, to taste
½	cup grated Parmesan cheese
	paprika

Preheat the oven to 400°F. Cook the scallops in boiling water for three minutes. Drain. Gently combine lobster, shrimp, and scallops together, and arrange in a shallow, greased baking dish. In a medium-size skillet, sauté the mushrooms in 3 tablespoons butter until lightly browned. Transfer to a medium-size bowl, and toss with the flour. Stir in the sour cream, 4 tablespoons softened butter, Worcestershire sauce, sherry, and salt and pepper. Pour the sauce mixture over the seafood, sprinkle the top with Parmesan cheese, and dust the entire mixture with paprika. Bake for 10 to 12 minutes or until bubbly. Serve over rice or noodles. Serves 6.

the overall salad price into the mid-$20s range. But such salads are complete meals and then some, and very healthy, to boot.

The lobster rolls here are legendary. They are, far and away, Arnold's top-selling item. First, there's Arnold's standard cold lobster roll with a generous portion of lobster meat tossed with a bit of mayo and served with a leaf of lettuce on a split-top bun. In a nod to southern New England, Arnold's warm lobster roll is served with warm, melted butter instead of mayo. And for the truly famished, try the jumbo lobster roll, which has twice the meat of the standard roll and can be had either warm or cold. All lobster rolls come with fresh coleslaw and french fries.

Wait, There's More!

Some other things to consider while you're at Arnold's: First, be sure to check out the fried seafood offerings, in case lobster isn't what you have in mind for lunch or dinner. Arnold's has some of the best deep-fried platters of clams, scallops, shrimp, oysters (and lobster!) on the Cape; each platter comes with generous sides of french fries and coleslaw, and the thin-cut onion rings make for a wonderful side to share with your dining mates.

Dozens of fresh-steamed bugs in Arnold's high-tech Rational steamer.

The raw bar features fresh oysters from Wellfleet Harbor just up the road. Stuffed clams are another popular raw bar specialty, as are the native clams on the half shell and the peel-and-eat gulf shrimp. Excellent crab cakes come from the kitchen, topped with guacamole and served with a side of summer salsa.

No trip to Arnold's is complete without stopping by the ice-cream window on the side of the building. They've got everything from hard- and soft-serve ice cream, sundaes, and Italian ice, to homemade brownies and fresh-baked chocolate chip cookies. This is a popular stop for those pedaling up and down the adjacent Cape Cod Rail Trail. There's plenty of open-air seating right next to the window, much of it shaded by Arnold's trademark yellow-and-white canopy.

Then there's the miniature golf. Arnold's 18-hole course was actually designed by a golf architect and features streams, ponds, waterfalls, a treasure chest, and facsimiles of historical buildings around Eastham. Even if you don't care to play, it's fun to watch young duffers navigate the scenic course while you nosh at Arnold's outdoor dining areas.

They say the harder you work, the luckier you get. With all the labor and love that Nate Nickerson has poured into Arnold's over the years, he's one lucky guy. And we all reap the benefits of his well-earned good fortune.

The Friendly Fisherman

The **Friendly Fisherman is housed** in a modest, shingled shack on the east side of Route 6 in North Eastham on the way to Provincetown. What started as a seafood market some 20 years ago has blossomed into a fine little eatery with a shaded picnic area and an adjacent package liquor store, in case you want to BYO and partake with lunch or dinner.

Co-owners Janet and Alana Demetri (mother and daughter, respectively) work tirelessly to keep up with the orders for lobsters in the market and at the shack window. The Friendly Fisherman has a long-standing reputation as one of the best places to get fresh fish on the Cape. They've also always had strong connections with many of the local lobstermen, who fish the ocean side of the outer Cape and bring the best of their catches to the Fisherman's cold-water tanks every day during the busy season from May to October.

4580 State Highway, North Eastham, MA

508-255-3009

www.friendlyfishermaneastham .com

Open early May to mid-October

The Best Fish in Town

The Friendly Fisherman sprang into being when Janet and her husband, Michael, opened as a fish market in the spring of 1989. They quickly became known for their consistently fresh fish, and tourists and locals alike came to depend on the modest market for their seafood needs. Lobsters were always part of the mix, with a couple of aquamarine cold-water tanks next to and behind the counters and display cases.

A small addition was put on the side of the shack a few years after Friendly Fisherman opened, and the Demetris began cooking up lobsters and deep-fried seafood and serving the fare through a takeout window where diners could pick up their food and enjoy it at the 20 or so picnic

Owners Janet (left) and Alana Demetri showcase a couple of 8-pound lobsters.

tables scattered around the side and the back of the building. With its tree shade and its colorful lobster buoys and fish nets on the surrounding wooden fence, it's a pleasant spot to enjoy your repast, set back from the road in a quiet setting. Michael passed away in 2006, and Alana, who had already spent plenty of time working at the shack as a teen, stepped up and joined her mother in running the place.

Have Some Lobster at Friendly Fisherman

The most popular lobster dish at the Friendly Fisherman is the lobster roll, which consists of a generous portion of chilled lobster meat tossed with a bit of mayo served on a leaf of romaine lettuce and tucked into a toasted, split-top bun. It's simple, yet satisfying and loaded with the good stuff that makes lobster rolls the coveted treat that they are.

One summer day a couple of years ago, celebrity chef and television personality Rachael Ray stopped by the Friendly Fisherman on her way back to Boston from Provincetown. She ordered up a lobster roll and went gaga over it, raving about the roll in her magazine, especially the copious amounts of sweet lobster meat that seemingly buried the lettuce and bun beneath it. (Ray, by the way, is a Cape Cod native who really knows her local seafood.)

The Friendly Fisherman's well-manicured fish market facade.

Monsters of the Deep

The other big seller in the lobster category is Friendly Fisherman's shore dinner, which consists of a hard-shell lobster (you pick the size), a side of melted butter, an ear of corn, and some of the shack's homemade coleslaw. In addition to serving up lobster through the takeout window, Janet says they sell "a ton" of cooked whole lobsters over the seafood market counter to customers (mostly regulars) who take them home to eat. There's no charge for cooking the lobsters, and the Friendly Fisherman staff will also crack the claws and split the tails for you, if you wish.

The cold-water tanks at Friendly Fisherman occupy a good amount of the floor space in the seafood market and can hold up to 2,000 pounds of lobster; the supply is constantly replenished throughout the day. All the lobsters are locally caught by two independent lobster boats plying the "back side" (ocean side) of the Cape off Provincetown. In addition, the Demetris employ the services of an independent scuba diver, who goes after big lobsters in deeper water—bugs that often weigh 10 to 15 pounds or more.

What Else Is There?

If lobster doesn't happen to be your thing, try some of the excellent deep-fried seafood that has helped make the Friendly Fisherman one of the premier, if lesser known, shacks on the Cape. The whole-belly clams are light and sweet and full of fresh-clam flavor. The sea scallops are also excellent, with firm

The Friendly Fisherman has all your seafood needs, and then some.

meat and flavorful breading; they're sourced locally, so they're super fresh. And the fillets in the fish-and-chips platter come from the fresh daily catches of haddock and cod and other deepwater fish that are filleted throughout the day in the seafood market.

So if you happen to be bound for P-town or the Cape Cod National Seashore for a day at the beach, be sure to stop by the Friendly Fisherman for a bite to eat or some super-fresh fish and shellfish to cook up at home. This place has all the down-home warmth and, yes, friendliness that you should expect to find at any fine lobster shack or seafood emporium on the Cape or anywhere else.

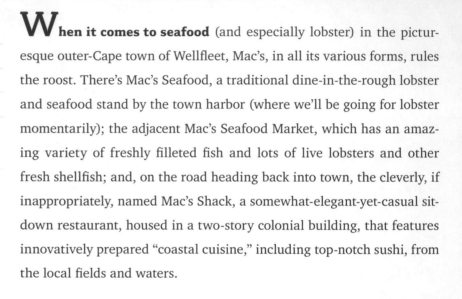

Mac's Seafood

✕ Town Pier, Wellfleet, MA

☎ 508-349-9611

🦞 www.macsseafood.com

Open May to late September

When it comes to seafood (and especially lobster) in the picturesque outer-Cape town of Wellfleet, Mac's, in all its various forms, rules the roost. There's Mac's Seafood, a traditional dine-in-the-rough lobster and seafood stand by the town harbor (where we'll be going for lobster momentarily); the adjacent Mac's Seafood Market, which has an amazing variety of freshly filleted fish and lots of live lobsters and other fresh shellfish; and, on the road heading back into town, the cleverly, if inappropriately, named Mac's Shack, a somewhat-elegant-yet-casual sit-down restaurant, housed in a two-story colonial building, that features innovatively prepared "coastal cuisine," including top-notch sushi, from the local fields and waters.

In the Beginning, There Was a Market ...

The Mac's Seafood story begins in 1995 when brothers Mac and Alex Hay opened a modest seafood market next to the town pier in Wellfleet. Their dedication to purveying and promoting the local bounty of the sea set them apart from many other seafood markets, which shopped far and wide for the best deals they could find for their inventories.

The market became a popular go-to place for locals to pick up fresh lobsters, fish fillets, locally sourced oysters and clams, and scallops for enjoying at home. Summer visitors quickly caught on, and the market hummed along through the boom times of the late 1990s.

As often happens in the seafood-market business, requests from customers for freshly cooked seafood were made on a regular basis. Given Mac's location by the town dock and next to a public beach, it was kind

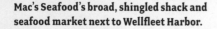

Mac's Seafood's broad, shingled shack and seafood market next to Wellfleet Harbor.

of a no-brainer to install some deep fryers and cooking pots for a classic shack setup. Thus was Mac's Seafood born.

Mac's Seafood Today

When you go to Mac's Seafood now, you'll quickly notice that the shack portion has taken over the front of the one-and-a-half-story building, with its order and pickup windows and extensive wallboard being the most noticeable features of the place. The seafood market has taken a backseat of sorts around the corner of the building, but it still hums with activity, as people keep coming back for the freshest of local seafood.

Lobster seekers will find plenty to like in Mac's Seafood's boiled lobster dinners and clambakes. The dinners come with good-sized bugs starting at 1½ pounds, then jumping to 1¾, 2, and 3 pounds. The dinner version comes with drawn butter and your choice of corn on the cob or boiled red potatoes. The clambakes supersize each lobster dinner by throwing in a generous bag of steamed clams or mussels.

The lobster roll features handpicked meat lightly tossed in seasonings and served in a split-top bun. And there's a Lazy Man's Lobster Roll that contains 5 ounces of lobster meat sautéed in butter, ladled into a grilled hot dog bun, and accompanied by fries and coleslaw. The lobster bisque, which comes by the cup or the bowl, is thick with fresh-picked lobster meat that's blended into a creamy, sherry-infused base.

Mac's Shack: A Shack in Name Only

Mac's Shack is a wonderful, whimsical place about ¼ mile up the road from Mac's Seafood as you head back into Wellfleet from the town pier. Though it may not be a shack in the traditional sense, it's a great place to stop for a sophisticated bite to eat.

Mac Hay has taken an old colonial house hard by the road and dressed it up into a casual restaurant with a raw bar, a sushi bar, a bar bar, and an extensive menu of wonderfully inventive local seafood done up in an amazing variety of ways.

Perhaps the biggest surprise of the place is the "roof art" that you see only when coming back from the town pier or after pulling into the parking lot. If this doesn't say "Come in for some fresh seafood," what does? Mac's Shack is located at 91 Commercial Street in Wellfleet (call 508-349-6333, or visit www.macsseafood.com/macs_shack.asp).

A Glorified Clam Shack

Mac's Seafood has evolved in the past several years into what some refer to as a "glorified clam shack." Along with the deep-fried seafood and lobster dinners on the menu are some relatively bold offerings, in keeping with Mac Hay's desire to continually promote upscale and unusual foods made from local ingredients. Mac's may be the only lobster/clam shack that sells sushi rolls, supplied by the sushi chef of Mac's Shack, just up the road. And there are some very inventive wraps with tuna, falafel, shrimp, and organic salmon drizzled with exotic sauces such as ginger soy sauce and soy vinaigrette. Not your typical shack fare.

Continuing in this vein, Mac's has come up with an array of seafood burritos that have proven to be very popular. Try grilled sea scallops, fried cod, or grilled shrimp. Each burrito comes stuffed with

Mac's sandy, beachside picnic tables are a great place to enjoy shack fare.

Spanish rice, black or refried beans, homemade salsa, cheese, and sour cream. Also from south of the border come Mac's quesadillas, which contain many of the same fine ingredients as the burritos, only flattened into a grilled flour tortilla with lots of cheese. You can also get seared tofu in either your burrito or quesadilla.

Wellfleet is renowned for its oysters, and the raw bar at Mac's Seafood serves them up by the half dozen and dozen. The same goes for locally sourced littleneck clams. Another item of interest is Portuguese kale, a mildly spiced, tomato-based stew that is served by the cup or by the bowl.

Sunsets on the Beach

Mac's is right next to a small town beach, and the dining area consists of a bunch of picnic tables scattered over a sandy stretch between the shack and the water's edge. There are gorgeous views of the boats in Wellfleet's fabled harbor and more distant views of Cape Cod Bay. The sunsets in early evening are not to be missed, as the big red solar orb seems to slowly drop into the bay and day fades to night. The atmosphere is festive, with people coming down from town and boaters stopping by for a meal or a snack before motoring home. Come for the food, stay for the sunset, and you're pretty much guaranteed to leave with a smile on your face.

The Lobster Pot

Few seafood restaurants in New England have the history, the tradition, and the cachet that the Lobster Pot of Provincetown has. From its iconic neon-lobster signage on the front of the building to its 40-foot-long exposed kitchen-prep area to its two stories of window-wrapped dining rooms overlooking Cape Cod Bay and the Provincetown Harbor, this place packs 'em in seven days a week in-season.

╳ 312 Commercial Street, Provincetown, MA

☎ 508-487-0842

www.ptownlobsterpot.com

Open mid-April to December

From Shack to Seafood Restaurant

The story of the Lobster Pot as it exists today really begins with the arrival of Joy McNulty in the 1970s. A single mom with four young kids, Joy arrived in Provincetown from upstate New York in a VW bus. She landed a job waitressing, then running a restaurant called the Crown & Anchor. Eventually she bought the Lobster Pot, a shack by the harbor and beach in downtown Provincetown. In the intervening years, the "Pot," as it's referred to locally, has grown into a behemoth seafood restaurant that stretches from busy Commercial Street all the way back to the edge of Provincetown's harbor.

Joy has been the driving force behind the Lobster Pot's expansion and growth, and her son Tim, who has been involved in the business since he was a teen, has transformed the Pot's kitchen and menu into one of national renown. Tim was instrumental in redesigning the kitchen into an open galley that is in full view as you pass between the hostess stand and the dining rooms in back. The seawater-filled lobster tanks are in the front end of the Pot and are glass-sided for your lobster-viewing pleasure.

The Lobster Pot's distinctive neon-lit exterior on Provincetown's busy Commercial Street.

The Namesake Lobster Still Holds Its Own

The menu at the Lobster Pot is extensive and varied, with some fairly highbrow items like oysters Rockefeller and crab Provençale, but lobster and lobster rolls remain some of the best-selling items at this Provincetown institution.

Take the boiled lobster dinners. Each features a lobster of your choosing between 1¼ and 2 pounds, with larger ones available upon request. The dinners come with boiled red potatoes. Any lobster dinner can be upsized to a clambake, which includes red potatoes, corn on the cob, steamed mussels, and your choice of the Pot's famous clam chowder, the Portuguese soup, or the lobster bisque.

Other lobster dishes include a wonderful pan-roasted lobster that's flambéed with brandy, then roasted in the oven. The baked stuffed lobster features a 1¼-pound bug stuffed with sautéed onions, celery, and Ritz crackers, blended with shrimp, scallops, and crabmeat. Out-of-the-shell lobster dishes, for those who wish to forgo the battle of the shell,

---

TIM'S LOBSTER POT CLAM CHOWDER

Head chef Tim McNulty began making clam chowder at the Lobster Pot when he was a teenager over 30 years ago, and he's been making it in increasingly large quantities over the years (close to 80 gallons per day during high season at this point). His chowder is classic New England style, thick and creamy and chock-full of diced potatoes and fresh clam meat.

In recent years, Tim's chowder has won radio station WCOD's "Chowdahfest" competition four years in a row, making it, in many peoples' opinions, the best chowder on the Cape. Tim has a number of variations on his clam chowder recipe, but this is the basic one, which is also the simplest and the most popular.

INGREDIENTS

3	tablespoons butter		½	teaspoon ground white pepper
1¾	cups onions, medium dice		¾	cup butter
1½	cups peeled potatoes, medium dice		1	cup all-purpose flour
1	pound large sweet sea clams, diced		1½	cups milk
3	cups clam juice, canned or jarred		½	cup light cream
2	cups fresh clam juice			salt to taste (optional)

In a soup pot, melt 3 tablespoons butter and sauté onions until just translucent. Do not brown. Add the potatoes, clams, juices, and pepper. Bring to a boil, then simmer until potatoes are cooked (about 20 minutes). While potatoes are simmering, prepare the roux: in a second pot, melt the ¾ cup butter and, with a wire whip, stir in the flour. Smooth with the whip. Cook on low heat until potatoes are done, then stir roux into pot with potatoes. Bring this pot back to a boil before removing from heat. (Whenever a roux is added, it must be brought back to a boil or it will go rancid.) Heat the milk and cream on the side, then add to the chowder, or add enough hot chowder to the cold cream until the cream is the same temperature as the chowder base, then add to the rest of the base. This is called *tempering*. Salt to taste, if desired. Makes 9 cups.

include lobster scampi, lobster Newburg, and a Lazy Stuffed Lobster, with fresh lobster meat baked in the oven with seafood stuffing and served with red potatoes. Another inventive choice for either an appetizer or an entrée is lobster ravioli. The oversized ravioli squares are bathed in a Parmesan cream sauce, then topped with a panko-Parmesan crust for a cheesy crunch.

The Pot's lobster roll is famous, and they serve tens of thousands during the busy summer season, especially during the lunch hour. The roll contains a generous portion of all-knuckle meat mixed with mayonnaise, scallion, and finely chopped celery on a toasted bun. It comes with a scoop of potato salad. There's also a crab-salad roll that's seasoned and served in the same fashion. You can't go wrong with either one.

Lobster rolls comin' up!

The Dining Experience at the Lobster Pot

Unlike most lobster shacks, the Lobster Pot is a sit-down, full-service restaurant that usually has long waits just to get to the reservation stand, located some 30 feet inside the front door. Once you've put in your name and received a plastic-lobster pager, you can try and find a spot in the crowded and popular second-floor Top of the Pot bar or go back outside to check out the street scene on busy Commercial Street.

When you're summoned, you'll settle into a table in one of the two large dining rooms in the back of the Lobster Pot, both of which have wonderful views of the harbor beyond. The dining rooms are loud and convivial, and the drinks flow freely, especially in the evening. Though the dining rooms are by no means fancy, the food is quite upscale and inventive, and that mix of informal and sophisticated is part of the appeal of the Pot (and one of the main reasons that the long waits for a table are almost always worth it).

The Lobster Pot is a Provincetown institution, and if you happen to arrive when there's a long line snaking out the door, ratchet up your patience quotient, queue up in the back of the line, and prepare yourself for the best that Provincetown has to offer in the way of fine dining in a casual atmosphere.

Townsend Lobster & Seafood

85-87 Shankpainter Road,
Provincetown, MA

508-487-5161

www.townsendseafood.com

Open late May to mid-October

Do you think there's a chance this place serves lobster?

Provincetown's busy, crowded Commercial Street is a lot of fun to explore, to check out the shops (and fellow shoppers), and to take in the overall carnival atmosphere that makes this festive town at the tip of the Cape the wonderful and unique place that it is.

When it comes time to eat, however, and you want lobster—and you don't want to fight the downtown crowds to get a seat in one of the many jammed restaurants—head on over to Shankpainter Road, which intersects Commercial Street, and walk a few blocks away from all the hubbub to Townsend Lobster & Seafood. It's an off-the-beaten-path treat for those who love truly good local seafood at reasonable prices in a low-key atmosphere.

Like a Theme Park

Townsend is owned and run by Chris Townsend, a bearded, energetic lobsterman who was raised in Provincetown. For 25 years, his parents were harbormasters for the town's busy waterfront, and Chris grew up along the docks, fishing and helping out his parents.

He also spent good portions of his youthful summers at a burger and snack stand on Shankpainter Road. As a kid, Chris would catch bluefish and sell them to the owner of the stand, then take his earnings and spend them at the go-cart track and ice-cream shop next door. "It was like a theme park to me," he says today, reminiscing about this great hangout that would one day coincidentally become the location of his lobster shack.

In the late 1980s Chris went off to college at Keene State in New

Hampshire. When he was a senior, he was assigned a project to come up with a plan for launching a new business. He knew immediately what he would do. Having spent so much time on the Provincetown waterfront, Chris drafted a plan to buy a lobster boat, do some commercial fishing, start selling his lobster wholesale to local restaurants and seafood markets, then open a modest lobster and seafood shack of his own right on his hometown docks. When he graduated in 1992, he went straight back home and began to build his dream business in the place that he loved most.

After fishing and wholesaling for 10 years, he secured some space in a small shack right on the docks, covered the exterior walls with lobster buoys of all different kinds, and hung out his shingle as a place to get fresh-cooked lobster right off the boat. Deep fryers were soon installed, and Townsend's became the go-to place for seafood in the rough on Provincetown's waterfront.

Eviction, Then Resurrection

One day in early 2009 the Townsends received a phone call from the new owners of the waterfront property they leased. They were informed that Ma and Pa Townsend were out as harbormasters, and Chris would have to vacate his dockside restaurant spot. Chris searched about feverishly for a new location and came across the old food-stand of his youth, whose property had come up for sale. After several months of wrangling with the banks, Chris

Owner Chris Townsend (left) and his barkeep father, David.

TOWNSEND'S LOBSTER BISQUE

Years by the waterfront helped the Townsends develop an enviable recipe for lobster bisque that now has a cult following in Provincetown, with regulars coming from New York and Boston every year to get a cup or bowl.

INGREDIENTS

2	bunches scallions, finely chopped
½	cup vegetable oil
1	cup butter
2	cups flour
5¾	cups clam juice
1½	cups dry sherry
1	pound lobster meat, chopped
2	tablespoons Old Bay seasoning
3	tablespoons tarragon
	salt and pepper to taste
	hot sauce, to taste (optional)
8	cups half-and-half

Cook the scallions in oil and butter until soft. Whisk in the flour until a smooth paste forms. Add the clam juice and cook until thickened. (Do not boil.) Add sherry and lobster meat and cook for two to four minutes. Turn off the heat, add the seasonings and hot sauce (if desired) and stir well. Add the half-and-half and heat slowly to proper serving temperature. Makes 8 large servings.

took possession of the property and set about relocating and expanding his lobster shack into the seafood emporium that it is today.

Though it may look a bit less like a shack than its predecessor on the docks, Townsend's is every bit as authentic in its cooking and its procurement of seafood as it ever was. Chris remains a lobsterman, and he goes out most mornings in-season to check,

empty, and bait his traps. Townsend Lobster & Seafood now boasts an airy seafood market, a clean, bright order counter, a full-service bar, and a couple dozen indoor booths and tables along with several picnic tables out front. Word is starting to spread about this alternative seafood spot close by downtown P-town's crazier scene.

Home of the Lobster Bake

Townsend's menu is straightforward lobster-shack fare with an emphasis on the fresh lobsters that Chris brings to port nearly every day. The most fulfilling lobster dish on the menu is the Lobster Bake. You get a 1¼-pound fresh lobster, a cup of chowder, half a dozen steamers, half an ear of corn, and a dinner roll for a very affordable price. The lobster roll consists of fresh-picked lobster meat lightly tossed in mayo and seasoned with a bit of tarragon and celery.

The lobster bisque here is beloved by locals and has them stopping by frequently for a cup or bowl and a glass of wine or tap beer at the full-service bar, which is tended by Chris's loquacious and entertaining father, David. Another taste treat is the baked stuffed clam, which contains half a pound of Townsend's famous clam-filled stuffing baked in a good-sized sea clamshell.

Townsend's may not have the outward tourist-town charm or the prestige of a Commercial Street address, but it won't be long before people who really love fresh lobster and a good bargain make this place a happening spot on the Provincetown dining circuit.

Lobstering, Anyone?

Chris Townsend is a lobsterman most days of the week, going out on his boat to check and bait his traps and haul his catch back to shore. It's a rough but rewarding life, if you like being at sea; and if you'd like to get a taste of what it's like catching lobsters, read on.

Three times a week, Chris takes people out with him on his lobster boat, the *H/V Trevor Kane*, so they can experience what it's like fishing for lobsters off Cape Cod. The one-and-a-half-hour-long excursion takes you out to visit Townsend's traps, where you can help haul them in and watch as Chris harvests his catch.

You also get a tour of the harbor and great views of Provincetown from the water. The educational trips, which are appropriate for adults and older children, have been named a top pick for kids' activities on the Outer Cape by *Cape Cod Life* magazine. The cost is $25 per person, and a maximum of six people can go at a time. Be sure to call in advance to reserve a spot (508-487-5161).

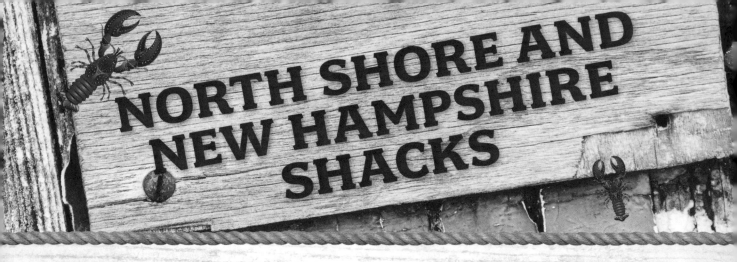

NORTH SHORE AND NEW HAMPSHIRE SHACKS

Boston's North Shore is known far and wide as the birthplace of the fried clam and the home to perhaps the three best clam shacks in the world: Farnham's, Woodman's, and the Clam Box. Yet the North Shore, including Cape Ann and the towns of Gloucester, Rockport, and Essex, also serve up some of the finest lobsters anywhere—and in the grand, informal "shack" tradition, to boot.

How can you beat getting a whole boiled lobster at a stand-up counter, then taking it out to a rough-hewn picnic table and diving into your feast? It's an almost primal experience, yet hundreds of thousands of people do just that all along Boston's North Shore all summer long. The classic Roy Moore Lobster Company and Rockport's Lobster Pool are world-famous for their lobster in the rough, and of the aforementioned clam shacks, Farnham's and Woodman's also do a brisk business in lobsters and lobster rolls. (The Clam Box makes a nice roll, also.)

Moving up the coast and over the border into New Hampshire, the mood changes a bit, and things get (if it's possible) even more informal at the lobster-shack magnets along the Granite State's short but lively coastline. From the twin shacks across the street from one another in Seabrook to the dueling shacks along the shores of Rye Beach, there's a time-honored tradition in New Hampshire of hitting the beach on a hot summer afternoon, then having a lobster or two before heading home.

Read on to learn the particulars—and prepare yourself for some of the finest in-the-rough lobster eating in all of New England.

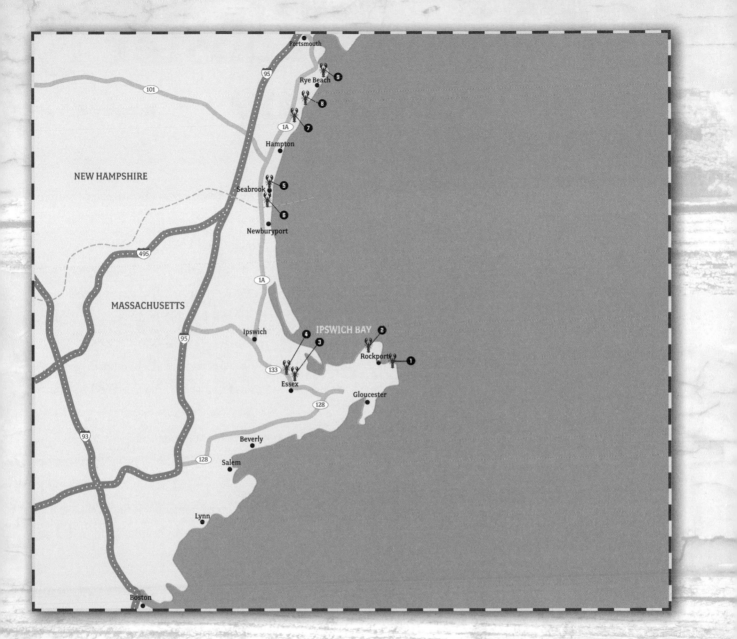

Roy Moore Lobster Company

39 Bearskin Neck, Rockport, MA

☎ 978-546-6696

Open late March to late October

This is a great place to begin our lobster quest on Boston's famed North Shore—at a place so informal and so much fun, it might be said to embody everything a lobster shack should be.

Roy Moore Lobster Company is smack-dab in the middle of Rockport's historic, artsy Bearskin Neck waterfront district, housed in an impossibly small, shingled shack with a low pitched roof. It's wedged tightly between two other weather-beaten structures. Without its cedar-shingled front and the tasty New England victuals inside, Roy Moore Lobster might be mistaken for a merchant's stall in a crowded bazaar in some far-off land.

At first, you can't believe such a famous place can be so tiny. But just step inside and make your way to the order counter next to the lobster tanks, then walk through the minuscule kitchen and on through the back door and out onto the small yet cheery back deck with ten or so small tables along the edges. Everything here is small and fast—and a lot of fun!

The diminutive yet mighty Roy Moore Lobster Company.

It All Started with Roy Moore

Back in 1918, local fisherman Roy Moore started selling cooked lobsters out of this small shack on the crowded streets of Bearskin Neck in Rockport. Not all that much has changed in the intervening years. There has been a succession of owners, and current proprietor Ken Porter has been associated with Roy Moore Lobster since 1979, first as an employee, then as the owner beginning in 1989.

Ken is perhaps the most optimistic and accommodating of all the lobster-shack owners on the New England coast. He brings to his business tirelessly upbeat customer service and good cheer, and he's a constant presence in Roy Moore's cramped quarters from the spring opening in March until October 31, the last day of the season, making sure things run smoothly and that everyone has a good time.

Ken's wife, Karen, has played a big role in Roy Moore's success over the years, and she now runs Roy Moore's Fish Shack, a sit-down, full-service seafood restaurant about 100 yards up the street from Roy Moore Lobster. Their son John works with Ken at the lobster outfit, and their daughter Charlene helps Karen run the fish shack. It's a family that's totally devoted to Rockport's seafood dining scene, and they work hard to keep customers happy and coming back for more.

Roy Moore Lobster Company owner Ken Porter, serving up the chowdah.

Assembly-Line Lobsters

Roy Moore Lobster does something most other lobster shacks don't: they continually cook dozens of lobsters at a time, pile them up on a stainless steel countertop, crack their shells with a large knife on a wooden cutting board, and dole them out hot and fresh to customers as soon as they're ordered. There's rarely a wait for your lobster: it's handed to you, perfectly cooked, along with a cup of butter and any side dishes you may desire, all in the blink of an eye.

How can they do this? For starters, all the precooked lobsters are a uniform 1¼ to 1½ pounds, so they're all priced the same. In order to batch-process customers through their tiny operation, Roy Moore Lobster encourages these quick purchases by pricing the precooked bugs very competitively. (You can order larger lobsters, but they'll be more expensive and will be custom-cooked, which means there will be a wait.) Batches of just-boiled lobsters hit the stainless steel table every ten minutes or so during busy times, so they're as hot and as fresh as can be.

Roy Moore's lobsters are all from adjacent Rockport Harbor, where the local fishing fleet offloads their fresh catches daily on Roy Moore's dock out back. Ken says he has some 12 to 15 boats working exclusively for Roy Moore in the summertime, and he has cold seawater tanks that can hold 3,000 to 4,000 pounds of live lobsters at a time.

Famous Side Orders

The number one side dish to have with your lobster is a cup of Roy Moore's creamy, rich New England–style clam chowder. The broth is chock-full of minced sea clams and chunks of potato, and the chowder resides in a couple of good-sized cauldrons between the order counter and the back door. Be sure to order up and grab a cup on your way out to the deck in back.

Tucking into some bugs and beverages on Roy Moore's back deck.

Many of the other side dishes sit atop beds of shaved ice in front of the order counter, and you can pick them up when you order your lobster. Choose between shrimp cocktail, smoked salmon, smoked or peppered mackerel, or stuffed clams (the stuffies are served warm). You can also order a meaty, 5-ounce cold lobster roll that's fresh-picked, tossed with a bit of mayo, and served over a leaf of lettuce in a split-top bun. And there are some excellent, locally harvested oysters on the half shell, served with lemon slices and cocktail sauce.

The Dance on the Deck

Perhaps the biggest challenge at Roy Moore is securing a seat on the small waterside deck outside the back door. There are a limited number of old, wooden lobster-crate tables and benches in the cramped space, yet diners seem to sense the need for others to be seated, so people here tend to eat and run. During peak periods, Ken encourages diners to go out by the docks in back of the deck and use the lobster traps by the dock as makeshift tables and chairs. You can also sit and eat on the nearby seawall or wander up the street to a small park that overlooks Sandy Bay for a more picnic-like setting.

Back on the deck, there's a lot of squeezing by and polite excuse-me's as diners maneuver around in the limited space. It's like an impromptu dance with strangers, but once you've got a table, you're in good shape.

Don't let the tight fit put you off Roy Moore Lobster. It's still the best, funnest game in town and shouldn't be missed by any true lover of genuine lobster in the rough.

The Lobster Pool

Scenic Route 27 heads north and west out of downtown Rockport along the craggy Cape Ann coastline that defines this timeless part of northeastern Massachusetts. It's a beautiful drive that gets even better when a red-painted, expanded-cape-style building on the right comes into view just after passing Halibut Point State Park. That's because the red shed is Rockport's famous Lobster Pool, one of the great lobster shacks in this part of New England. And with five lobster traps nailed to its roof, it's pretty easy to recognize.

329 Granite Street, Rockport, MA

978-546-7808

www.lobsterpoolrestaurant.com

Open early April to late October

Serving Lobsters for Over 50 Years

The Lobster Pool first opened its doors in 1954 and has been serving lobster in the rough ever since. The shack has had several owners over the years but has never wavered from its commitment to serving fresh steamed lobsters and other seafood in a beautiful setting on northwest Rockport's Folly Cove.

Back in 1997, the husband-and-wife team of Thomas Tedesco and Myalisa Waring bought the Lobster Pool and kept the place as simple and unadorned as it ever was. It's always consisted of the main building, with an order counter and open kitchen up front, a couple of pine-paneled dining rooms in back, and a bunch of picnic tables in the grassy backyard overlooking the cove and Ipswich Bay. A bunch of large rocks provide a buffer between the water's edge and the Lobster Pool's outdoor dining area.

Enjoying some lobster and deep-fried seafood in the Lobster Pool's backyard.

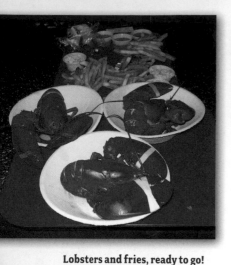

Lobsters and fries, ready to go!

Originally from different parts of Connecticut, Thomas and Myalisa summered with their families in the Rockport area when they were kids. They eventually met, married, and settled down in Rockport, then became owners of the Lobster Pool and, with their five children, made it the Tedesco family business. Thomas passed away in 2010, and Myalisa and their kids have soldiered on, keeping the place running smoothly.

LAZY LOBSTER PIE

Lobster Pool owner Myalisa Waring says this dish is one of the most popular on the menu.

INGREDIENTS

¼	pound fresh lobster meat
1	tablespoon butter
4–5	Ritz crackers, finely crumbled
	Seasoning of your choosing

Melt the butter in an 8-inch pie tin. Add the fresh lobster meat. Crumble the Ritz crackers into a bowl, and season according to your preference. Sprinkle the seasoned crumbs on top of the lobster meat. Bake in the oven at 400°F for 15 minutes. Serve. Yields 1 serving.

Fresh from the Steamers and Fryers

The menu at the Lobster Pool is straightforward shack fare. Lobsters start at 1¼ pounds and go up to 2 pounds and above. They're steamed in big pots on the stove in the kitchen, and they come with french fries and coleslaw. The lobster rolls are made from meat that's picked fresh on the premises each morning. You get a little more than 3 ounces of meat and a leaf of lettuce tucked into a split-top bun. The meat is unadorned, unless you ask for mayo, in which case they'll mix it for you on the spot. You can also request a side of melted butter instead. The Lobster Pool will sell upwards of two hundred of these tasty sandwiches on a typical summer day.

Lazy Lobster Pie is a Lobster Pool specialty that consists of fresh-picked lobster meat, lots of butter, and seasoned Ritz crackers, mixed and baked in a small pie tin in the oven. It's excellent comfort food on a chilly day.

The deep fryers churn out plenty of fried clams, scallops, oysters, haddock, sole, and shrimp all day long, either à la carte or as part of seafood plates with fries and slaw. Chowder comes in the clam and seafood varieties, either in a cup or a bowl. For those averse to seafood, the kitchen's grill does some tasty burgers, hot dogs, and grilled chicken sandwiches.

Thinking about having something lighter? Try one of the Lobster Pool's salads. There's a grilled chicken Caesar salad, a Greek salad with feta cheese and calamata olives, and a salad called The Rockporter, which features bleu cheese and walnuts.

There's one easy way to find the Lobster Pool: look for the traps on the roof!

Two Great Dining Options

A highlight of the Lobster Pool is the charming, mesmerizing ambience of its various dining areas. Indoors, the two dining rooms are warm and inviting, with blue-and-white-checkered tablecloths on the tables, windows overlooking the backyard and cove, and a small woodstove in one of the dining rooms that helps take the chill out of the air during the shoulder seasons.

As nice as the dining rooms are, the outdoor picnic tables are the place to be most of the time. There are a couple of tables on the side of the building and several in back, and lots of people simply take their meals and beverages out back (it's a BYO place for alcohol) and sit at a table or on the rocks by the water.

The view of the cove and bay are wonderful, and you can see the shores of New Hampshire and even southern Maine in the distance on a clear day.

Because the Lobster Pool is situated on the northwest edge of Rockport, right along the water, the sunsets viewed from the backyard are simply amazing. You're looking to the west/northwest, and in the middle of summer, the sun appears to melt oh-so-slowly into the sea.

Put this place down for dinner on a clear, balmy evening and be sure to arrive early to get a spot to enjoy the sunset. The food is great, and the view is even better.

JT Farnham's Seafood and Grill

✕ 88 Eastern Avenue, Essex, MA

☎ 978-768-6643

🦞 Open early March to late November

JT Farnham's is in Essex, Massachusetts, on Route 133, known locally as the "Clam Highway" because a 10-mile stretch of the road connects three of the best clam shacks in the world—and Farnham's is one of them. Housed in a long, narrow, two-story wood-frame structure wedged between the highway and a salt marsh, Farnham's appears to be an unlikely place to find world-class seafood. However, don't be fooled by appearances.

Famous for Fried Clams

Farnham's has been around in one form or another since the early 1940s, and the contemporary story line picks up in the mid-1990s when current husband-and-wife owners, Joseph and Terry Cellucci, bought Farnham's and spiffed it up a bit by expanding the kitchen and dining areas.

Farnham's had always been known as a great place to get fried clams and other seafood, and the Celluccis stuck with the original recipe, tweaking it a bit along the way. One of their secrets is that they use super-clean cooking oil that has some animal fat mixed in with it to deliver extra flavor. They are also very picky about the clams they accept from local purveyors. Farnham's has been featured on Guy Fieri's *Diners, Dives, and Drive-Ins,* on the Food Network, and their clams are the primary reason for the glowing national coverage.

Some fine-looking sandwiches out of Farnham's kitchen, ready to eat.

Deep-Fried Lobster (and Steamed Ones, Too)

Sticking with the deep-fried motif, Farnham's is one of only a handful of shacks that offer deep-fried lobster. It's a simple process of breading

Farnham's picnic tables out by the salt marsh are highly coveted on busy days.

and deep-frying the lobster meat, which makes the lobster taste that much richer and sweeter. Some consider deep-frying lobster meat to be over the top in terms of richness. But it's really worth a try because you get all the meat in a 1½-pound lobster without all the work, and with your choice of two side orders of fries, onion rings, or coleslaw.

The regular boiled lobster is done on the stovetop, so your bug gets personal attention from the cook staff, and it also comes with fries, rings, or slaw (pick two). The lobster roll is a meaty one that comes unadorned on a split-top bun. You may have mayo and/or melted butter on the side and mix them in, if you wish. There's no lobster bisque at Farnham's, but there are a few fine chowders: clam or haddock or a Manhattan-style spicy scallop version. But the chowder of choice is the brazenly named "Best Seafood Chowder." It's loaded with clams, haddock, shrimp, scallops, and lobster meat. A 12-ounce bowl will set you back some 10 bucks, but it's worth every penny.

Dining and Driving Tips

Farnham's is small and it's famous, so you can expect to encounter crowds during the busy summer season and on weekends in the spring and fall. Parking can be a challenge. There's only a small lot on the side of the building, capable of holding a dozen cars or so, and there's limited street parking across the way. You may have to circle around a few times until a spot opens up in one of these places, but you'll soon forget the hassle of parking after you've sampled Farnham's fare.

If you're tempted to park on the street in the clearly marked no-parking areas, be forewarned that the local police may ticket you. However, they're also known to call Farnham's in advance to alert customers that they'll be cruising by soon, giving scofflaws a chance to move their vehicles. (That's thoughtful!)

Once you're (legally) parked, you queue up in the order line and wait your turn. At this point, you may wish to have someone in your party stake out a place to sit either indoors or outside at a picnic table. The indoor dining room is a cozy, wood-paneled gem with picture windows overlooking the salt marsh in back, and there's also a counter with several stools for diner-type seating.

The tables outdoors give you the best view of the mesmerizing marsh that stretches unimpeded to the sea ½ mile away. You're wedged between the parking lot and the edge of the marsh, but it's a bucolic scene that sometimes offers glimpses of shore birds and other wildlife while you're eating.

This place is a gem among gems on the Clam Highway, and though it may take you some time to get from your car to your fresh-cooked meal, you'll be glad you hung around to sample the lobsters and clams and other treats that Farnham's has to offer.

Farnham's long, narrow building sits right next to Route 133, the Clam Highway.

Woodman's of Essex

Woodman's is where the fried clam is said to have been invented in July 1916, when on a lark Lawrence "Chubby" Woodman cooked up a batch of breaded, fried, whole-belly clams in his roadside fry pot. The New England seafood world hasn't been the same since, and Woodman's has become an institution in the world of fried clams and other types of seafood.

What's less known about this shack of shacks is that it serves up *tons* of boiled lobsters throughout the spring, summer, and fall. It's a great place to order up a bug and devour it in Woodman's festive, wood-paneled and -tabled dining room or out back at a picnic table in the field by the meandering Essex River.

121 Main Street, Essex, MA

978-768-2559

www.woodmans.com

Open year-round

Home of the Roadside Lobster Stand

In addition to laying claim to being the originator of the fried clam, Woodman's has another distinguishing characteristic: its colorful, lively, open-air, street-front lobster stand. You can pick your own lobster right out on the street and watch it cook up in one of the large, gas-fired, brick-encased outdoor cooking pots that sit underneath an awning in front of Woodman's main building on Route 133.

The lobster setup resembles a roadside produce stand, with a vendor hawking his wares to passersby—only here it's gorgeous, scarlet-red, half-cooked lobsters spread out on a stainless steel table

Woodman's roadside lobster stand features a constant stream of fresh-cooked lobster to choose from.

done in large batches of 20 to 25 lobsters at a time before they're set out on the display table to tempt Woodman's customers.

It can get pretty lively on the street, and Woodman's employees play to the crowd, especially to curious children. The uncooked lobsters are kept in a large seawater tank next to the cookers, and kids are invited to step up and touch the live crustaceans that employees take from the tank. Geoffrey Woodman, who passed away several years ago, used to be the reigning king and emcee of Woodman's lobster stand, keeping up a nonstop banter and pulling pranks, like pretending to cut off his finger, to the shock and delight of his curbside audiences. Suffice it to say that having lobster at Woodman's is a lot of fun.

More Fine Seafood from Woodman's

The portal through which all fried-clam seekers must pass at Woodman's is the front door, which is right next to the lobster stand. Be prepared: if you come at a busy time, you may have to spend up to an hour in line on the street before gaining access to the inside order counter for deep-fried seafood and other good stuff. Once you're inside and you can see the large menu above the counter, make note of the deep-fried lobster tails, a Woodman's specialty. The tails come with fries and battered onion rings for an amazing deep-fried lobster feast.

There's also a meaty, cold lobster roll that's very large, quite pricey, and very popular. It's made from fresh-picked lobster meat and served on a toasted,

Serving up fresh-cooked lobsters in front of Woodman's on a very busy Mother's Day.

that's covered with shaved ice. You pick your bug, they pop it in the pot for a final couple of minutes of cooking, fish it out with a long-handled net, crack it with a kitchen knife, and you're all set.

All the lobsters are weighed in advance of cooking, and their weights are marked on one of the claws with an indelible grease pencil. The pre-cooking is split-top bun. The lobster roll comes with potato chips or, for a couple of bucks more, french fries.

The Clams and Rings are Tops

The big draw here, of course, are the world-famous clams. Dubbed "Chubby's Original Fried Clams," Woodman's has stayed true to the inventor's recipe, which calls for freshly shucked soft-shell clams to be given a quick milk wash, followed by a dredging in a tub of finely sifted corn flour, then deep-fried in liquid lard. It's this last step that gives Woodman's clams (and their other deep-fried seafood) its uniquely rich and distinctive flavor. This isn't something you should eat every day, but a plate of Woodman's fried clams every now and then will do you no harm, and your palate will definitely thank you.

Woodman's onion rings are the standout among side dishes. They're battered, then fried, which gives them a wonderfully sweet crunch. Also worth trying are Nana Bessie's Famous Clamcakes, deep-fried balls of clam-infused dough that make for a great appetizer or side dish.

Beyond the Clams and Lobsters

There's a full bar available in the main dining room, where you can step up and order a drink (alcoholic or otherwise) while you wait for your food. The pickup window, located across from the beverage stand in the main dining room, offers a glimpse into Woodman's busy kitchen, where a bank of deep fryers bubbles all day long. All the kitchen food is served in

You can find some peace and quiet at the picnic tables in back of Woodman's.

cardboard Miller beer case holders--a handy conveyance, given the large portions that come with nearly every deep-fried order.

Upstairs from the main dining room, you'll find an attractive raw bar that's open in the summer. Outside in back of the main building is a cute little ice-cream stand, and there's even a gift shop that's well stocked with lobster memorabilia and the usual array of T-shirts, coffee mugs, and items promoting all the fun things to see and do around Essex.

Yes, Woodman's is world famous for its fried clams, but people in the know come here in droves for the fresh-cooked lobster, also—queuing up on the street, picking out a good-looking bug, and enjoying it in the informal, somewhat chaotic atmosphere that makes the Woodman's dine-in-the-rough experience oh so worth it.

Brown's Lobster Pound

407 Route 286, Seabrook, NH

☎ 603-474-3331

🦞 www.brownslobsterpound.com

Open year-round

On the Route 286 approach to Seabrook, New Hampshire, and its fabled beaches, there are two large, low-slung lobster shacks, one on each side of the road, looking almost like sentries surveying all those heading to and from the oceanfront ¼ mile to the east. Of the two, Brown's is the oldest and longest established, and it's on the left-hand side as you head east toward the water. Let's go there first.

You should be able to recognize Brown's right away while traveling down the road because it's, well, brown. Actually it's more a goldenrod color with rustic red and white trim. The name, however, derives from the founders of Brown's, which is currently in its third and fourth generations of running the business.

Hauling 'Em, Then Selling 'Em

Back in 1947, Hollis Brown and a friend were laid off from factory jobs in Seabrook, so they bought a truck and started hauling lobsters down from the Pemaquid region of Maine and selling them in northern Massachusetts and southern New Hampshire. They bought their lobster for 35 cents per pound and sold them for 40 cents.

A year later, they opened a lobster pound in Hampton, New Hampshire, by the Taylor River and sold lobsters from that location for the next two years. In 1950 they moved down the road several miles to a spot on the Blackwater River in Seabrook, where the tidal waters were saltier and better for keeping lobsters. This spot is where Brown's stands today.

In the spring of 1952 Hollis and his partner opened a lunch bar in their modest lobster shack, serving fried seafood, lobster rolls, steamed

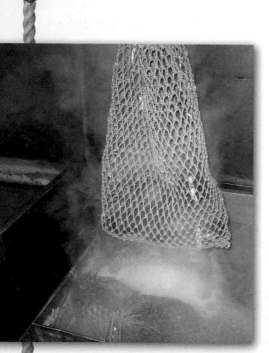

A freshly boiled lobster coming out of the gas-fired cooker at Brown's.

clams, and sandwiches in addition to their live and cooked lobsters. They built a large addition on the west side of the building that rested on pilings above the water and gave customers a place to sit and eat and enjoy the scenic river and marshland to the west.

Customers could also pick their own lobsters from the cold-water tanks inside the shack then have them cooked up on the spot. Hollis got the concept for his eatery from a similar place he had seen in Pemaquid, Maine. He bought out his partner in 1957, and Brown's has been a family business ever since.

Bruce Brown Sr., longtime owner of Brown's Lobster Pound, with two of his granddaughters.

Lobsters on a Large Scale

Over the years, Brown's has refined its shack to meet the demand of a constant flow of hungry travelers coming to and from the beach. During the winter months in the 1950s and 1960s, Hollis constructed more than 80 sturdy, solid wooden picnic tables and benches and installed them in Brown's enclosed post-and-beam dining room and on the outdoor deck, which dangles over the river.

The gas-fired lobster cookers in the main portion of the shack are a sight to behold. They sit next to the cold-water tanks (you can still pick your own lobster, if you wish), and the cookers can handle over a hundred lobsters at a time. Hollis also pioneered a lobster ID system decades ago that is still used today. When you order your lobster, you receive a small wooden paddle with a number written on it. Your lobster is then plopped into a netted drawstring sack with the corresponding number on a wooden float, and your bug is dropped into the cooker. Hold on to that paddle, because that's the only way you can claim your feast when your number is called.

On a busy summer day, there may be hundreds of diners in the hall and on the deck, noisily chattering away and tucking into their seafood repasts. It's a really festive atmosphere and a wonderful way to wrap up a day at the beach.

Other Goodies at Brown's

In addition to boiled lobsters, Brown's offers a full complement of fresh seafood, nearly all of it taken from fisheries just up the road in Maine, where Brown's still gets its lobsters. From the deep fryers, you can enjoy fried whole-belly clams, clam strips, scallops, shrimp, lobster tails, and haddock, along with generous portions of french fries and crispy onion rings. Brown's double-washes its seafood before frying, which means it's immersed in an egg wash followed by a dredging in flour followed by another wash and then a trip to the cracker-crumb bin. The end result is moist, crunchy, flavorful seafood that really satisfies.

Brown's also has a meaty lobster roll, with chilled lobster meat tossed in a bit of mayo and served on a leaf of lettuce in a split-top bun. The meat for the rolls is picked fresh throughout the day, as Brown's is constantly cooking lobsters in its vast pots.

To whet your appetite while waiting for your lobster dinner or lobster roll, try a cup or bowl of the creamy, spicy lobster bisque. This flavorful version contains finely chopped lobster meat and a hint of sherry—a nice way to begin your meal.

Speaking of sherry, Brown's is a BYO establishment, and you'll see families and groups of friends hauling in coolers full of beer and wine and setting them beside their tables. If you prefer anything else to drink (soda, iced tea, juice, or bottled water), you'll have to buy it from Brown's, as their BYO policy doesn't extend to nonalcoholic beverages.

Beware of Mother Nature

Brown's sits astride and over the extremely tidal Blackwater River. Each day, the river rises and falls several feet, and if you happen to be there at the right time, you can almost detect the ebb and flow occurring before your very eyes. Depending on the time of day and tide that you're there, you may be staring down at muddy flats or warily eyeing the water level as it creeps dangerously close to the floor of the deck.

Brown's dining room has been known to flood over the years, and during the blizzard of 1978, when the storm conspired with the tide tables to cause a gigantic surge of

Brown's cavernous, raucous BYO dining hall on a busy summer day.

Brown's sits atop wooden pilings alongside the Blackwater River.

water into the river, the eatery was almost lifted off its pilings and washed away. Hollis Brown's son and current owner, Bruce Brown Sr., remembers receiving a phone call from the police chief, informing him of the impending deluge. Bruce and other family members went down to the restaurant and opened all the doors to relieve pressure on the structure. "The water in the dining room was waist-deep," he recalls, years later. When asked by the police chief what to do next, Bruce simply said, "It's in God's hands now."

The restaurant survived the storm, and the Browns eventually installed four "portholes" in their dining room floor to let the occasional incursion of floodwater escape. When they do take on water, the crew at Brown's opens the hatches, mops down the floors, and reopens when everything is clean and dry once again, usually within several hours of the deluge.

Nature can also be kind. The marshland to the west of Brown's is filled with avian wildlife, which makes for some good bird-watching at the right times of year. And the sunsets viewed from the deck on long, languorous summer evenings can be breathtaking. So stock your cooler, gather your family and friends, and head on down to Brown's for an afternoon or evening of adventure and fun on the rising and falling Blackwater River.

Markey's Lobster Pool

420 Route 286, Seabrook, NH

☎ 603-474-2851

www.markeyslobsterpool.com

Open year-round

Across the street from Brown's is Markey's Lobster Pool, the new kid on the block (if you can call 40 years old "new"). Though newer to the scene than Brown's, it's equally popular with tourists and locals, and it serves up hundreds of pounds of succulent boiled lobster on busy summer days and nights, along with some excellent deep-fried seafood.

Life on the Blackwater River

Markey's was founded in 1971 by Tom Markey Sr. and his wife, Christine, along with their son and current owner, Tom Markey Jr. The new lobster stand offered the younger Tom, who'd just been discharged from the armed services, the prospect of gainful (and very busy) full-time employment. With Brown's across the street as a model, Markey's started small, with a modest one-story building that boiled lobsters and fried up seafood.

It didn't take long for things to get busy during the summer months, with tens of thousands of people coming and going to and from the nearby Seabrook, New Hampshire, beaches on busy, two-lane Route 286. Even in those early days, there would be a line out the door, and that's still the case today, even after a few expansive additions were put on Markey's over the years to accommodate the crowds.

Like at Brown's across the street, the Markeys found the salty, tidal Blackwater River to be the perfect place from which to draw water for their cold-water lobster tanks and their gas-fired cookers. It's always fun to go out onto Markey's shaded back deck and check out the level of the river, which ranges from up to the gunwales when the tide's coming in to

Markey's lobster cooker can hold up to a hundred lobsters at a time.

a bunch of mudflats and puddles just over the edge of the deck during low tide.

The restaurant grew from a modest shack to a megashack in fairly short order, and today Markey's can seat hundreds of hungry diners in its enclosed, white-and-blue dining hall and large back deck. With its faded indoor-outdoor carpeting and whitewashed wood-plank walls, the indoor dining area has the look and feel of a 1970s rec room. It's a very comfortable spot where customers relax in what the Markeys like to describe as their "beach-casual" atmosphere.

Beach casual it most certainly is. Lots of customers are in bathing suits, shorts, tank tops, and other beach attire, and the atmosphere is always relaxed and fun. The Markeys have made friends with many of their customers over the years, and Tom Jr. and his wife, Joyce, spend plenty of time chatting with regulars in the dining room when they're not back in the kitchen helping to cook the food.

Markey's back deck is a great place to hang out over the Blackwater River.

The Lobster Pool

There never was a lobster pool per se at Markey's. Instead, when you first walk through the front door, you're confronted with several large cold-water tanks and an order counter for anyone interested in having boiled lobster. The tanks are fed a constant stream of fresh seawater from the Blackwater River, and the water is chilled to between 40° and 46°F to keep the lobsters in good form. There are hundreds of lobsters swimming in the tanks at any given time, and they're sorted by size to expedite selection and cooking.

Also behind the counter and a safe distance from the cold-water tanks is Markey's stainless steel gas-fired cooker, which can hold up to a hundred lobsters at a time. Markey's often caters clambakes and lobster boils, and the massive cooker comes in handy on such occasions. Hanging suspended above the cold-water tanks is a simple chalkboard that lists the daily prices of the lobster.

You're more than welcome to choose your own lobster; otherwise, just specify the size you want, and one of the servers will pluck one out, pop it into a netted sack, and drop it into the cooker (also filled with constantly refreshed seawater) for a 9- to 12-minute boiling. Each sack has a numbered wooden block attached to the drawstring that corresponds to a claim number you'll receive at the lobster counter. They'll call your number when your bug is ready, and you can claim your feast at the same place where you ordered it. They will split the tail for you with a knife and crack the claws, in addition to giving you crackers to assist with the knuckles and other challenging parts.

There's More

If you or anyone in your party plans to have deep-fried seafood or chowder, turn to the left and join the line of hungry diners queued up to place their orders at the kitchen counter. You'll find some delectable fried clams and scallops and tasty chowders as well as more-pedestrian items such as hamburgers and hot dogs. You can also purchase soft drinks and other nonalcoholic beverages at the food counter, if you wish.

Should you care for a brew, just take the two steps up into the main dining room, where there's a small service bar that offers beer and wine by the glass. It's also a steamer bar, where you can order succulent steamed clams or mussels by the pound and enjoy them with broth and drawn butter.

The most recent addition to Markey's marquee of food choices is a raw bar, which is situated next to the lobster stand. There you can order up freshly shucked oysters and clams or a shrimp cocktail.

Where to Eat at Markey's

Once you've ordered and assembled your repast, you have two basic choices for dining at Markey's. First is the massive indoor dining hall, with its low-slung ceiling and its sliding glass windows that admit breezes off the surrounding marshlands. It's always cheery and full of laughter and conversation during busy times, and the tables are plentiful and spacious. Some three hundred people can fit into this space, making it a good choice, should you be with a large and raucous party.

The other option is to grab a table on the riverside deck in back of the building, which stretches along and above the river. This is a better choice for a more quiet and reflective meal, though at certain times the atmosphere can get rocking here as well. It's a great place to take in the acres of marsh grass across the river that stretch unimpeded to the ocean's shore about ¼ mile away.

Regardless of what you choose to eat or where you choose to enjoy it, you'll find that Tom and Joyce Markey and their daughter Lindsey will welcome you with open arms and do all that they can to convince you to come back to their beach-casual shack time and again.

Curious kids love to check out the lobster tanks at Markey's.

Rye Harbor Lobster Pound

✕ Rye Harbor, NH

☎ 603-964-7845

Open mid-June to late September

Rye Harbor Lobster Pound co-owner Sylvia Cheever.

AS YOU APPROACH RYE HARBOR there's a row of small shacks along the right-hand side, each one hawking various goods or services to passersby. One shack offers whale-watching and other sight-seeing trips on boats berthed in the harbor; another displays an array of nautical gifts. Then there's Rye Harbor Lobster Pound, an oh-so-small, oh-so-humble, and oh-so-tasty little lobster shack that's front and center in this collection of shacks, proudly flying a lobster flag from its front porch, letting everyone know they've got the good stuff inside.

This modest shack is owned and run by Nate Hanscom and his daughter, Sylvia Cheever. Nate originally built the shack for his wife in 1996, and the two of them cooked lobsters and served lobster rolls to people as they came and went to and from the adjacent harbor. Business has almost always been good, and Nate twice added 10 feet of kitchen space to the back of the stand.

Nate's wife passed away a few years ago, and Sylvia came on board to help her father keep the successful enterprise going. Like a breath of fresh air, Sylvia has introduced an amazing array of inventive, almost exotic, lobster dishes that belie the size of the place. From a cold lobster gazpacho—filled with fresh vegetables, lobster stock, lemon and lime, and a generous garnish of fresh lobster meat—to a recently introduced lobster alfredo pizza, there are some amazing things happening in this tiny kitchen.

But the signature dish of Rye Harbor Lobster Pound is its self-proclaimed "infamous hot, buttered lobster roll." It's an anomaly in this part of the world, where most lobster rolls are served chilled and mixed with mayo. Sylvia sautés her lobster meat in lobster stock, butter, and sherry, and she heaps it onto a toasted, split-top roll. This fine sandwich won Best Lobster Roll honors at a recent Hampton Beach Seafood Festival, where numerous larger lobster shacks and restaurants vie for top honors. Could there be a slow shift toward hot rolls along the New Hampshire coast? Stay tuned—and in the meantime, be sure to try some lobster gazpacho!

LOBSTER ROLL ALERT!

Ray's Seafood Restaurant

🍴 1677 Ocean Boulevard, Rye, NH

☎ 603-436-2280

🦞 www.raysseafoodrestaurant.com

Open early January to late November

Rye Beach, in the northern portion of New Hampshire's abbreviated Atlantic coastline, is a busy place in the summer. Lots of beachgoers park along the ocean side of Route 1A and clamor over the berms, which separate beach from road in most places, to enjoy a day in Rye's surf, sand, and sun. A very casual atmosphere prevails in this section of mostly upscale Rye, with lots of families in SUVs and middle-age bikers on Harleys seemingly reliving the glory days of their youth.

There's a certain working-class spirit to the area, and it's best seen and experienced at a couple of large lobster and seafood shacks that sit on 1A across from the beaches. Heading north out of Rye Harbor, the first one you'll encounter is Ray's Seafood. You can't miss it; it's two stories tall and as blue as the sea.

Water in the Basement

Ray's Seafood was founded a little over 50 years ago by local entrepreneur Ray Parker. He was an affable host, selling mostly lobsters and deep-fried seafood to his customers while also cooking up whatever else they asked for. The shack's menu grew to include such disparate items as steak, spaghetti, pork chops, tacos, egg rolls, barbecued chicken, and more.

When Ray passed away some 25 years ago, he willed the restaurant to his hardworking manager, who kept it going until 1986, when the boiler in the basement blew and the place burned down. At that point, she decided to retire, and her son, Andy Widen, the current owner of Rays, took over.

It's hard to drive by Ray's roadside sign without stopping in for a bite.

A lobsterman by trade, Andy put on his carpenter's belt and had the restaurant rebuilt from the ground up. The original Ray's was below ground level in a basement-type space with beach apartments on the floors above it. From time to time, waves from the ocean across the street would kick up and over the road and flood Ray's basement space, with much of the water settling into one corner of the restaurant. Ray's management and customers took it in stride and stayed on the other side of the basement where it was nice and dry (if a bit dank). The new Ray's was transformed into an aboveground, two-story eatery and painted a distinctive, deep, dark blue, which you can see from miles away as you approach on 1A.

Ray's current manager, Steve Chud, came on board around the time of the rebuild, initially as a carpenter pounding nails. He and Andy formed a bond, and Steve stayed on. He now runs the entire operation, from the kitchen to the order window to the second-floor bar that overlooks the marsh out back. Andy took a new tack with the eatery when it reopened in August 1987, gutting the menu and focusing back on the lobster and seafood items, and it's been a lobster and seafood place ever since.

Lobsters at Ray's

Andy owns two lobster boats that supply virtually all of the lobsters that Ray's needs on any given day. The boats are docked just down the road in Rye Harbor, and the fresh lobster catch is trucked in daily.

Steve says the 1- and 1¼-pound lobsters (often sold as twins) are the most popular lobster item on the menu. In addition, there are about half a dozen other lobster dishes, including:

Big Blue, a 12-foot-tall wooden chainsaw sculpture, presides over Ray's back parking lot.

- Lobster baked stuffed mushrooms, a great way to start your meal
- Spinach artichoke dip, a concoction that's whipped together only in the summer
- Baked stuffed lobster, a 1¼-pound lobster with extra lobster meat and a Ritz-cracker crumb coating over the tail portion
- A lobster pasta dish, made by Steve, using stewed tomatoes, lobster meat, fresh grated cheese, and angel hair pasta (available during autumn months only)

Lobster rolls may be had either hot or cold, the hot version featuring 4 ounces of lobster meat sautéed in butter and cream sherry and served in a toasted, split-top bun. The cold roll is claw and knuckle meat only, mixed with mayo and served on a toasted, buttered bun.

Ray's keeps its lobsters in a large shed in back of the restaurant. Fresh seawater is pumped constantly from the tidal marsh out back, so the lobsters retain their liveliness and their tasty saline flavor. Lobsters are steamed at Ray's in a large chowder steamer that's been converted for lobster cooking. It's purged of sand every day, guaranteeing grit-free lobsters at all times. (The chowder, by the way, is made in a couple of separate, large stovetop pots on a daily basis.)

There is also a wide variety of deep-fried seafood and baked seafood dinners. Lobster pie is another popular item, and Ray's keeps a bunch of them frozen for takeout. A lot of Ray's customers are regulars who have been coming for years, and some families have three generations of devotees, which is always a hallmark of good, steady, consistent food and service.

Say Hi to Big Blue

In addition to the blue-hued main building that houses Ray's, there's another blue object worthy of special attention. Big Blue is a 12-foot-tall wooden chainsaw sculpture of a lobster standing on its tail in the back portion of Ray's parking lot. This behemoth was carved by world-famous chainsaw sculptor Ray Murphy of Hancock, Maine, and shipped down to Ray's, where it was painted blue to match the building. Kids love checking out Big Blue as well as the adjacent hands-on aquarium where tide-pool creatures such as starfish are on display.

Keep Ray's Seafood in mind if you're spending a day at the beach in Rye. It's a lively place with a lot of character—and lobster pretty much any way you want it.

The Hampton Beach Seafood Festival

Each September, on the weekend following Labor Day, the seaside town of Hampton Beach, New Hampshire, rolls out the red carpet for one of the largest and most fun seafood festivals in New England.

The Hampton Beach Seafood Festival (www.hamptonbeachseafoodfestival.com) got its start in the late 1980s, when a group of Hampton-area merchants and restaurateurs decided to put on a waterfront festival to promote local businesses and seafood. After a slow start, the festival grew over the years, eventually taking over the entire downtown area of Hampton Beach, with large tents and entertainment venues set up on the waterfront to house all the food, live music, and other goings on.

Today the festival draws nearly 150,000 people over its three-day duration. There are food booths featuring area restaurants and specialty food purveyors (mostly seafood), a beachside stage where live music plays throughout the festival, culinary chef demos, a Kiddieland tent, fireworks, and a lobster-roll-eating contest.

But the big draw is the food, and there's plenty of it. It's a great way to sample lots of the local fare (especially lobster!) and to spend some time outdoors in sun and sand before the winds of autumn begin to blow.

A fresh batch of lobster rolls ready for Hampton Beach Seafood Festival's hungry customers.

Petey's Summertime Seafood and Bar

Another great oasis on Route 1A in Rye Beach is Petey's Summertime Seafood and Bar, a lively place across from the beach and next to a small tidal creek that winds beside and behind Petey's and its adjacent parking lot.

Petey's is a two-story funhouse, and like Ray's down the road, it has a full bar on the second floor, with great views of the beach across the street. This shack may win the award for the most (and most colorful) collection of lobster-trap buoys anywhere. They hang from the road sign out front, dangle all over the sides of the building, hover overhead in some of the indoor rooms, and cover the sides of the outbuildings that wrap around the back of the shack. All of them are branded with the Petey's name, and though Petey is a working lobsterman himself, you know he doesn't tag his traps with so many different colors and designs. Nonetheless, just one glance at Petey's garish display of buoys tells you there's got to be plenty of good lobster inside.

Humble Beginnings

Owner Petey Aikens Jr. founded his namesake shack in 1990 in a little one-story shanty on a small traffic circle to the north, away from the beach and closer to the center of Rye. He kept the menu simple with selected deep-fried items and lobster. (Aikens has lobstered since he was young, so he split his time, as he does today, between lobstering and running the restaurant.)

✕ 1323 Ocean Avenue, Rye, NH

☎ 603-433-1937

🦞 www.peteys.com

Open year-round

Petey's is part full-service reataurant, part dine-in-the-rough lobster joint.

Petey's has more colorful lobster buoys than any other lobster shack in New England.

Down along the beach on Route 1A, a timeworn restaurant named the Harbormaster came up for sale in the late 1990s. Petey had worked part-time while in high school at the Harbormaster, so he was familiar with the place and thought it would make a great spot for an expanded version of his shack in town.

He bought the place and set about fixing it up, keeping the shell of the building and adding a carryout/ice-cream window on the south side by the creek. He renovated the upstairs lounge and remodeled the indoor seating areas to make them more appealing to Petey's (and Harbormaster's) regular customers. The place has been a success ever since. Aikens still lobsters most days in the summer, and his sister, father, and other family members help keep the wheels turning at Petey's throughout the day.

Lobster As You Like It

Aiken, of course, supplies most of his own lobsters. When things get really busy in the middle of summer, he supplements his catch with that of a friend who also lobsters out of Rye Harbor. And when things get *really* busy, Aikens will truck in some more from another friend in Maine.

When you order a lobster here, it's steamed in a large stainless steel steamer, which seals in the moisture and the flavor of the lobster meat and cuts some time off the cooking process. Petey's has what they call their Clam Bake Dinner, which consists of a 1-pound lobster, a pound of steamed clams, corn on the cob, french fries, coleslaw, and the chowder of your choice.

The baked stuffed lobster, which features Petey's secret seafood stuffing and a cup of chowder, is a popular choice. And there's the increasingly popular Lazy Man's Lobster, a 1½-pound lobster de-shelled, with drawn butter and a cup of chowder on the side. The lobster roll is served cold, tossed in mayonnaise, and tucked into a toasted, top-split bun. For those who will only take their seafood breaded, try the deep-fried lobster tails with butter.

Three Kinds of Chowder

The chowders at Petey's are famous, having won local awards on several occasions. You have your choice of three different kinds: clam, haddock, or seafood. These chowders are made fresh daily in immense cauldrons on the stovetops, and even when the thermometer outside heads toward triple digits and people pour into Petey's for some relief from the heat, there's always strong demand for steaming, hot chowder in cups and bowls.

The clam chowder is made in the traditional New England style—thick and creamy, with big chunks of potato and clams within. The seafood and haddock chowders are more in the Maine vein—milky and complex with plenty of seafood and fish included.

Of Jamaican Punch and Helipads

In the evenings, Petey's second-floor dining area and lounge, with its bird's-eye view of the beach across the way, really gets rocking, and the house-drink Jamaican Punch certainly adds to the festive atmosphere. Made with rum and various fruit juices, one has to be careful, as a couple of these tasty concoctions can creep up on you. So have fun, but be judicious in your consumption.

Every good shack should have something unique about it, and at Petey's, that would probably be the helipad out back. A helicopter pilot keeps a small chopper parked there for his occasional excursions and for the flying lessons he conducts from time to time. In addition, a Petey's customer will occasionally fly in for a meal, landing out back on the flat, grassy pad. So don't be surprised if you hear the *thwop* of helicopter blades while enjoying your lobster at Petey's. It's just one of several surprises that makes this place the special hangout that it is.

SOUTHERN MAINE SHACKS

Okay, now we're entering serious lobster country. Once you cross the Piscataqua River bridge on I-95 and enter the state of Maine, a whole world of possibilities opens up. Maine is synonymous with the red crustacean, and there is probably no better place to indulge yourself in a freshly cooked lobster or two plucked from the lobster trap earlier that day.

Southern Maine, which stretches from the border town of Kittery to Portland, Maine's largest city, is one of the most trafficked stretches of coast in the state when it comes to tourism, beach bumming, outlet shopping—and eating lobster! There are a wide variety of possibilities, from tiny mom-and-pop joints with only a picnic table or two outside to a massive dock in downtown Portland where hundreds eat lobster and other seafood and quaff their favorite beverages.

In between these extremes are some excellent lobster pounds and dine-in-the-rough places, such as the somewhat fancy Barnacle Billy's in Ogunquit, the bare-bones, tradition-rich Bayley's Lobster Pound in Pine Point, and the shack with the million-dollar view—Lobster Shack Two Lights in Cape Elizabeth.

Within a relatively short distance, you can find all sorts of lobster-shack experiences, each one with its own distinctive feel and flavor. Plan to spend at least a couple of days (and several meals) exploring southern Maine's coast, using U.S. Route 1 as your main thoroughfare. It's a great introduction to the lobster capital of the world.

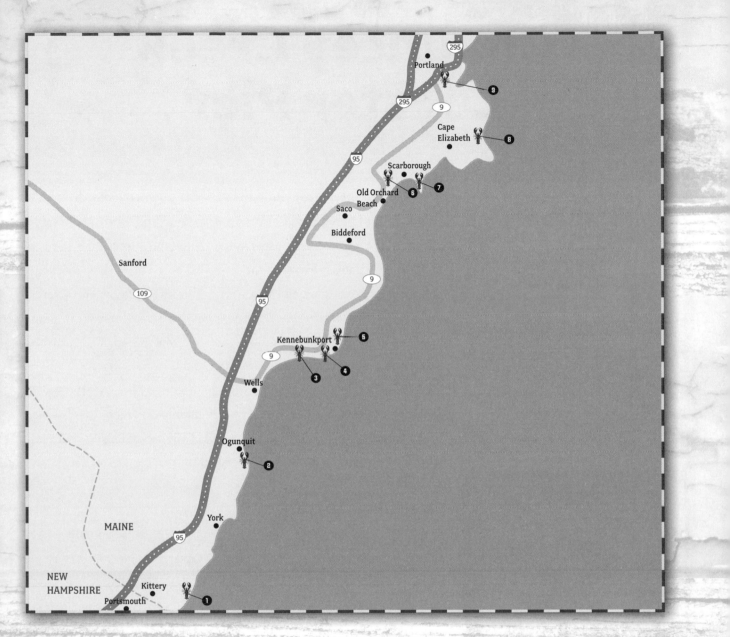

Chauncey Creek Lobster Pier

16 Chauncey Creek Road, Kittery, Maine

☎ 207-439-1030

🦞 www.chaunceycreek.com

Open mid-May to mid-October

Kittery, Maine, is best known as a border-town, outlet-mall mecca, with dozens of brand-name stores positioned up and down Route 1 and lots of traffic and tourists, especially in July and August. It's hard to imagine the contrast between this crowded scene and what lies just a few miles to the east, along the waterfront in Kittery Point, the quieter, more residential part of town. Well-appointed homes tucked in pine-forested enclaves look out on quiet, rocky coves dotted with pleasure craft resting at anchor in the sparkling waters.

While traveling on winding, two-lane Route 103 through this quiet, scenic part of Kittery, be sure to hang a right onto Chauncey Creek Road, which will take you in short order to one of the nicest lobster shacks in all of Maine: Chauncey Creek Lobster Pier.

Straddling the Creek

Chauncey Creek is pretty much a creek in name only. It's actually a narrow inlet connected to nearby Pepperell Cove. The creek is very tidal, rising and falling some 10 feet, twice per day. This allows big boats, some up to 50 feet in length, to navigate the creek—if they time it right. Why would they want to do this? To dock at Chauncey Creek Lobster Pier and come ashore to enjoy some fine lobster and other tasty fare from the sea.

Back in the 1920s, a couple of enterprising fishermen floated a building up the creek from Kittery, placed it on pilings along the side, and set up a fishing dock that was well protected from the ravages of the nearby ocean. Three brothers, Herbert, Charles, and Eddie Lithiam,

Chauncey Creek Lobster Pier is one of the premier lobster shacks in southern Maine.

began using the dock as a home port and as a place to service fishermen in need of bait and gas and a spot to offload their catches.

Lobsters were part of the daily take at Chauncey Creek pier, and Herbert started cooking up some of the catch on the dock in the late 1940s, serving fresh-cooked lobsters to the locals, who enjoyed the creek-side eatery. He began with two small cookers and two picnic tables. Lobster rolls, tuna salad, egg salad, and potato chips soon followed, and Chauncey Creek Lobster Pier was born.

Eight Hundred-Plus Meals a Day

Flash forward to the present, and the quaint little lobster stand from 60 years past has grown into a thriving enterprise that serves eight hundred customers, sometimes more, per day on a brightly painted, festive pier that runs some 200 feet along the northern bank of Chauncey Creek. Current owner Ron Spinney, a third-generation direct descendant of Herbert Lithiam, has run Chauncey Creek for the past 28 years. He and his wife, Jean, bought the shack from his parents, George and Claire, in 1984. Ron and his family have transformed Chauncey Creek into a destination shack. It has a huge following of lobster lovers that hail from Boston to California and all points between, many of whom come to the pier several times per season.

When you pull on to Chauncey Creek Road, the creek soon comes into view through the trees off to the right. Then you begin to see scores of cars parked on both sides of the narrow road ahead and eventually a couple of youthful parking attendants who help direct you to the best spots to park in order to get to the pier (and to avoid parking on private

A humongous order of fresh-cooked bugs ready for feasting.

property). Once you've ditched your vehicle, proceed to the CHAUNCEY CREEK LOBSTER PIER sign and walk down the steps and the gangplank that lead to the sunny pier straddling the creek some 20 feet below street level.

The first thing you'll notice are all the colorful, glossy wooden picnic tables that line the pier from one end to the other. Painted variously in shades of red, green, light blue, beige, and peach, they're usually packed with diners enjoying a day outdoors. Every spring Ron and his crew sand each of the 42 tables, then they repaint them with bright, high-gloss, marine-grade paint. These days, very little is left of the old fishing dock, as most of the pier space has been converted into dining areas that range from totally exposed to the elements to semi-enclosed with a roof overhead to shaded tables beneath a large tent on the south end of the pier.

The Food Huts

There are three "huts," or places where you can place your food order, each dispensing a different type of delectable. Once you descend to the pier from street level and plant your boots on the deck, turn left and behold the lobster hut, where cold-water tanks hold the day's offerings and where you can pick out your own lobster or simply specify which size you want. Ron gets his lobsters from Canada, receiving massive shipments every other day. He claims that the hard-shell, cold-water lobsters from the northern waters are better for eating. The 1½- and 1¾-pound hard-shell lobsters are the most popular—always full of firm lobster meat and just the right amount for one lobster-craving individual.

The middle hut takes food orders for virtually everything else, which includes chowders, steamed mussels or clams, seafood rolls, hot dogs, and side dishes, such as cole-slaw, corn on the cob, french fries, and onion rings. There's very little in the way of deep-fried seafood at Chauncey Creek, as they prefer to focus on the lobster specialties for which they're best known.

The third hut contains a small raw bar, where you can get oysters on the half shell, cherrystones, and boiled, chilled, peel-and-eat

Fresh lobsters being lowered onto the pier.

gulf shrimp. It also holds a couple of deep fryers and Chauncey Creek's five vast lobster cookers.

Lobster is clearly the most popular item here, and the lobster roll adds to the overall popularity at Chauncey Creek. They sell more than ten thousand lobster rolls each season to those who love the taste of lobster but don't want to grapple with the hard shells and the lobster crackers and the bibs that are part of the whole-lobster experience. Chauncey Creek's recipe for their lobster roll consists of fresh, chilled lobster meat mixed with Miracle Whip, a little bit of onion powder, and a dash of fresh lemon juice. It's served on a toasted hamburger bun (a bit of a variation from the norm) piled high with 5 ounces of lobster meat and served with potato chips and pickle slices.

There are also some excellent pies baked daily, so save room for a slice of pie or a generous portion of Chauncey Creek's famous cheesecake.

BYO—Big Time

There's BYO and then there's *BYO*. Bringing your own is a big deal at Chauncey Creek, and we're not just talking about beer and wine. You are more than welcome to bring your favorite libations, and you'll see many fellow diners hauling in coolers of beer and bottles of wine and other spirits, as it's all part of the fun at Chauncey Creek.

Additionally, you're welcome to bring any side dish you wish to complement your meal, as long as it doesn't duplicate anything that's on Chauncey Creek's menu. And you're free to lay out any tableware you want to bring along, including plates, glasses, silverware, tablecloths, candelabras, whatever. Some people really dress up their tables, offering a stark contrast to the very informal, woodsy surroundings. But it's all in the spirit of having a good time.

Ron recalls perhaps the ultimate BYO at Chauncey Creek, which occurred several years ago, when a couple rented the pier for their wedding rehearsal dinner.

Chauncey Creek's spacious deck affords great views of the boats on the water.

For the evening's entertainment, they hired a piano player and rented a full-size grand piano, which was lowered from Chauncey Creek's street-level loading dock down to the pier using the pier's industrial-strength winch. The music that night must have been grand indeed, echoing off the waters and the pine-tree forest some 100 yards across the creek on the opposite shore.

Sittin' on the Dock of the Creek

One of the most enjoyable things to do at Chauncey Creek is to sit back and watch the amazing variety of boats and other watercraft that cruise by the pier throughout the day, especially at high tide. You'll see lots of sleek kayaks skimming by, with paddlers waving to the appreciative crowd on the deck. There are canoes, skiffs, the occasional small sailboat, and plenty of cabin cruisers, many of which tie up to the pier and come aboard for a lobster or a roll or a little liquid refreshment on dry land. Don't be surprised if you see a wind surfer or two plying the creek's waters while you dine.

There is perhaps no better (or quicker) way to kick off your trip to Maine than to get off I-95 or Route 1 after crossing the Piscataqua River bridge and snaking your way down to this peaceful pier perched on the creek that isn't really a creek, yet at the same time is so much more. Chauncey Creek Lobster Pier sets the bar high for lobster shack expectations that await you on the rest of the Maine coast, all the way from Kittery to Canada.

Barnacle Billy's

50-70 Perkins Cove, Ogunquit, ME

☎ 207-646-5575

www.barnbillys.com

Open mid-April to mid-October

Ogunquit is the epicenter of tourism in southern Maine in the summertime—and with good reason. It's a quaint, charming, walkable town filled with great restaurants, wonderful shopping, and cultural amenities that bigger towns and even small cities could only hope to have.

Barnacle Billy's of Ogunquit may be the only lobster shack anywhere that offers valet parking. Why, you ask? Just try and find a parking spot on Perkins Cove (where the shack is located) or anywhere in Ogunquit, for that matter, on a summer day. Valet parking may seem like an unnecessary luxury, but it is in fact a necessity down near the water here.

Fifty Years and Still Going Strong

The year 2011 marked the 50th anniversary of Barnacle Billy's. Owner Billy Tower (aka Barnacle Billy) first opened his doors in 1961 when he purchased a store that had been an art supply and gift shop in the Perkins Cove section of town, and he's been boiling up lobsters and serving up seafood to the tourists and the locals who inhabit this seaside hamlet ever since.

A friend of Billy's had owned the shop and hated running it, so he made Tower a great offer to take over the property and transform it into a dine-in-the-rough lobster joint. Billy, who had been lobstering for more than a decade, saw a great opportunity, accepted the offer, and hasn't looked back.

Barnacle Billy's was a success from the beginning for two reasons: First, there was a steady stream of well-heeled tourists constantly coming up the coast from places like Boston and New York, and most of them

Barnacle Billy's is the premier place for lobster in Ogunquit.

Boiled versus Steamed Lobster

There are two basic ways to cook lobsters: boiling them in water or steaming them in a pot or steamer. Each method has its fans and skeptics.

When you boil a lobster, the creature is totally immersed in a pot of rapidly boiling water, which is then returned to a boil and left to bubble away for 10 to 15 minutes, depending on the size of the lobster. Most lobster shacks that boil their lobsters use salty water from the sea, which they claim adds to the overall maritime flavor. If seawater isn't available, then highly salted water is recommended. Nonbelievers in this method claim that the meat in the lobster may get water-logged because it spends so much time immersed in the cooking pot.

The steaming method calls for putting an inch or so of sea- or salted water in the bottom of the pot, heating it to a boil, then placing the lobster inside, with the lid firmly on top. Alternatively, a number of lobster shacks use the more high-tech and efficient method of steaming their lobsters in a stainless steel convection steamer. Fans of steaming claim that steamed lobster meat retains its firm, succulent texture and flavor better than the boiling method. Opponents of steam claim that the natural flavor of the sea may be steamed out of the lobster, leaving the meat less flavorful than the boiling method.

When you go out for lobster, ask what method each shack uses to cook their bugs, then take your own personal running survey and decide which method you prefer. As with many things in life, it pretty much boils (or steams) down to what works best for you.

wanted to enjoy a lobster or two while vacationing on the Maine coast. Second, Billy developed a killer menu that has pretty much stayed the same since the shack opened. People keep coming back and telling him how much they appreciate that the place hasn't changed over the years and they can always count on Barnacle Billy's to deliver great food in a relaxing atmosphere.

It also doesn't hurt that the shack is located on a small harbor attached to Perkins Cove. The harbor and cove are surrounded by stately homes and upscale hotels. There is also a unique, wooden, hand-crank-operated pedestrian bridge over the channel that connects the harbor to the cove. Billy, who is now in his 80s, says the channel used to be a creek, but after it was dredged, larger pleasure craft quickly began filling the harbor and were a boon to his business.

It's Raining Paprika

Someone at Barnacle Billy's must really likes paprika; many of the dishes are dusted with the burnt red Hungarian seasoning. It's on top of the chowder, the lobster rolls, and several other items, and the effect is a pleasant one, both for the eye and the palate.

Lobster remains the most popular item on the menu. Billy's gets theirs from Atwood Brothers of St. George, Maine, and from nearby York Lobster. They sell hard-shell lobsters for as long as they can get them. The lobster roll also sells in big numbers. It's a cold salad roll that consists of lobster meat, a bit of mayo, a dash of mustard, and a sprinkling of chopped celery for crunch (and, of course, paprika!). The traditional Maine-style clam chowder, made with milk instead of cream, also is a crowd pleaser.

One interesting item that Billy's has had on the menu from the beginning is the barbecued rotisserie chicken. They've got a brick rotisserie setup in the kitchen that can roast as many as 16 chickens at a time, and the birds come out plump and juicy. Steamed clams are popular, as is Billy's famous rum punch, which they sell by the hundreds of glasses on busy summer days.

Barnacle Billy's Et Cetera

Billy's two sons, Court and Tim, run the day-to-day operations of the business, along with their sisters, Cathy and Meg. It's a family business in every sense, and Barnacle Billy's customers benefit because the Tower family takes impeccable care of the place, seeing to every detail to make sure that things run smoothly and customers keep coming back.

The business has been so successful over the years that Billy opened a somewhat fancier sit-down, full-service restaurant next door named Barnacle Billy's etc. If anything, you might think that the "etc." should be applied to the less fancy dine-in-the-rough original, but Billy's has remained true to its roots. Though the buildings and grounds of both Barnacle Billy's are quite polished and snappy looking, the atmosphere remains relaxed at both, and you'll feel comfortable in casual dress regardless of which one you decide to frequent. (Both have the aforementioned valet parking.)

Too many cooks don't spoil the broth at Barnacle Billy's.

The Lay of the Land at Billy's

Upon entering the original Barnacle Billy's, you find yourself in a warmly lit, comfortable, pine-paneled order area with a counter stretching the length of the room along the left-hand side. There are several workers, mostly young men, in starched-white cook's garb and crew-neck Barnacle Billy's t-shirts ready to take and prepare your order on the other side of the counter. There's no menu save for the one on the chalkboard by the counter. You'll probably notice that the prices are a bit dear at Billy's, but you get what you pay for, and here you're getting a first-rate in-the-rough lobster-dining experience.

Once your order is placed and you have your claim number, you can either linger by the counter or descend several steps into another pine-paneled room, this one filled with tables, a cozy fireplace on one wall, and a service bar for beer, wine, and spirits. The room is lined with windows overlooking the deck outside and the harbor beyond, and it's a good choice for rainy or blustery days.

A Most Unusual Pedestrian Bridge

The best place to park yourself, however, is on the deck outside, which overlooks the harbor and its handsome boats and offers an excellent view of the odd yet captivating wooden pedestrian bridge that arches high in the air over the channel and is cranked up frequently to let masted boats pass in and out. Billy says that George H. W. Bush, who lives about 15 miles to the north in Kennebunkport, comes down

Lobster rolls with Billy's trademark paprika.

on his boat with family and friends (and his Secret Service entourage) for lunch every week or so in the summertime. The Bushes and the Towers are good friends, and there's always an open table for the elder statesman and his dining companions.

There's no need to queue up to the service bar if you want something to drink. Waiters will take your order once you've settled down at a table. You still have to go inside and claim your food when your number is called, but your beverage needs will be attended to by the young, cheerful college-student waitstaff. So while you're here, waiting for some of the finest fresh seafood southern Maine has to offer, order yourself a rum punch and enjoy the bliss that Perkins Cove and Barnacle Billy's have to offer. It's a beautiful spot in a beautiful town—and it has valet parking. Lobster shacks don't get much swankier than this!

The Clam Shack

⚒ 2 Western Avenue, Kennebunk, ME

☎ 207-967-3321

🦞 www.theclamshack.net

Open early May to mid-October

"**I'm** **king of the lobster rolls!**" proclaims Clam Shack owner Steve Kingston (à la Leonardo DiCaprio in *Titanic*) while standing on the roof of his modest eatery during the recent filming for an episode of the Travel Channel's popular *Food Wars* program. Kingston's lobster roll was pitted against that of Alisson's Restaurant, which sits some 500 feet away over a short bridge spanning the Kennebunk River in downtown Kennebunkport, Maine.

Given Steve's normally more modest demeanor, it's a bit surprising to see him make such a bold and dramatic proclamation—and on national television, no less. Yet, if you think about it, he may very well be what he claims, as the Clam Shack's famed lobster-roll sandwich has won state and even national awards for its freshness, its honesty, and its unbeatable texture and flavor. This man may very well need to be crowned some day.

Names Can Be Deceiving

Make no mistake about it: the Clam Shack serves up some excellent deep-fried seafood with its simple yet mouthwatering offerings of fried whole-belly clams, clam strips, deep-sea scallops, haddock, and shrimp. And the onion rings, french fries, and homemade coleslaw make for excellent sides that round out the various seafood plates very nicely.

But it's the Clam Shack's lobster that keeps popping up in the extensive media coverage that the

Clam Shack owner Steve Kingston tending to the lobster cooker.

eatery has received over the years. There's good reason for this, and a lot of it has to do with the Clam
Shack's lobster roll, a sandwich that dates back to the
shack's early days, when it was just a seafood market.

The Clam Shack's Origins

The Clam Shack started as an offshoot of a seafood
market that was founded in the late 1930s. The market was purchased by Richard Jacques in 1968, and
he added a small food shack to the side of the building. The shack is perched over the edge of the Kennebunk River, right next to the road and bridge that
traverses the narrow stream. Thus was born the
Clam Shack, where Jacques proceeded to fry up local
clams, scallops, and fish and at the same time added
a tasty lobster roll to the menu.

Jacques's lobster roll was a bit different from others in that he served his lobster meat on a toasted,
hamburger-style bun instead of the traditional split-
top hot dog roll. People seemed to like it, and for
decades the Clam Shack thrived in its downtown location, building a reputation among tourists and locals
alike for its excellent fried seafood and its tasty, if
unorthodox, lobster-roll sandwich.

Flash-forward some 30 years, when local ice-
cream shop owner and paper wholesaler Steve Kingston was driving through town on a snowy December
day. He noticed a FOR SALE sign in front of the Clam
Shack, and he saw then and there an opportunity
that would grow into a lifetime passion. Steve bought
the Clam Shack and the adjoining seafood market,

The Clam Shack's award-winning lobster roll and its signature
hamburger bun.

and he opened the following spring, full of hope for
prosperous times to come.

That first year—as locals and summer regulars
held their collective breath to see what the new guy
would do to the place—Steve wisely changed very
little, in order to establish trust with his base of loyal
customers. In fact, over the years, not that much has
changed at the Clam Shack, as it continues with its
philosophy of doing only a few things but doing them
very well. After a bumpy first couple of years, the
Clam Shack hit its stride, and it's been a perennial
success ever since.

The Lobster Roll Today

The lobster roll at the Clam Shack continues to be one of the most popular items on the menu, and Steve has made a few tweaks to the roll over the years. First, he started an exclusive agreement with Reilly's Bakery in nearby Biddeford, Maine, to do a special hamburger-style bun, which has become the shack's signature style for its sandwich. The special buns are delivered fresh six times per week during the busy season, and the Clam Shack is the only place you can get them.

The Clam Shack serves its lobster rolls two ways: with a touch of mayonnaise slathered on the top bun or with some warm butter drizzled directly onto the lobster meat. Or, if you desire, you can have both. Either way (or both ways), you really can't go wrong.

The lobster preparation is key to the sandwich's success. Steve has two to three local lobstermen who work exclusively for the Clam Shack, delivering fresh catches every day. When the lobsters arrive from nearby Cape Porpoise, they are immediately placed and sorted in the shack's burbling cold-water tanks in the back. The rear portion of the shack is suspended over the river, and you can see the water below through the narrow cracks between the floorboards. Fresh seawater is drawn through a pipe at high tides and pumped directly into the cold-water tanks, keeping the lobsters in their native saltwater habitat.

There is a large cooker next to the tanks that is capable of holding dozens of lobsters at a time. When the bugs are boiled, they're placed on a screen rack to cool down, then they're moved to a stainless-steel-countered picking area in a room between the cold-water tanks and the seafood market.

The Clam Shack packs 'em in all summer long.

The Ice House

One thing Steve discovered over the years is that fresh-picked lobster meat is best when it remains at a constant temperature of 32°F. To accomplish this, the Clam Shack forgoes traditional electric refrigeration and instead opts for an icehouse, with a large ice-making machine serving as the coolant. When the lobster meat is picked and divided into individual portions (one whole 1-pound lobster—tail, claw, and knuckle, plus one or two more pieces—per sandwich), they are put in plastic cups, capped, and placed into a cooler filled with ice cubes, then covered with more cubes. This keeps the temperature constant, and the ice distribution is checked throughout the day to ensure proper coverage.

Why go to all this trouble? When you taste a lobster roll at the Clam Shack, you'll know why. It's the freshest, tastiest lobster roll meat you'll experience virtually anywhere. It's a lot of hassle and extra expense, but for Steve it has created a large and devoted following of lobster-roll lovers who keep coming back for more.

Soft-Shell Meat Is Best

Once again going against the prevailing wisdom in the lobster-eating world, Steve believes that soft-shell lobster meat makes for a better-tasting lobster roll. He says this is due to the fact that a molting (soft-shell) lobster has more seawater between its relatively diminutive body and its newly formed larger outer shell and that this seawater buffer keeps the meat sweet and salty tasting as opposed to more densely packed hard-shell meat. Some people, particularly lobstermen, also prefer soft-shell meat to the hard-shell variety, but this group is in the minority. Try both kinds of lobster meat, and you can decide for yourself.

Whole Lobsters at the Clam Shack

In addition to the highly popular lobster roll, the Clam Shack boils up numerous whole lobsters each day for consumption in the small dining areas inside the market and just outside on benches and boxes—or, more likely, for takeout to be eaten at home. Lots of local families will order dozens of lobsters for summertime parties, and Steve is only too happy to oblige. The whole lobsters typically come in 1-, 1½-, and 2-pound sizes. Steve says that on a busy summer day, between the lobster rolls and whole lobsters, the Clam Shack will cook and sell over 500 pounds of lobster.

In the summer of 2007 the Clam Shack was called upon to supply lobsters for a dinner at the home of famed local resident George H. W. Bush. The former president was hosting a meeting between his son President George W. Bush and visiting Russian dignitary Vladimir Putin. The dinner was dubbed the "Lobster Summit," and it brought tons of collateral attention to the Clam Shack, especially from European media.

So if you're in Kennebunkport and you're thinking of having a whole lobster or a lobster roll, don't let the Clam Shack name throw you off. You'll get some of the best lobster anywhere at this little stand by the Kennebunk River. Oh, and by the way, the Clam Shack won the *Food Wars* lobster-roll challenge. Surprised? You shouldn't be.

Cape Pier Chowder House

79 Pier Road, Cape Porpoise, ME

☎ 207-967-0123

🦞 www.capeporpoiselobster.com

Open early April to late October

As you motor north on Route 9 out of downtown Kennebunkport, in a few miles you'll come to the hamlet of Cape Porpoise, a charming and less crowded part of Kennebunkport township that has a grocery store, a couple of churches, a few restaurants, and not much else. It's more representative of the quieter side of coastal Maine, so if Kennebunkport proper seems too busy and touristy for your tastes, Cape Porpoise may be just the antidote you're looking for.

There are two wonderful lobster shacks in Cape Porpoise—one by the water and the other on Route 9 as you continue to head north out of town. Let's go to the waterfront shack first.

A Shack on the Harbor

Like so many lobster shacks in Maine, the Cape Pier Chowder House is an outgrowth of the lobster fishing that occurs on the adjacent dock—in this case, from the Cape Porpoise town pier located at the end of Pier Road. Cape Pier Chowder House is tucked between the town dock and the landward side of the harbor.

You can find the chowder house and pier by veering off Route 9 onto Pier Road and following it as it snakes through a couple of residential areas and around the edge of scenic Cape Porpoise harbor. The road eventually dead-ends in a small parking lot that is shared by the pier and the shack.

Since the Cape Porpoise pier is a working dock, you'll find lots of lobstermen's pickup trucks in the small parking lot during morning and

Cape Pier's lobsters are off-the-boat fresh. midday hours, making parking a bit of a challenge for the lunchtime

crowd. There are attendants in the summertime for an adjacent high-end restaurant in a blue house; they can direct you to the nearest public parking spots in case you're having trouble finding one.

Simplicity Rules

Cape Pier Chowder House is owned by Allen and Wanda Daggett. Allen spends most of his time tending to his lobster wholesaling business. He buys lobsters from local fishermen on the pier, processes them at his small plant in town, and resells his lobster meat to numerous local businesses. He also keeps Cape Pier Chowder House stocked with fresh live lobsters right off the boat.

The sun-splashed dining deck at Cape Pier Chowder House.

Wanda handles virtually everything in the dockside shack, doing much of the cooking and watching over her staff of three or four workers on busy summer days. Cape Pier is a very simple operation: you walk inside the small building, order at the counter, then grab a seat at one of the dozen or so shaded picnic tables outside on the deck overlooking the harbor, or you can sit at one of the six tables indoors next to the counter.

In either spot, there's plenty to look at while you wait for your food to be prepared. Outside, you have the harbor, which is bustling with lobster boats

coming and going during high tide. Inside, the walls are lined with historic photographs of Cape Porpoise harbor and many of the boats and piers and characters that have inhabited the inlet over the past century.

The menu is spare and direct—several seafood platters, a small selection of sandwiches and rolls (the lobster roll is especially good), a couple of excellent chowders and stews, and, of course, lobster.

Cape Pier's cold-water tanks sit right next to the order counter, and you can select your own lobster from the day's fresh catch and wait for it to be boiled up and delivered to your table. Wanda prefers to boil her lobsters in tap water, believing that, as the day goes along and more lobsters are cooked, the water takes on the fresh, unadorned flavor of lobster shells and meat. So one might deduce from this theory that the best-tasting lobsters would make their appearance at dinnertime. Truth to tell, the midday ones taste just as good.

Life on the Pier

One of the great things about being right next to the town dock is you can see the fleets of lobster boats in action. Throughout the day, they pull up, offload their catch (mostly in early afternoon), get fresh bait from the bait house on the dock, and fuel up for their next trip out to sea. You can witness much of this from the safety and comfort of a picnic table on Cape Pier's deck. It's an education in how the lobster business works, and it makes you appreciate your lobster meal that much more.

Be sure to check out the colorful mural painted on the side of an abbreviated fence that separates the shack from the parking lot. There's also a whimsical wooden cutout of a 3-foot-tall lobster waving from an old wooden trap that's nailed to the shack's roof. Enjoy your time at Cape Pier, and be sure to take a stroll on the town dock before leaving to check out the numerous lobster traps stacked along the edges and to gaze off the end of the dock at the picturesque Goat Island lighthouse about ½ mile away. It's as picture-perfect as the New England coast gets.

This whimsically painted fence greets you as you approach Cape Pier's dining deck.

Nunan's Lobster Hut

Is a hut the same thing as a shack? In the case of Nunan's Lobster Hut on Route 9 in Cape Porpoise, the answer is a resounding *yes!*

Nunan's is one of the most storied and authentic lobster shacks in southern Maine, given its deep roots in the area and its three-plus generations of Nunan family members who have been running the place for some 60 years. Just gazing upon the brown and yellow and rusty red wooden exterior of the hut makes you want to roll up your sleeves, tie on your bib, and pull up a chair or bench at a table within. The relaxed, screen-porch-type atmosphere at Nunan's is warm and inviting, and the menu couldn't be simpler: lobster, lobster, and more lobster.

✂ 9 Mills Road, Kennebunkport, ME

☎ 207-967-4362

Open early May to mid-October

It All Started under a Tree

According to family legend, George Nunan, who had been a fisherman off the Grand Banks for years in the 1920s and 1930s, returned to his hometown of Cape Porpoise to take up lobster and mackerel fishing. He plied his trade for a dozen or so years from the late 1930s until the early 1950s, when he hit upon the idea of cooking up some of his lobster catch and selling it to the neighbors and passersby. He dragged a cooking kettle out into his front yard, set it up under an old elm tree, fired it up, and started boiling lobsters. The price of lobster in those days was a bit less than today: Nunan would sell one lobster to a customer for $1.25 and charge 80 cents for each additional lobster the customer ordered. Sadly, the elm tree (along with the $1.25-per-lobster price) is no longer in existence.

It wasn't long before Nunan's front-yard setup was overwhelmed

Richard "Yogi" Nunan, co-owner and lobsterman.

with lines of hungry and expectant customers, so he emptied out his workshop next to the house and made it into a small kitchen for cooking lobsters. He also had a nearby garage moved to the side of the workshop and converted it into a dining room. In the intervening years, the Nunans have tacked on a few additions to the rear of the dining room, so now there's a series of long, narrow rooms that extends back toward the marsh at the rear of their property. Nunan's kitchen is still in the same spot and building as George's original converted workshop.

George's son Clayton took up lobstering, and he joined the family business in those early days, fishing by day and cooking by night. Clayton wed in 1956, and his wife, Bertha, began helping out at Nunan's. Bertha started as a waitress, and eventually she was pressed into additional service, baking pies for dessert. In the ensuing decades, her pies became legendary—especially the blueberry. The Nunans estimate that she baked some 80,000 pies over the years while she continued to hop tables (for a while, anyway) and raised the Nunans' two sons, Richard (better known as Yogi) and Keith.

The Bertha Years

George passed away in 1972, and Clayton followed two years later. With two young sons, Bertha soldiered on, keeping Nunan's running with the help of family and friends. Bertha became the face of Nunan's for the next couple of decades, and many longtime customers have fond memories of the years when she was at the helm and an ever-present fixture at the hut.

Yogi and Keith both became lobstermen, growing into the business and taking over many of the cooking chores after long days at sea. Each of them has married, and both their wives work at Nunan's as well. Yogi's wife, Terri, began working at the hut in 1974, and she now runs the dining room and overall operations. Keith's wife, Kim, who also works in the dining room, has been with Nunan's since 1994. She took over pie baking from Bertha, who bequeathed the business to her sons and daughters-in-law in the mid-1990s. Sadly, Bertha passed away in 2009.

Yogi's son Jonathan has his own lobster boat and fishes for Nunan's, so the fourth generation appears to be getting in line to help keep the family business going. In fact, Jonathan and his wife just welcomed their daughter, Paige, into the world. She is the first female born into the Nunan family since the late 1800s. Will she or won't she lobster some day? Stay tuned.

We Catch 'Em, We Cook 'Em, We Crack 'Em, You Eat 'Em

That's the motto at Nunan's, and you can count on them to stand by it. From ocean to plate, the Nunans are involved in every step of your lobster experience.

For your Nunan's lobster dinner, you basically have four choices: a $1\frac{1}{8}$-pound lobster, two $1\frac{1}{8}$-pounders, a $1\frac{1}{4}$-pounder, or a $1\frac{1}{2}$-pounder. All are boiled to perfection and come with melted butter,

Nunan's, with its cook shack on the left and its dining room on the right.

previously mentioned blueberry, there are apple and chocolaty Toll-House-cookie pies and special pies of all sorts baked on a regular basis. Strawberry shortcake is another standout dessert choice, along with brownies and blueberry cobbler.

Nunan's has a small but satisfying wine list from which you may order a glass or bottle of nearly every vintage on the list. There's also an interesting lineup of half a dozen or so local beers and the usual sodas, juices, lemonade, and Nunan's own root beer.

A Back-Porch Atmosphere

a bag of potato chips, a dinner roll, and pickles. The lobster dinners come on circular metal trays that resemble deep-dish pizza pans. They're very useful when it comes to containing the shells that inevitably pile up once you tuck into your bug.

If you're not in the mood for lobster, you're not out of luck. Nunan's grills up a very good 12-ounce Delmonico steak that comes with a tossed salad, baked potato, and dinner rolls. There are also some simple sandwiches, such as grilled hot dogs and hamburgers, PB&J, tuna salad, grilled cheese, and an open-face grilled chicken sandwich.

To round out the lobster offerings, Nunan's picks lots of fresh lobster meat each day and uses it in their meaty lobster roll, in a healthy lobster salad that comes with lettuce and fresh vegetables, and in an excellent lobster stew that's rich and creamy and loaded with fresh lobster meat.

Pies are a must at meal's end. In addition to the

One of the truly special things about Nunan's is the intimate, cozy, breezy, back-porch-type atmosphere in its long, narrow dining area. Windows are hinged along their top frames and are raised and hooked to the ceiling, allowing cool breezes to come in off the marshes in the evening (Nunan's is only open for dinner). There are lots of historical photos of Nunan's and its customers lining the dark, wood-paneled walls throughout, and all sorts of lobster buoys and pulleys and other nautical curiosities dangle from the ceiling. It's a warm and charming place to enjoy a meal.

The Nunans have been welcoming regulars and first-timers for more than 60 years, and it looks like they're ready to keep going for many years to come. Be sure to check this place out when you're in the Kennebunkport area. It's a great place to have a truly genuine coastal-Maine lobster-eating experience.

Ken's Place

207 Pine Point Road,
Scarborough, ME

☎ 207-883-6611

Open May through October

Pine Point Road in Scarborough, Maine, is the highway to the sublime (Pine Point) and the somewhat ridiculous (tourist-crazed Orchard Beach). Situated strategically on this thoroughfare and catering to the crowds heading to and from both destinations is the large yet unassuming Ken's Place, a modern-looking eatery with a long history of serving lobster and other seafood to generations of tourists and locals alike during the busy spring, summer, and fall seasons. Today, Ken's handpicks up to 150 pounds of fresh lobster meat in its kitchen and sells as many as 120 whole cooked lobsters per day in the middle of summer. These stats make Ken's Place a major lobster magnet in southern Maine.

It Started in a Garage

Back in 1927, local clam digger Ken Skillings opened a seafood stand in his garage a little farther down Pine Point Road from Ken's current location, and he and some friends started frying up clams and clam cakes and selling them to the tourist traffic that had already begun to stream down the road on a regular basis. Skillings eventually got the business out of his garage and into a small stand on the road a bit closer to the beach than its current location. He added boiled lobsters to his menu around 1947.

As Skillings neared retirement age in the early 1960s, he sold the business to the Bergeron family, who kept it going and eventually moved the shack to its current location in a gray, wooden roadside stand on the west side of Pine Point Road about a mile from Pine Point proper and the northern edge of Orchard Beach. They added enclosed front

Ken's Place on Pine Point Road in Scarborough, Maine.

and side dining areas, which greatly expanded the indoor seating, and the displaced picnic tables along the building's sides were relocated to a shady pine grove out back, where they remain to this day and where numerous local families go for a quiet repast.

Enter Dave Wilcox

As the Bergerons tired of the rough-and-tumble seafood business in the late 1990s, they put Ken's Place up for sale. Dave Wilcox, a seasoned restaurant manager in the Portland area who was eager to have his own business, jumped at the chance to buy Ken's, and his effect on the place was immediate. Wilcox revamped and cleaned up Ken's and brought a tireless work ethic to the establishment. Within several years, business had quadrupled, and it's been busy ever since. Thin, wiry, and always on the move, Dave sets the pace and the level of expectation for his 60-odd part-time summer employees, most of whom are local teens and college students. Ken's customers reap the benefits of all their hard work and hustle.

A Lobster by Any Other Name . . .

Lobster comes in many forms at Ken's Place, and Dave prides himself perhaps most in the fact that so much lobster meat is picked fresh here each day. There's a workstation with stainless steel counters and sinks and cutting boards that's devoted exclusively to cracking and picking freshly steamed lobsters for lobster rolls, lobster stew, and a large and tasty lobster salad. Lots of high-volume places like Ken's order their lobster meat pre-picked from local wholesalers because they don't have the time to do the picking. Dave believes firmly that it's worth the extra time and effort to pick his own meat, and it shows in the finished product.

More than 150 pounds of lobster meat is picked fresh each day in the summertime.

The lobster roll at Ken's is lean and spare, with 3 ounces of lobster meat tossed in Hellmann's mayonnaise and/or served with drawn butter on the side. The meat is spread over a thin, crisp piece of lettuce and wedged into a toasted split-top bun. It's very affordably priced at $10.99 for the roll alone and $12.99 with french fries, coleslaw, and pickle slices.

The lobster stew is made in limited-quantity batches several times during the course of the day. Lobster base and seasonings are heated in a steamer, then removed and tested until the temperature is right. Simultaneously, light cream is heated to a similar temperature, and when it's ready, everything, including the fresh-picked lobster meat, is mixed together for one last warming. The meat is then separated from the broth, and servings are set up with the properly generous amount of lobster meat being added to each cup or bowl of stew. The end result is a creamy, flavorful stew with lots of lobster in each serving.

There's an excellent lobster salad at Ken's that's as healthy as it is tasty. It comes with a whopping 6 ounces of fresh-picked lobster meat on a bed of lettuce. That's just the beginning. Also included are tomato and cucumber slices, green pepper, sliced cheese, a hard-boiled egg, pickle slices and pickle chips, and a generous scoop of homemade potato salad. This is, of course, a meal unto itself.

The lobster stew at Ken's is carefully prepared and measured to guarantee plenty of lobster meat in each serving.

Finally, there's the whole lobster. Dave steams his lobsters using a handy, compact, stainless steel steamer that's tucked beneath one of the many counters in Ken's busy kitchen. Dave believes steaming keeps the moisture and the flavor in the lobster meat, and it only takes about five minutes from the time you order your lobster until the time it's ready. The whole lobsters are $1\frac{1}{8}$ pounds and are served as singles, as twins, and as dinners that come with drawn butter, french fries, coleslaw, a roll, and a pickle.

Where to Dine at Ken's

Ken's Place is an old-fashioned dine-in-the-rough operation with a couple of order windows and three pickup windows strung along the enclosed front portion of the building. Once you've ordered and you have meal in hand, you can grab a table in any of the three indoor dining areas—one right opposite the food counters and two smaller ones flanking the building. Classic rock is piped in all day long through speakers in the ceilings. These rooms may be a good choice on a brutally hot day, but it's a bit dark inside, so give some thought to going out to the picnic tables in front or to the pine grove in back. Dine-in-the-rough seafood always seems to taste better outdoors.

For those who prefer something a bit more exotic in the way of food and drink, Ken's has a nice raw bar in one corner of the front dining area. You sit on bar stools at a full-service bar, where you can order oysters and clams on the half shell and chilled jumbo gulf shrimp in addition to your favorite libation. The raw bar is a constantly busy spot, from lunch hour right up until closing. It's a favorite hangout for local boaters and beach regulars.

Dave has done a splendid job of building a large and loyal local clientele who come to Ken's throughout the season and don't seem to be scared off during the busy summer months. They do, however, have two favorite times to visit in the shoulder seasons: On Mother's Day hundreds of families come to Ken's for a meal, when clam cakes are particularly popular. And on closing day of every year, well over two thousand locals pack the place to say goodbye and to enjoy one last meal before hunkering down for the winter. It almost makes you wish that the constantly working and hustling Dave would consider staying open year-round. Feel free to make the suggestion.

Bayley's Lobster Pound

Bayley's Lobster Pound is perhaps the oldest continuously run family lobster operation in all of Maine—or so co-owner Susan Bayley claims. The pound dates back to 1916. Can anyone beat that? Regardless of whether it's the oldest or not, it's certainly one of the busiest when it comes to selling live and fresh-cooked lobsters and lobster rolls. Speaking of which, the Bayleys also claim to have invented the lobster roll—read on.

✗ 9 Avenue 6, Scarborough, ME

☎ 207-883-4571

🦞 www.bayleys.com

Open mid-March to mid-January

Lobsters in Suitcases

Bayley's got its start in 1916 when Steve Bayley and his wife, Ella, made the move from Wells, Maine, north to the Pine Point section of Scarborough so he could take a job at the Snow clam-processing plant. At that time, the Pine Point area boasted some of the richest clam beds in Maine. With extensive tidal flats that yielded thousands of soft shell clams each day, the place was a natural for the clam business. (Though the beds are not as fruitful as in years past, there are still some small concerns in and around Pine Point that dig clams on the flats and sell them to local markets.)

Bayley started lobstering on the side to help support his family, and he bought a small shack in Pine Point just down the road from the local lobster cooperative. Soon he began to distribute lobsters to restaurants and seafood markets, which welcomed having a new dealer in the area. He would often ship his catch to nearby restaurants and seafood markets by rail with the lobsters riding in barrels.

On occasion, Steve's lobster take would exceed demand from his

A netted sack full of fresh-cooked bugs.

Bayley's owners Bill Bayley (left), daughter Sue Bailey, and Vinnie Clough.

local customers. Rather than take a loss on the excess inventory, he and his partner would grab a few suitcases, load them up with live lobsters and seaweed, and hop the local northbound train to sell the lobsters in nearby Portland. The company's methods of lobster transport have become a bit more sophisticated over the years, but the suitcase story remains an important, if amusing, legacy of the nearly century-old business.

The Invention of the Lobster Roll

Bayley's also claims to have invented the lobster roll (Maine's version, anyway), and here's the story: From

time to time, Steve Bayley had excess lobster inventory, and when he didn't feel like riding the rails with lobsters as stowaways in his suitcases, he would have Ella cook them up and use them to supplement the Bayley family larder. Steve developed a craving for what he called a "lobster sandwich," which consisted simply of lobster meat placed between two pieces of white bread. He was not a big fan of bread crusts, so he had Ella trim them off his sandwiches.

Ella eventually grew tired of the crust-trimming chore, so she started putting the lobster meat in an untoasted, split-top, New England–style hot dog bun. Thus was the lobster roll as we know it today brought forth into the world. To this day, Bayley's doesn't toast its lobster-roll buns.

Regardless of whether or not the Bayleys actually were the inventors of the lobster roll, they certainly make a fine one, selling more than five hundred per day out of their retail seafood market in July and August. Many of the customers are locals who walk over for a roll nearly every day in-season, but plenty also drive in to Pine Point and jockey for a parking spot in Bayley's small lot in order to score a roll and sit out on Bayley's dock to enjoy it.

Lobsters through the Kitchen Window

From time to time Ella Bayley would boil up some lobsters from the pound and sell them to neighbors and friends, dispensing them through her kitchen window and collecting money through the same portal. This

---

MAINE'S ORIGINAL LOBSTER ROLL

Whether or not Bayley's claim to be the originator of the lobster roll is true, one thing is for certain: this major player in the lobster business has a very simple and winning recipe for their version of the sandwich.

INGREDIENTS

1	pound fresh lobster meat
1/3	cup mayonnaise
5	hot dog rolls

Cut the lobster meat up into bite-sized pieces. In a bowl, mix the lobster meat with the mayonnaise until the meat is thoroughly coated. Fill the hot dog rolls with the lobster meat mixture. Serves 4–5.

turned into a nice little side-business, and the afore-mentioned lobster rolls were soon added to the menu.

The Bayleys have supplemented their lobster wholesaling business with fresh-cooked lobsters, lobster rolls, and other seafood dishes ever since, and they have a loyal following of locals who stop in frequently and order up lunch, dinner, and snacks at the recently remodeled seafood market at the front of the building. The market features all sorts of fresh fish displayed in glass cases, and there's a tempting list of cooked seafood items for takeout. Clam chowder, haddock chowder, and lobster stew, all made fresh daily, are popular, and there are Maine crab rolls and Maine shrimp rolls to add variety to the lobster offerings.

Rather than passing cooked lobsters through the kitchen window, Bayley's now has a couple of sheltered, open-air, cold-water tanks next to the seafood market, where you can pick your own lobster and Bayley's will cook it up for you at no charge. In a room just in back of the open-air tanks are a few good-sized, gas-fired lobster cookers that almost always have stringed bags of lobsters boiling up in them and an extra cold-water tank that holds phone orders from customers who will be by later in the day to pick them up.

There's a beautiful new dock in back of Bayley's that snakes its way out into the marshy cove, and the view across the water (or mud flats at low tide) is spectacular. You may see numerous local lobster boats moored in the cove, and you get a great view of

Bayley's back deck looks out onto beautiful Jones Creek.

the expansive tidal flats that stretch more than a mile toward Scarborough.

Dining on the new dock is a bit of an adventure, as the only place to sit is on the benches that are built into the dock's railings. You need to balance your meal on your knees and lap as you tuck into your lobster. A plan was in place to have some new picnic tables installed all along the dock in time for the 2012 season. But the Bayleys say that customers don't seem to mind the absence of tables. They just sit out there with their lobsters in their laps and rip into them while enjoying the beautiful view over the marsh grass. Some even park themselves on the low concrete wall that separates the open-air tanks from the parking-lot area.

Bayley's Big Backroom Operations

Bayley's prides itself in shipping fresh lobsters and seafood all over the country, and they're one of the best at doing it. When they first started overnight shipments via the US Postal Service in the 1980s, they used cardboard liquor-case boxes and seaweed to pack their lobsters. To keep the bugs chilled while in transit, they would put one or two pint-size plastic bottles containing frozen seawater into each package. When Bayley's eventually switched to more modern methods of refrigerating their packages, some customers complained, having grown accustomed to thawing the seawater in the plastic bottles and using it in the boiling process to add more flavor to their lobsters.

In addition to the seafood market and the lobster tanks and cookers adjacent to it, there's a massive array of cold-water tanks in a warehouse-like building in back of the market where Bayley's keeps virtually all of its lobsters for wholesaling. Every day, numerous lobstermen drop off their catches for weighing and processing. Going farther back into the Bayley complex, you'll find a lobster-picking room, a fish-cutting room, and a couple of large deep-freeze units for much of the chowders and other prepared foods that Bayley's sends out to retailers.

Bayley's is currently in the third and fourth generations of family ownership. The founder's grandson, Bill Bayley, lives above the pound in a small apartment, and Susan (Bill's daughter) and her husband, Vinnie Clough, live in the house right next door. So, the three co-owners never stray far from the Bayley "family farm."

The Bayleys have played a major role in the lobster business and in lobster shacks throughout Maine for almost a hundred years, and we should all be grateful for the family's commitment to the lobster world. And if they really did invent the lobster roll, and there's a good chance they did, we owe them an even greater debt of gratitude.

BAYLEY'S LOBSTER NEWBURG

Bayley's has been in the lobster business for nearly a hundred years, and when they offer a recipe for lobster Newburg, you know it has to be good. Fresh steamed asparagus goes particularly well with this dish.

INGREDIENTS

6	tablespoons (¾ stick) butter
3	tablespoons flour
1½	cups half-and-half
3	beaten egg yolks
1	pound fresh lobster meat, cut into bite-sized pieces
3	tablespoons sherry
1	tablespoon fresh lemon juice
	paprika

In a skillet over medium heat, melt the butter, then stir in the flour to form a smooth paste. Add the half-and-half slowly, stirring constantly until thick and bubbly. Pour half of the mixture into a bowl with the egg yolks, then return the portion with yolks to the skillet. Mix everything together, then stir in the lobster meat. When the lobster has heated through (about 2 to 3 minutes), stir in the sherry and lemon juice. Serve immediately over white rice, patty shells, or toast points. Garnish with paprika. Serves 4.

Lobster Shack Two Lights

Lobster Shack Two Lights is known far and wide as one of the finest and most scenic places to enjoy lobster and other fine shack food by the sea. It's not an easy place to find, but it's worth the effort it takes to get there, not only for the tasty seafood but also for the magnificent ocean view from the shack's many picnic tables that sit right by the rocky shore.

225 2 Lights Road, Cape Elizabeth, ME

☎ 207-799-1677

www.lobstershacktwolights.com

Open late March to late October

Once a Shack, Always a Shack

Lobster has been served in one form or another from this locale since the 1920s, when it was a modest seaside shack known as the Lobster Shop. Lobster rolls were all the rage here for the first few decades, and the eatery hummed along, catering mostly to locals from the Cape Elizabeth area and curious day-trippers from Portland.

A baker named Jim Ledbetter and his wife, Ruth, bought the Lobster Shop in 1968 and renamed it the Lobster Shack. "Two Lights" was added to the name later in order to distinguish the place from all the other lobster shacks up and down the coast; it refers to two nearby lighthouses.

The Ledbetters remodeled the shack, then added a gift shop in a separate building in 1974. They also expanded the menu to include deep-fried seafood and lots of desserts, mostly in the form of pies that Jim would bake in the ovens on the premises. Lobsters and lobster rolls remained an important part of the menu, as they do today.

Eventually, Lobster Shack Two Lights passed into the hands of the Ledbetters' daughter, Martha, and her husband, Herb Porch, who ran it until their son, Jeff, and his wife, Katie, took over in 2005; they have been running it ever since.

A whimsical wind sculpture, left, and Cape Elizabeth light, right.

Lobster Shack Two Lights is in a residential area that would never allow such an operation to be where it is today, except that Two Lights has been grandfathered in to the neighborhood. They are allowed by ordinance to operate only 30 weeks per year and at very specific times, opening in late March and closing in late October; and their hours of operation are limited to 11 AM to 8 PM (8:30 PM in July and August). Despite these restrictions, which the Porches don't seem to mind, the place is buzzing throughout each year's brief window of opportunity.

GPS Comes in Handy Here

Cape Elizabeth is a beautiful peninsula of land south of Portland, with rocky shores, famous lighthouses, and rolling farmlands stretching inland from the sea. In order to find your way to Lobster Shack Two Lights, GPS should be your first choice and your best friend. You'll need to navigate your way down a few scenic, curving country roads that will bring you to Two Lights State Park.

It may sound like you've arrived, but you're still not quite there yet. You need to drive by the park entrance and follow a narrow, two-lane road about a mile or so into a quiet residential neighborhood. There are

Two Lights' breezy picnic area has a great view of Casco Bay and the open ocean.

no road signs telling you to continue forward. Just when you're certain you've missed the turnoff, you'll find yourself dead-ending into the parking lot for Lobster Shack Two Lights at the end of the road. It's not easy to find, but you'll be so glad you did.

About That View . . .

From the parking lot, you ascend about a dozen steps to the shack and its outdoor dining area, which consists of a couple dozen picnic tables perched on the edge of a rocky shore that offers an amazing view of the ocean straight ahead and the entrance to Casco Bay to your left. It really is an arresting experience, especially on a warm, sunny day, to stand there and absorb the magnificent view. At high tide, the waves crash on the rocks below, and at low tide, some of the braver diners clamor over the rocks (at their own risk) to explore tide pools and get a closer look at the water.

The view looking inland is also pleasant, with the two lighthouses, each about a quarter mile from the shack, standing sentinel over this part of the coastline. The west tower is decommissioned and no longer functioning, and the east tower has an automated light. In addition, there's a small foghorn station right next to the Two Lights dining area that emits audio blasts every 30 seconds or so when the weather is even the slightest bit foggy, which adds to the maritime atmosphere of the place.

Award-Winning Lobsters and Lobster Rolls

Though the deep fryers do a brisk business here, it's the lobster you'll want to have while visiting Lobster Shack Two Lights. The Porches personally pick up their lobster each morning at New Meadows Lobster in Portland and drive it to the shack. Klenda Seafood in South Portland supplements this with fresh-picked lobster meat, mostly for lobster rolls, during the busy summer season.

The lobster dinner consists of a boiled lobster, french fries, coleslaw, and a home-baked biscuit. Drawn butter is served on the side. If you're really hungry, go for the twin lobsters for twice the fun.

The lobster roll at Two Lights has won the *Portland Press-Herald*'s Best Lobster Roll award so many times that the Porches have lost count. What makes the lobster roll here so good? For starters, it's the freshness of the lobster meat. It's served chilled on a toasted split-top bun with a little bit of shredded lettuce between bun and meat. Second, the Porches add a dollop of extra-thick real mayonnaise on top of the meat, and you can either mix it into the meat yourself or remove it and go straight for the good stuff. The mayo here is extraordinary and well worth mixing into the sandwich; however, if you prefer, you may get your lobster roll with drawn butter on the side or naked (no butter, no mayo). They'll do it any way you request, though most people opt for the house style with the schtickle of mayo on top.

There's also a great lobster stew here that's quite pricey. But that's because it contains an extraordinary amount of lobster meat, making even a cup of the stew a meal in itself.

The Best of the Rest

Fried clams here are particularly good, as are the clam cakes and hand-cut onion rings. For those not inclined to eat seafood (or any form of meat), there are burgers, hot dogs, and a veggie burger as well as various salads.

Speaking of salads, Two Lights has a nicely prepared lobster-meat salad that comes with a generous portion of lobster meat and a good-size pile of lettuce and fresh-sliced vegetables.

Pies, mini-pies, whoopie pies, strawberry short-cake, cookies, brownies (all home-baked) and a very tasty Grape-Nuts pudding make dessert a must-have here. Given the baking background in the Ledbetter/Porch family, you'll find it hard to resist the strategically placed, glass-fronted dessert display case stuck in the middle of the order counter.

There's a cute little dining room just off the order-counter area that's filled with antique nautical kitsch, but with the view and fresh sea breezes available at the picnic tables outside, dining outdoors is the way to go. Nowhere else in Maine will you be able to get so close to the open ocean while having lobster in a wonderful setting such as this. So fire up your GPS and set out for this gem by the sea for an unforgettable meal—and an unforgettable view to match. Don't forget the camera!

Portland Lobster Company

180 Commercial Street, Portland, ME

☎ 207-775-2112

🦞 www.portlandlobstercompany.com

Open early May to late October

The city of Portland is a lively, vibrant place these days, with one of the most heralded dining scenes in the country. No wonder. Located on a deepwater harbor in Casco Bay and filled with winding, narrow streets and lovely brick buildings, Portland has become the focal point of Maine's artistic and commercial communities and a place where innovative and unusual restaurants are welcomed.

The waterfront area in downtown Portland is packed with restaurants, shops, boat tours, and entertainment venues. It's a scene of constant activity, especially in the summer. So it's only fitting that there be a great outdoor seafood place right in the midst of all this fun, and the Portland Lobster Company fits the bill.

Get Crackin'

Portland Lobster Company came into being a little over 10 years ago when four local businessmen decided to buy out a restaurant on the docks and open an informal lobster shack right on the waterfront. The idea was to serve fresh Maine lobster in the midst of Portland's bustling downtown and to do it in a fun way, with dining in the rough and lots of outdoor seating on the dock so that patrons could soak up all the sunshine and good vibes that Portland has to offer.

At one of their early planning meetings, the four new owners were brainstorming over a platter of

Portland Lobster Company's Downeast Feast.

freshly cooked lobsters. Among the items on their agenda: come up with a catchy slogan for the place. One of the owners commented in an offhand way that they'd "better get crackin'" on all the work they needed to do. They looked at their lobsters, then at each other, and pretty much decided on the spot that "Get Crackin'" would be a great catchphrase for their new place. The slogan has stuck, and it's on everything from the menus to the T-shirts to the placemats to the ads in the local papers.

From Farm to Fork: Buying Local

After a few years, the four owners found that they had differing views of how to run the shack, which was a side-business for each of them, and so they put Portland Lobster Company up for sale. Dave Pulido of nearby Cape Elizabeth bought the place and gave it the focus it needed to become a success.

Though he didn't change a lot at first, he did start a push to buy all of the shack's raw food materials from local farmers and fishermen. This was in keeping with a movement among many Portland restaurants to source their food from nearby—make the distance from farm to fork as short and quick as possible. Dave's daughter-in-law owns an organic farm in Cape Elizabeth, and it's been a steady supplier of fresh vegetables and fruits.

Portland Lobster gets its seafood from Harbor Fish, a wholesale and retail purveyor that is also on Portland's waterfront; and their lobsters come from a family of lobstermen across the bay in South

A Taste of the Lobstering Life

Among the numerous cruise boats that disembark from the wharves around Portland Lobster Company's pier, perhaps the most apropos is Lucky Catch Cruises. This outfit takes passengers out for 90-minute excursions on the 40-foot *Lucky Catch* commercial lobster boat to witness lobster traps being pulled from the bottom of the bay, emptied and baited, and lowered back overboard.

It's an eye-opening experience, seeing how lobsters are caught and all the different things that come up in the traps. You'll witness various lobster-fishing techniques, learn the difference between hard-shell and soft-shell lobsters firsthand, and hear about conservation efforts undertaken by Maine lobstermen to keep the lobster population at large and healthy levels.

Perhaps the best part is when you return to the dock: you can purchase lobsters at the wholesale, "boat" price from the *Lucky Catch*'s haul, then take your bugs over to Portland Lobster Company where, for several dollars more, they'll steam them and throw in corn, potatoes, and coleslaw for a complete lobster feast. (Call 207-761-0941, or visit www.lucky catch.com.)

Portland. All this fresh produce and seafood means that some very interesting specials come out of Portland Lobster's kitchen on a regular basis, and it keeps the locals coming back to see what's new and exciting on the menu. The buy-local credo even extends to

The view down Portland Lobster Company's lengthy dining pier.

the beer served in the shack's large and busy bar area, with only locally brewed beer being offered on tap, usually about half a dozen different types at a time.

Dining on the Dock

Portland Lobster Company is blessed with a long dock that's lined with two rows of colorful picnic tables painted rusty orange and a bunch of round, umbrellaed tables with tall stools for seating in the bar area. It's a great place to enjoy your repast, have some locally brewed beer, do some people watching, and check out all the activity on Portland's waterfront.

When it comes to ordering, lobster should be at the top of your list. The Lobster Dinner features a lobster between 1 and 2 pounds (you choose), along

---

BACON BOURBON SCALLOPS

Portland Lobster Company rolls out this tasty dish as a special on a regular basis. It's fun to make and oh-so-tasty to eat.

INGREDIENTS

2 cloves garlic	3 ounces bourbon
2 teaspoons fresh parsley	1 pound fresh jumbo scallops
2 tablespoons butter	6 ounces thick-cut bacon (preferably apple wood–smoked or similar)
2 tablespoons extra virgin olive oil	
1½ tablespoons brown sugar	⅓ cup heavy cream
¼ cup fresh chopped shallots	Pinch of salt and pepper

Lightly sprinkle salt and pepper on scallops. Heat butter and olive oil in pan on high heat until almost smoking. Add scallops and bacon to pan and sear quickly, about 30 seconds on each side. Make sure not to lift or move scallops while searing. Remove scallops and set aside. Add garlic and shallots to pan, and sauté until they soften. Add bourbon, and carefully ignite to burn off alcohol. Once flame subsides, add brown sugar, heavy cream, and 1½ teaspoons fresh parsley. Reduce until desired consistency is reached. Pour over scallops and garnish with remaining parsley.

Serves 2 to 3

with baked or french-fried potatoes, coleslaw, corn on the cob, and a dish of melted Cabot's butter. You can take it up a notch with the Downeast Feast, which gives you everything in the Lobster Dinner, plus a bag of steamers and a cup of chowder. Twin Lobster Dinners are also available.

Portland Lobster Company's lobster roll has won the "Best of" award from the *Portland Phoenix* alternative weekly for two years running. This popular roll (some 30,000 are sold each summer) features fresh-picked lobster meat

Portland Lobster Company sits right at the base of downtown Portland.

(they pick twice daily at PLC), a bit of fresh lemon juice, a few drops of Cabot's melted butter on the toasted bun, and a dollop of mayo on the side, if you wish. It also has a thin leaf of organic romaine lettuce between the split-top bun and lobster meat.

The lobster bisque here is extraordinary—very thick and creamy with fresh-cut chives and a small chunk of lobster-claw meat floating on top, a sure sign that there's plenty of lobster flavor in the bisque. There's also a lobster stew that's laden with fresh-picked meat; you can get it served in a bread bowl for a couple of dollars more.

There are also some very large and tempting deep-fried seafood platters of various types and a daily fresh-fish special that comes with a garden salad

and corn on the cob. Locally harvested peekytoe crab, more commonly known as Atlantic rock crab, is also featured in a variety of dishes, from crab cakes to a crab roll to a tasty crab and avocado wrap.

There's one last thing to lure you down to Portland Lobster Company: live music. This place jumps with live bands and soloists every night in the summertime and throughout the day on Saturdays and Sundays. So even if you've eaten someplace else, consider stopping in, grabbing a stool at a table, quaffing a local brew or two, and listening to some fine music on Portland's hopping waterfront. Portland Lobster Company is your one-stop place for food and fun in Maine's artsy, bustling cultural capital on the dock-lined shores of Casco Bay.

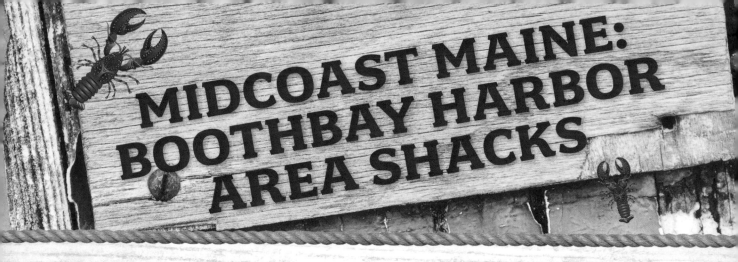

MIDCOAST MAINE: BOOTHBAY HARBOR AREA SHACKS

Once you're free of the metropolitan pull of Portland, you begin to enter what many consider to be the "real Maine." The accent here is more pronounced (LL Bean is in the town of "Freepawt"), and the coastline, with its lengthy peninsulas and dozens of islands and coves, really begins to show itself as the craggy, rock-strewn, pine-forested wonderland that characterizes Maine.

From the maritime city of Brunswick (home of prestigious Bowdoin College) to the eastern reaches of Boothbay Harbor, there are a number of long, narrow peninsulas of land that snake downward from US Route 1 to the sea. These stalactites of land are separated by broad, tidal rivers and picture-perfect inlets and coves.

You can navigate the region by driving up and down the twisting, turning two-lane highways that more often than not dead-end in a small port town or village by the sea. This is lobster country, where many outfits like Five Islands Lobster Company, Holbrook's Lobster, Boothbay Lobster Wharf, and Harraseeket Lunch & Lobster started as fishing docks, then eventually evolved into the lobster shacks that they are today.

Take your time as you travel in this scenic part of Maine. In addition to the lobster and other fine seafood to be enjoyed throughout the region, you'll discover lots of little towns and villages that have retained much of their maritime history and charm. It's a welcome throwback to simpler times.

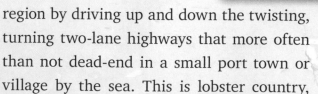

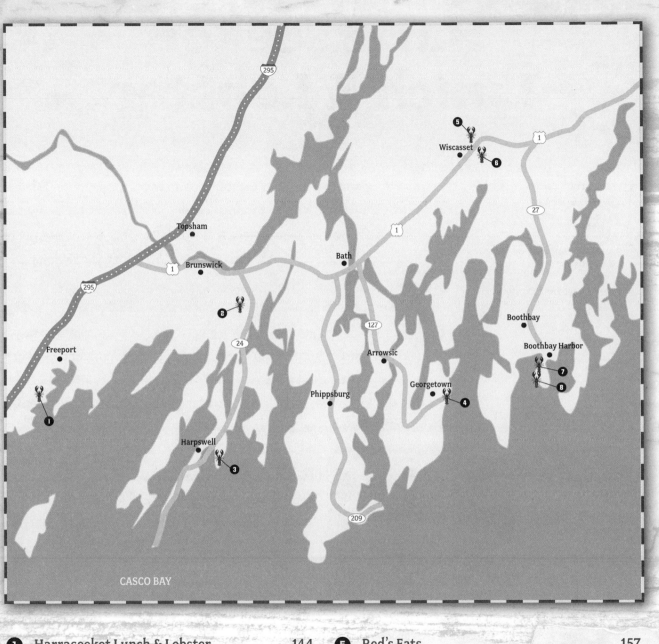

CASCO BAY

Harraseeket Lunch & Lobster

🍴 36 North Main Street, South Freeport, Maine

☎ 207-865-3535

🦞 www.harraseeketlunchand lobster.com

Open early May to mid-October

Like Lobster Shack Two Lights some 20 miles to the south, Harraseeket Lunch & Lobster can be a real challenge to find. As you're driving through tree-shaded neighborhoods in South Freeport, full of handsome houses and trimmed lawns, you'll be convinced that you're going the wrong way.

Worry not. Just like at Two Lights in Cape Elizabeth, local zoning laws prohibit the posting of any signs on the well-kempt streets leading to the shack, so you sort of have to take a leap of faith and just keep going straight down Pine Street and Main Street and let them lead you into the waiting arms of Harraseeket Lunch & Lobster next to beautiful South Freeport town harbor.

Harraseeket's lobster stand overlooks the scenic harbor.

It All Began with Lobsters

Way back in 1970, Regis Coffin and her then-husband, John, opened a modest lobster pound in South Freeport harbor on the Harraseeket (pronounced harrah-SEE-kit) River as a place to sell John's daily lobster catch from his boat. They set up shop in a little building next to the harbor, installed some cold-water tanks, and began pumping seawater straight from the harbor into and out of the tanks inside the pound.

They steadily built a solid base of wholesale customers, like restaurants and seafood markets, and they also sold live and cooked lobsters to the locals. A few picnic tables were installed alongside the pound so people could enjoy their lobsters right there if they so desired.

Lobsters led to steamers, which led to deep-fried clams and other seafood, and before long, Harraseeket's was a hopping place with a steadily growing reputation and clientele.

Lobsters to the Left, Fried Food to the Right

Pretty much from the beginning, the lobster pound and fry shack have been kept separate and are run almost as distinct operations. When you arrive at Harraseeket's and park in their side lot (a bit of a challenge during busy lunch and dinner hours), the first things you'll encounter under the festive blue-and-white-striped canopy on the front of the building are the fry shack and ice-cream/dessert ordering windows. Large signs inform you that, if you're here for lobster, you should go around to the harbor side of the building, where there's another window specifically for bugs. (Lobster rolls are served at the fry shack, by the way, and not at the lobster window.)

While on your way to the lobster window, you're treated to a splendid view of South Freeport Harbor, which is filled with commercial and pleasure craft of all shapes and sizes. Though you're on the southern, sun-exposed side of the building, you're still under the blue-and-white canopy that wraps around the front and side of the building, so you won't roast in the sun while waiting to order.

Sidle up to the window and take a peek into the

pound's extensive array of cold-water tanks, where each day's fresh lobster catch is stored. The menu here is brief and to the point, but there's one item you should consider above all others: the Lobster Delight. This complete meal is advertised on a sign right next to the window, and the

Heed the sign telling you where to go for lobsters at Harraseeket.

combo consists of a 1-pound boiled lobster, 12 steamers, and an ear of corn on the cob for a price somewhere in the vicinity of $21.95. It gives you a little bit of everything and leaves you wanting for nothing. On the outside chance that you do crave more, however, you can also get boiled crabs or red potatoes or steamed corn à la carte.

Brendan Alterio is the director of lobster operations at Harraseeket, which means he oversees everything happening in the pound, and he also manages the fleet of 10 lobster boats that fish exclusively for Harraseeket. Throughout the day, you can watch the boats tie up at the dock next to the lobster pound and offload their catches before departing with fresh traps and bait. It's an up-close, authentic look at lobster fishing and all the hard work it entails. Trucks pull up on the other side of the pound at regular intervals to pick up the day's catch and deliver it to Harraseeket's

Brendan Alterio, head of lobster operations at Harraseeket Lunch & Lobster.

local wholesale and retail accounts. Watching all this activity as an accompaniment to your meal really does make that lobster taste all the better.

The lobster pound opens at 7 AM each day, four hours before the fry shack window, in order to accommodate customers who wish to grab some lobsters fresh off the boat and take them home to cook up in the evening. Harraseeket will also pack your lobsters in your cooler if you wish to take them with you, or they'll sell you a handy transport box with coolants in case you don't have a cooler with you. This is truly your one-stop lobster shop.

Dining Options

There are a few choices if you plan to stick around and enjoy your lobster on the premises. First, the maroon-colored picnic tables in front of Harraseeket's are certainly the most popular place to dine. Many of the tables are shaded beneath the large awning, and if you prefer to enjoy the warmth of the sun, there are several more tables out in the open.

Over by the walkway to the lobster pound and facing the beautiful harbor to the south are about half a dozen stools and a counter stretching along the wrought-iron fence that separates Harraseeket's from the water below in the harbor. This is a great perch for dining and soaking up some sun and watching the boats come and go.

Finally, there's an enclosed dining room with antique-style wooden tables and chairs situated between the fry shack in front and the lobster pound around back. If you order a lobster at the pound and take a seat in the dining room, they'll pass it to you through an interior window so you don't have to circle the building to pick it up. Harraseeket's hosts private parties in the dining room when advance arrangements are made.

The shack is a BYO establishment with regard to alcoholic beverages; no soda or other nonalcoholic beverages can be brought in from the outside. Harraseeket's will gladly sell you a wide variety of soft drinks, juices, and other beverages. There are also some wonderful ice cream treats and home-baked desserts, including Harraseeket's famous whoopie pies, available at the window next to the main food-ordering area.

As shacks go, Harraseeket's is quite elegant, with its striped awnings and its slick picnic tables and nicely appointed dining room. But it's a dine-in-the-rough shack nonetheless and well worth a visit any time you're in the Freeport area.

Gurnet Trading Company

✕ 602 Brunswick Road, Brunswick, ME

☎ 207-729-7300

🦞 www.gurnettrading.com

Open year-round

Once you pass through Brunswick, Maine, and start heading south toward the ocean, you've entered what many consider to be the real threshold of Midcoast Maine. In this part of the world, you're probably better off in a boat if you're trying to travel from one lengthy peninsula to another. It can be just a ½-mile trip across a river or inlet from one town to another, compared to a 20-mile-or-more, up-and-down journey by car to achieve the same thing.

But that's part of the fun of exploring this part of the Maine coast. There are lots of interesting villages, shops, and eateries to check out—and some wonderful lobster shacks at the far ends of these spits of land, ready to cook you up a fresh-from-the-water lobster feast that will make your driving efforts well worth it.

One little gem of a shack lies in the southern reaches of Brunswick, yet it's worlds apart from the rarified atmosphere of Brunswick's Bowdoin College campus—the Gurnet Trading Company. Hard by the side of Route 24 and housed in a hutlike structure that looks like it belongs in the Pacific Northwest, the Gurnet Trading Company is a fun little spot that has close ties to the local lobster and scalloping industries, and it offers some fine lobster and other seafood in its funky indoor and outdoor dining areas.

From Junkyard to Lobster Pound

All good lobster shacks have their roots in the lobster-fishing business, and Gurnet Trading Post is no exception. Owners Julie and Brian Soper can trace their families back several generations and find nothing but

Gurnet's snazzy T-shirt design captures the spirit of the place.

fishermen—lobstermen who set their traps from sailboats, ground fishermen who hauled tons of haddock and cod from the Gulf of Maine, and, in the case of Brian's current occupation, scuba divers gathering sea scallops and urchins. In addition, the Sopers own a pier in nearby Cundys Harbor that services some 15 lobster boats—fueling them up, selling them bait, and buying their catches at the end of each day.

The fishing business in Maine has always waxed and waned, depending on the abundance or scarcity of various species. The Sopers have fished for just about everything you can think of in their part of Maine, and in an attempt to hedge their bets and diversify a bit without getting too far from what they know best, they decided to open a seafood market.

Shopping around for a location, they came across a junkyard filled with old cars and machinery on

The playful entrance to Gurnet's is hard to resist.

Route 24 a few miles south of downtown Brunswick. Their family and friends thought they were crazy when they bought the place. They had the old stuff hauled away and went about cleaning up the site and building a rough-hewn wooden shack no more than 10 feet from the two-lane road and hard by Buttermilk Cove to the rear.

Set amid a stand of hardwood trees and decorated inside and out with vintage lobster buoys and other nautical items, it's a cozy little spot that's hard to pass by without stopping to check it out. Soon after opening the market, Julie had a hankering to add a kitchen to the place, which they did, and the Sopers have been cooking up lobsters and other seafood dishes ever since.

Inside the shack are a couple of cold-water tanks filled with freshly caught lobster from the Sopers' pier down in Cundy's Harbor. There's also a small but well-stocked glass-fronted case displaying all sorts of locally caught seafood. Between these two displays is an order counter with a handwritten chalkboard menu overhead listing all the steamed, fried, and chowdered items available from the kitchen.

Everything Comes Fresh from Casco Bay

There's an amazing variety of fresh seafood harvested from nearby Casco Bay that's available at Gurnet, starting with the lobsters. You can pick your own from the tanks, and the cook staff will steam it up for you and serve it to you à la carte or as part of

MAMIE'S SEAFOOD CASSEROLE

Julie Soper's mom, Mamie, came up with this recipe for Gurnet's seafood casserole, which she served for years at family get-togethers and on special occasions. It's now a prized item on the menu at Gurnet's, when available. There's plenty of good seafood (including lobster) in here, and it's excellent comfort food for any time of year.

INGREDIENTS

½ cup breadcrumbs	2 tablespoons butter
¾ cup crumbled saltine crackers	1 pound haddock
½ cup grated cheddar cheese	1 pound Maine shrimp (or small-shrimp equivalent)
½ cup cream of shrimp soup	½ pound cooked lobster meat
½ cup whole milk	¾ pound sea scallops (sliced in half, if large)
¼ cup grated Parmesan cheese	¼ cup melted butter

Mix together the breadcrumbs, crumbled saltines, and grated cheddar cheese and set aside. In a separate bowl, mix the cream of shrimp soup, milk, and Parmesan cheese. Melt 2 tablespoons of butter in the bottom of a 9- by 13-inch baking pan. Layer the haddock on the bottom, add a light layer of breadcrumb mixture, then sprinkle half the shrimp and lobster, then more breadcrumb mixture, then the scallops and the rest of the shrimp and lobster, then top off with the rest of the crumb mixture. Pour the soup/milk/Parmesan mixture over the top, then pour the melted butter over everything. Bake at 350°F for 1 hour until golden and bubbly. Serves 6–8.

a complete dinner. There's a Downeast Feast, which consists of two 1-pound lobsters, 1 pound of steamed clams, a choice of coleslaw or potato salad, and a dinner roll. If that's more than you can handle, try the Lobster Delight, with one 1-pound lobster, ½ pound of steamers, and coleslaw or an ear of corn. Lobsters at Gurnet come in 1-, 1½-, and 2-pound sizes, and larger ones are available upon request.

An excellent opener for any meal is Gurnet's homemade chowder, which comes in two varieties. There's the clam chowder, done in the milky, sweet Maine style and loaded with whole-belly clams—something you don't find very often in clam chowder. Gurnet, by the way, buys its clams from local diggers

Gurnet's rustic interior is open year-round for dining.

and shucks them in its certified back-room processing area, so they're as fresh as can be. The other chowder choice is a fine haddock chowder, loaded with generous chunks of fish that the Sopers buy daily from local fish cutters.

The deep fryers are busy with freshly shucked clams, Maine shrimp (Cundy's Harbor has a large fleet of boats that go shrimping in the winter), and the prized deep-sea scallops that Brian retrieves regularly from the sea-floor. A seafood casserole is the pride of Gurnet's, but it's only available when the Sopers can get enough fresh lobster, shrimp, scallops, and haddock to make it exactly the way they feel it should be made. If they run out of anything on the menu, off it comes for that day. They won't truck in seafood from anyone except their local sources. So be prepared to have a backup selection in case they've run out of what you want.

A Stroll around the Grounds

Indoors at Gurnet's, by the counters and tanks, there are several round-topped tables and stools for year-round dining. There are also plenty of lobster-themed items and other kitsch for sale, stacked between the exposed wall studs on rough-hewn wooden shelves. Feel free to do a little shopping while you wait for your food.

Outside, there are a few tables under umbrellas by the front door for smaller parties. The main eating area is about 20 yards away and partially hidden

Lobster is a big deal at Gurnet Trading Company.

behind some large rocks that separate the half a dozen or so picnic tables from the parking area. This is a pleasant spot to sit and gaze through the trees onto Buttermilk Cove. There's a boat launch across the narrow cove where the clammers who service Gurnet's put in and take out their boats each day.

Gurnet's recently blazed a trail down to the cove, where they installed a dock to which customers can tie up and come ashore for a meal. Another recent innovation, which almost seems like overkill for a place this size, is the high-tech customer-notification system that the Sopers procured to let customers know when their food is ready. You now receive a buzzer (in the form of a toy lobster) to let you know when to pick up your order. You usually see such things at larger, more sophisticated places, but the Sopers decided to get some for Gurnet's so they wouldn't have to keep walking over to the picnic area to shout out order names and numbers. Just set your plastic bug down on your table and wait for it to start vibrating and flashing, then go and fetch your fresh-cooked food.

Though Gurnet's has the roadhouse feel of a place that's just between here and there on the highway, it's definitely worth a special trip for lunch or dinner, so be sure to add it to your list of destinations when you're in this part of Midcoast Maine.

Morse's at Holbrook Wharf Lobster

The story of this shack in the **Cundy's Harbor** section of Harpswell, Maine, is part of a larger story of a community pulling together to rebuild its waterfront and save it from private development. It's a story of careful planning, fund-raising, lobbying, and all the hard work it takes to rebuild piers and wharves and buildings that eventually brought life back to this centuries-old fishing community.

In 2005 local citizens of Cundy's Harbor formed a group called the Holbrook Community Foundation, aiming to refurbish the area's aging waterfront, which had fallen into disrepair over the years. They established goals to rebuild the docks and wharf, refurbish the general store and a gallery in a historic house across the street, and to completely modernize the seasonal eatery that had resided for years as Holbrook Wharf Lobster at the base of the main pier.

984 Cundys Harbor Road, Harpswell, ME

207-729-9050

Open late May to early September

A Dream Fulfilled

In 2009 the waterfront reopened to great fanfare. One of the centerpieces of the new development is the newly refurbished lobster shack, with its exciting menu and lots of outdoor seating that wraps around three sides of the building, offering great views of Cundy's Harbor and the New Meadows River and pine forests on the other side.

The waterfront and adjacent properties are owned collectively by the foundation, and they lease the shack space to the Morse family, who also own an unusual lobster shack drive-in just up the road in Brunswick. The Morses have tacked their name onto the traditional Holbrook Wharf name for the waterfront shack—hence, "Morse's Holbrook Wharf

There's plenty of seating along the side of the wharf at Holbrook's.

Holbrook's varied and colorful menu is on display by the order window.

Lobster." The old sign for Holbrook Wharf Lobster is still hanging above the order window.

Kathleen Morse and her husband run the shack, the adjacent general store, and the gallery in the house across the road; and they lease all three buildings from the foundation. In just a couple of years, they've been able to establish themselves as a destination eatery worth the lengthy drive to get to it. Their familiarity with the lobster business has helped them get the place up and running quickly, and they don't have to go far to get super-fresh lobster and other seafood.

Start with the Salads

Though this is a lobster shack by name, perhaps one of the best, most tempting things is the array of full-dinner salads that take center stage on the menu. These greens-based dishes are garnished with a variety of seafood and chicken. Each salad features a mix of three spring greens along with three fruits (typically strawberries, blueberries, and orange slices) and a generous sprinkling of feta cheese and nuts.

Seafood add-ons include steamed lobster or crab meat lightly mixed with mayo; fried scallops; fried haddock; or fried petite Maine shrimp. You can have your chicken topping either grilled or deep-fried. The house toasted-sesame-and-poppy-seed dressing is the way to go. These are no mere dinner salads; they're meals unto themselves and well worth considering.

For those seeking fresh lobster, Morse's Holbrook's steams theirs and serves them with steamed clams, if desired, for a shore dinner with the usual add-ons. The lobster roll comes in two sizes: regular, which is served on a hot dog bun, and a smaller, less expensive version, which comes on a finger roll.

Deep-fried seafood is popular here, especially the local sea scallops. Be sure to try the small yet sweet-tasting deep-fried Maine shrimp, which you can order as part of a dinner plate or in a roll. The locally caught haddock can also be fried up as part of a dinner or between buns in sandwich form.

Plan to Stick Around

The number one reason to drive all the way down to this enchanting little waterfront is to sit out on the dock at Morse's and enjoy the view of the harbor and the woods and waters across the way. Try and grab one of the two tables at the end of the wharf's pier, as they have unobstructed views of the entire gorgeous scene. And when you've had enough of the great food and the view, check out the adjacent general store or the funky gift shop, housed in a garage on the other side of the wharf.

The foundation has done a good job preserving this waterfront, and you can't go wrong spending an afternoon exploring and enjoying the fresh seafood to be had in this quaint harbor town.

Five Islands Lobster Company

Many lobster connoisseurs consider Five Islands Lobster Company to be hands-down the best lobster shack in Maine—or anywhere else, for that matter. Why?

Start with the lobsters. They come from the deep, cold water that nearly surrounds the Five Islands section of Georgetown, Maine, on the edge of Sheepscot Bay. The deep, dark, and frigid waters close to shore are considered ideal for propagating large numbers of healthy, meaty lobsters, and their proximity helps local lobstermen bring them to shore and market quickly. Numerous lobster boats have made the Georgetown wharf their home port (Five Islands Lobster is situated on the town dock), and there are fresh lobsters arriving throughout the day.

Then there's the view. When you first approach Five Islands, after driving south nearly 15 miles down a winding, wooded, two-lane highway from Bath, Maine, you're greeted with an elevated view overlooking Five Islands Lobster Company, the beautiful cove that it sits on, and an amazing view of the five namesake islands ½ mile or so offshore, many covered with thick evergreens and dotted with rocky shores and stately homes. Even on an overcast, foggy, or rainy day, the view from Five Islands' pier and decks doesn't disappoint.

Throw in the excellent deep-fried and grilled fare from the fry shack (*Down East* magazine declared Five Islands' deep-fried, whole-belly clams to be the best in the state) and the Annabelle's Ice Cream stand next to the fry shack, and you're going to find it mighty hard to get back in your car and leave this place.

╳ 1447 Five Islands Road, Georgetown, ME

☎ 207-751-5964

🐛 www.fiveislandslobster.com

Open early May to mid-October

Five Islands Lobster Company, at the end of Route 127 in Georgetown, Maine.

A couple of Five Islands's famous boiled-in-seawater lobsters.

Your Cheat-Sheet for Five Islands Lobster

Given that there are three or four different structures on the pier where Five Islands resides, it's easy to get confused when it comes time to order your food. You don't want to stand in a long line only to find that you're in the wrong place for what you want. Here's how to navigate your way around Five Islands Lobster.

The first building you'll encounter is the fry shack. It's the large, two-story wood-frame building with the pitched roof that's front and center on the pier and that has the large Five Islands Lobster Co. sign hanging over its front door. (It's actually the shack's rear door; the front door is around the corner. Confused already? Read on.)

If it's lobster you've come for (and it should be), you need to walk past the left side of the fry shack and proceed to a smaller, red-painted wooden shack directly in back of it. This is the lobster shack, and there's a small, faded, hand-painted sign over its front door that simply states: Lobsters. This is where you want to begin. Even if you plan to have other things, it's best to order your lobster first, since it takes the longest to cook, and all lobsters are cooked to order.

When you pass through the lobster door (it may take some time, as there's often a lengthy line stretching back on busy summer days), you'll find yourself at a counter where you need to make some big decisions: What size lobster do you want? Hard-shell or soft-shell? Do you want to "rent" a shell cracker? (It's about two bucks, refunded upon the implement's return; and it's highly recommended, especially for hard-shell lobsters.) Do you want an ear of corn or some red potatoes thrown into the netted cooking bag with your lobster, to be boiled in the same tasty seawater? How about a pint of steamers or a side of homemade coleslaw? All these options are clearly stated on a multicolored chalkboard on the wall next to the register. There are also glass-fronted coolers loaded with soft drinks, iced tea, bottled water, and other beverages.

Order to your heart's content, then settle up with the cashier. (Good news—they accept Visa and MasterCard—not usually the case in the lobster-shack world.) You'll be given a wooden, hand-painted, miniature lobster buoy that resembles a large dreidel and has a plastic-coated card chained to it, inscribed with the name of a local boat, like *Anna Lee* or *Lucky Catch*. When your lobster is ready, a server will bring it out on a tray and call out the boat name, at which time you hand over your buoy and get your meal.

The Lovenest Grill

While you're waiting for your lobster to cook, head back over to the fry shack to order anything else you may wish to have while dining at Five Islands. This building is nicknamed the "Lovenest Grill," because fishermen supposedly used it for trysts with their secret lovers after coming ashore and before heading home to their wives. There's no more hootchy-koo in the Lovenest these days—just simple, honest shack fare being grilled and fried up throughout the day.

Once you make your way into the fry shack (again, you may encounter a lengthy line on sunny summer days), there's an extensive chalkboard stating the items and costs of everything on offer. You place your order, settle up, and go outside with claim check and lobster-buoy claimer in hand. Grab a seat at a nearby picnic table, if you can. When your Lovenest food is ready, a window with wooden shutters and a wood-framed screen on the side of the building is thrown open by a young counterperson who will yell out your name. Ah, the anticipation!

Goodies from the Grill

It's said that the fryers at Five Islands produce some of the best deep-fried seafood in the area, if not the state. Certainly the fried clams have drawn high praise, and there's plenty of reason to cheer for much of the Lovenest's other fare. Take the fried scallops. They're locally sourced, large, plump, chewy, and full of deep-sea flavor. Deep-fried Maine shrimp are small yet sweet and lightly breaded.

The Lovenest Grill's order pickup window. Listen carefully for your name or number to be called out.

A Couple of Five Islands Witticisms

Five Islands Lobster Company prides itself on its sense of humor almost as much as it does on its fine lobster and other seafood. For example, take its slogan, which appears on some of the shack's promotional materials:

Maine's legendary "eat-on-the-dock-with-the-fishermen-but-best-avoid-the-table-by-the-bait-shack-door" summer dining and boats/islands/lighthouse-watching experience.

Quite a mouthful, yet certainly indicative of Five Islands' spirit. Then there's Five Islands' description of how to find the place, which appears on their website:

We are located approximately 14 miles from down-town Bath [Maine]. From Route 1 in either direction, take 127 south until it ends. As one local puts it: "Keep going until your hat floats, then back up a bit."

A little levity always makes the food taste better!

The fish-and-chips features fresh haddock or salmon, and there's a haddock sandwich at a very reasonable price. Other sandwiches include a lobster roll from meat that's picked fresh in the back room of the lobster shed throughout the day. Five Islands' "Somewhat Famous" crab-cake sandwich features two crab cakes that are virtually all meat, with no breadcrumb filler. Then there's Jenny's Special Sandwich, an unusual yet tasty combination of a grilled haddock fillet paired with a crab cake on top.

Homemade sauces for the sandwiches and grilled fish fillets (haddock and salmon) include Five Islands' innovative cilantro mayo, mustard dill, and a killer tartar sauce with fresh dill blended in. The fish chowder is a fine starter, filled with generous chunks of haddock in a milky, flavorful broth.

In the way of land-based cuisine, Five Islands has an excellent grilled burger that even seafood lovers will occasionally choose over all the fish and shellfish available on the menu. There are grilled hot dogs in natural casing, grilled cheese and chicken sandwiches, french fries, and homemade, hand-cut onion rings.

A Varied Dining Landscape

Five Islands offers several choices of places to dine once you've secured your lobster and your Lovenest fare. There is, of course, the dock right on the water in back of the shacks, which provides perhaps the best views of the working harbor and the lobster boats that come and go. This is the largest dining area, with some 20 solid wooden picnic tables lined up to the end of the pier. It's also where you want to be when they call names and numbers for food orders.

On the other side of the Lovenest is a deck extending over the rocky shore and affording views of the southwestern portion of the cove. It's a nice place for families and others seeking a quieter place to dine. Then there's yet another decklike area adjacent to this that's perched on dry land almost in front of the Lovenest's "back" door. This is another good choice for a more peaceful meal.

If none of this works for you (or all these places are filled with other diners), there are still a bunch of freestanding picnic tables a little farther away, alongside the parking lot. These tables offer a great view over the western portion of the cove and a glimpse of the open sea. With the rocky-shored islands and the expanses of sea before you, this may actually be the best place to sit.

Five Islands is BYO so be sure to bring your own beer or wine if you wish to partake. Sometimes there is live music on the main pier, and if you're there in the evening at the right time on the right day, you may see fishermen offloading their tuna catch right along the edge of the dock at dusk.

Five Islands may be a long ride down a narrow road that takes you well out of your way as you explore coastal Maine, but many have taken the detour and been really glad that they did. Take the time to check this place out for some of the best, most genuine lobster anywhere.

Red's Eats

🍴 41 Main Street, Wiscasset, ME

☎ 207-882-6128

Red's Eats, world famous for its lobster roll.

THIS LITTLE SHACK, perched on the western bank of the Sheepscot River on Route 1 in Wiscasset, Maine, is known throughout the state, the nation, even the world, as an amazing little eatery that's famous for basically one thing: its lobster roll. Red's bun-bursting, tin-foil-wrapped lobster sandwich creates huge lines of hungry patrons, massive traffic jams on the Sheepscot River bridge—and hundreds of satisfied customers each day, every summer, as tallied by such websites as Yelp, TripAdvisor, and Jane and Michael Stern's highly respected Roadfood.com.

What's all the fuss about? First, it's the depression-era ambience (if you can call it ambience). Red's Eats looks pretty much the way it sounds: small, informal, a little tattered around the edges, very inviting. It also has a trademark red-and-white awning over the front of its trailer-like facade.

But that's not where the name comes from. The shack is named after, Allen "Red" Gagnon, who took possession of the place in 1954, after the eatery had spent its first 16 years down in Boothbay Harbor. Red passed away a couple of years ago, and his children now run the place, led by daughter Debbie Cronk, who recently coauthored a book titled *Red's Eats: World's Best Lobster Shack*.

There's no indoor seating at Red's. You stand in a line that can take over an hour on most days to wind its way up the sidewalk on Route 1 and around the corner to the lone order window. You place your order, get your food on a plastic tray, and make your way around to the back of the eatery where there is a limited amount of outdoor seating at sturdy plastic tables and chairs.

All this may sound a bit nightmarish, but the big payoff comes when you unwrap and tuck into your lobster roll. There are mounds of lobster meat—as much as comes in a 1+-pound lobster—wedged into a buttered, lightly toasted, supersized New England–style hot dog roll. It really is a taste treat, and you can get your sandwich with either a side of mayo or melted butter (or both) to mix in with the meat. People may grumble and groan while standing in line, but most complaints melt away after the lobster rolls have been procured and enjoyed.

LOBSTER ROLL ALERT!

Sprague's Lobster

✕ 22 Main Street, Wiscasset, ME

☎ 207-882-1236

Open mid-May to mid-October

One sunny summer morning several years ago, Frank Sprague was sitting at a picnic table in front of his eponymous lobster stand on Route 1 in Wiscasset when he saw the broadcast journalist Katie Couric pull up in a massive SUV. She stepped out into the parking lot, squinting in the sunlight as she looked around, searching for something she couldn't seem to find.

Surprised and delighted to have a celebrity on his doorstep, Sprague hurried over and welcomed her to his place, offering to show her around. To borrow a line from the movie *A Christmas Story*, Sprague said Couric looked at him "like I had lobsters crawling all over me," then she proceeded to cross Route 1 to film a *Today Show* segment covering Red's Eats, which is directly across the highway from Sprague's.

A lesser man would have been hurt, even angry; but the bemused, pacific Sprague took it in stride. He has grown used to living in the shadow of his more famous neighbor, but that shouldn't diminish the stature or worthiness of Sprague's Lobster. This place is an excellent alternative to the madness that is Red's on a busy summer day. And if it's a whole boiled lobster you seek, Sprague's has it and Red's doesn't.

A Rolling Cooker and Seaweed

Sprague got his start in the lobster business in the 1970s as a caterer. At the time, he was working for the Dodge Inn, a local restaurant, and he eventually branched off and started catering on his own under the name "Sprague's Lobster." He became known locally for hauling around his 2- by 5-foot wood-fired lobster cooker, which he seasoned with ocean

The colorful, festive lobster shed at Sprague's Lobster.

water and seaweed, giving his boiled bugs a distinctively marine flavor. The "lobster bakes," as they were called, were sometimes very large affairs, with Frank cooking up more than a hundred lobsters at a time in his rolling cooker.

Eventually tiring of the gypsy life, Sprague rented a spot in 1988 next to a municipal dock on the Sheepscot River in Wiscasset. Some train tracks ran by the dock, and there was a depot where tourists on sightseeing tours switched from train to boat as part of the Rail-and-Sail tourist attraction in Wiscasset at that time. Bus tours would also pull in frequently for freshly cooked lobsters on the dock. These travelers and bunches of locals soon became Sprague's steady and loyal customer base.

A Stone's Throw from a Legend

Ten years later, the town built a newer, bigger dock a couple hundred yards upriver, right next to Route 1 and the bridge that spans the river. Sprague jumped at the chance to move closer to the action, right across the street from the legendary Red's Eats, and he's been on the same town dock next to Route 1 ever since.

Sprague's occupies approximately one-third of the wooden dock's expanse. He's got a fry shack, a lobster shack, and about 10 umbrellaed picnic tables in front of them. To the south on the dock, there's plenty more public deck space, with wooden chairs, more picnic tables, and splendid views of the Sheepscot River. A couple of smaller shacks sit across the dock from Sprague's, where T-shirts, pottery, and

Sprague's owner, Frank Sprague, in his custom-made lobster shirt.

other bric-a-brac are sold. Like the dock itself, the parking area between Route 1 and the dock is owned by the town. So anyone (including Red's customers, like Katie Couric) can park there.

What's Cookin'?

Let's visit the fry shack first, since it's first to greet you when you step onto the dock from the parking lot. The menu isn't huge, but it's appealingly varied between fried seafood baskets, grilled burgers and hot dogs, grilled cheese in a number of variations, and some killer seafood rolls.

As you approach the fry shack's order window, you can't help but notice a white signboard with red lettering that boldly advertises Sprague's meaty lobster roll—a full, a 1-pound (and then some) lobster's worth of fresh-picked meat, lightly tossed in mayo, and served on a buttered, toasted bun. This sign is clearly meant to catch the attention of any prospective defectors from Red's who may have grown frustrated with the long wait across the street. It's a worthy roll, in many ways every bit as large and good as Red's, so consider it a viable alternative to the superstar across the street. The lobster roll is Sprague's number-one-selling item, and they can probably thank Red's for making the sandwich synonymous with this stretch of Wiscasset.

The next most popular sandwich on the menu is Sprague's crabmeat roll. It's got loads of fresh-picked crabmeat, mixed with mayo and seasonings and tucked into a toasted bun. The fried haddock sandwich rounds out the seafood-sandwich offerings; you can also get the haddock in a generously portioned fish-and-chips basket.

Frank claims that Sprague's is one of the few places in Midcoast Maine that serves deep-fried clam fritters, a treat normally found more in the vicinity of Narragansett Bay in Rhode Island. Also from the deep fryers come excellent fresh, hand-cut french fries that go well with virtually every dish from the fry shack. And there's only one type of chowder—seafood—loaded with Maine shrimp and fresh haddock. For a dollar extra, they'll throw in some fresh lobster meat.

Low-Tech Fun

Some 40 feet away from the fry shack sits Sprague's lobster and steamers shack, where whole lobsters are kept in cold-water tanks and boiled up to order in fresh seawater. Sprague's gets its lobsters from local Wiscasset lobstermen and from the fleets of lobster boats in nearby Boothbay Harbor. (The meat for the lobster rolls comes fresh-picked daily from Atlantic Edge Seafood, a highly regarded wholesaler in Boothbay.) The most popular lobster dish is the aptly named Lobster Dinner, which features a 1-pound boiled lobster, 1 pound of steamed littleneck clams, corn on the cob, coleslaw, and a dinner roll, all for a price that usually hovers just north of $20.

If you plan to order a lobster or steamers, you must do so at the fry shack. When you place your lobster/steamer order, Sprague's low-tech communication system springs into action. The order slip is attached to a clothespin on a laundry line, then it's pulleyed from fry shack to lobster shack over the dining area for delivery to Frank, who boils up the lobsters from his perch next to the cooker. He knows when an order is coming because a large cowbell affixed to the laundry line peels loudly as the order slip makes its way overhead. (Franks says he used to have a string and two cans stretched between the shacks, to fake out the kids who asked how he knew when to cook the lobsters.)

Though Sprague's doesn't do nearly the business that its friendly rival across the street does, the shack holds its own. It has plenty to offer to the road-weary, lobster-seeking traveler who wants his or her food without the long waiting lines and who might find Sprague's sun-splashed town-dock deck a great alternative to the lobster-roll mayhem across the street. Did you hear that, Katie Couric?

The Lobster Dock

Boothbay Harbor is a lovely town at the end of Route 27, about a dozen miles south of Wiscasset, Maine. Boothbay is where the well-heeled come to unwind in the summer, and it's a great place to do it. The town's deepwater harbor is home port to many yachts and other stately boats, and the homes surrounding much of the harbor's shores are elegant, to say the least.

There are numerous restaurants and eateries in Boothbay Harbor, many of them upscale and fancy; yet quite a few are summertime casual, and they welcome tourists and locals of all stripes. Let's pay a visit to one of the best of the casual bunch—the Lobster Dock on the eastern shore of Boothbay's famed harbor.

✕ 49 Atlantic Avenue, Boothbay Harbor, ME

☎ 207-633-7120

🦞 www.thelobsterdock.com

Open mid-May to mid-October

From the Corporate Suite to the Kitchen Beat

The Lobster Dock is owned and run by the husband-and-wife team of Mitch and Dawn Weiss, who bought the restaurant in 2000. The Weisses were not your typical aspiring restaurateurs: both had well-paying, secure corporate jobs in eastern Connecticut—Mitch was a systems engineer for a large bank, and Dawn served as human resources director for a prestigious accounting firm. They had a couple of young children—and they also had a pipe dream to some day live in Maine, should the right opportunity present itself. So one rainy week in April 2000, while their kids were on spring break from school, they packed up the car and headed up to Maine to scope out possibilities.

They came across an ad for a restaurant that was up for sale in Boothbay Harbor, and they decided to check it out. Despite the rain and

The Lobster Dock's picnic area sits right by the harbor.

the cold and the gray April skies that cast a shadow over their visit, both saw the potential for something new and exciting. Long story short, they took the plunge, bought the place, and opened on Fourth of July weekend that same year.

They weren't totally lacking in restaurant experience when they purchased the Lobster Dock. Mitch had worked as a cook for several years at Red Lobster in his youth, and he also had chain-restaurant experience on the corporate side. And Dawn's human resources background proved invaluable in assembling a staff of 20 or so summertime workers needed to keep the place running smoothly and in setting up the financial structure for the new business.

The deck at the Lobster Dock is a lively place all summer long.

A Clean, Bright, Happy Place

Flash-forward to current times, and the Weisses' imprint on the business is distinctive. They redid the outdoor deck and completely rebuilt the outdoor lobster cookers and cold-water lobster tanks, which are an integral part of the new deck layout. Mitch also fully enclosed the indoor seating area at the rear of the shack overlooking Boothbay's harbor, giving diners a place to seek refuge in case of inclement weather and still enjoy their meal and the view. Perhaps the most apparent upgrade is the bright, red hue on all the picnic tables and benches, indoors and out, which are sanded then repainted annually with marine-grade paint. It just lights the place up and brings a cheery glow to the entire Lobster Dock experience.

Dawn has turned most of her attention to the restaurant's financials, while Mitch works in the kitchen and on the menu, refining the dishes that have been a hit with customers over the years and gradually adding some of his own to broaden the restaurant's repertoire.

Even with the spiffing up, the Lobster Dock remains a casual, seasonal, dine-in-the-rough place, where you order your food at a window near the front of the building, then walk around to the side and back to find a place to sit at one of the bright red tables. After ordering and settling up, you're given a plastic card with a number on it to place on your table, and your food is matched to your number and brought to you. The view of the harbor is amazing, especially on warm, sunny days.

LOBSTER DOCK'S SEAFOOD FRA DIAVOLO

This is Mitch Weiss's signature dish at Boothbay Harbor's Lobster Dock. There's a lot in here, and it all comes together very nicely. Try it at home, or better yet, motor up to the Dock and try the real thing!

INGREDIENTS

2 whole 1¼ lb. lobsters	2 bay leaves
¾ pound linguine, cooked and drained	½ teaspoon dry oregano
2 tablespoons olive oil	¼ teaspoon chili powder
4 garlic cloves, chopped	¼ teaspoon cayenne pepper
3½ cups marinara sauce	12 scallops, 10–20/lb. size, drained
¼ cup dry red wine	1 pound fresh mussels
½ teaspoon crushed red pepper	12 shrimp, 16–20/lb. size, raw, peeled, and deveined
½ teaspoon dry thyme	2 tablespoons fresh parsley, finely chopped
½ teaspoon dry parsley	Parmigiano-Reggiano, freshly grated
½ teaspoon dry basil	

Cook the lobsters for 15 minutes in salted water, cool and twist off the tail and claws. With a large knife, butterfly the tail down the back (red side) and spread open, then rinse under cold water. Lightly crack each claw and remove part of the shell, just enough to expose the meat and make it easy to eat. Discard lobster bodies.

Bring a large pot of salted water to boil, add linguini, and cook for 7–10 minutes or according to package directions. Drain the pasta and set aside. Meanwhile, in a large sauté pan over medium heat, add the olive oil and gently sauté garlic for 30 seconds (don't let it burn). Add the marinara sauce and wine. Then add the remaining dry ingredients and simmer on low for 10 minutes.

Next, add all of the seafood except for the shrimp. Cover and simmer for 7–8 minutes, just until the mussels open. Then place the shrimp into the pan so that they are fully immersed in the sauce. Simmer for 3 more minutes and remove from heat.

Divide the cooked linguini onto two plates. Gently pour some of the sauce from the pan on each plate of pasta. Center the lobster tail and two claws in the middle of each plate. Then place half the mussels around each plate and divide the remaining contents of the pan between both plates. Garnish with fresh chopped parsley and a side of Parmigiano-Reggiano. Serves 2.

There's almost always a pleasant din of chatter and laughter as people settle in to enjoy their meals and the overall camaraderie of the place. The good vibes here are infectious. And the Lobster Dock is a pet-friendly establishment, with two brightly painted tables in front by the parking lot that are reserved for those who wish to have Fido join them at mealtime.

The restaurant is built on the former grounds of Reed's Shipyard, a place where many large schooners were built in the late 1800s and early 1900s. There are remnants of the old shipyard's decking and foundations right next to the water. If you squint your eyes a bit while staring out into the harbor, you can easily imagine the creaking masts and billowing sails gliding by on graceful wooden ships, as they did over a hundred years ago. The Weisses also recently installed a small marina with 17 slips on their waterfront for customers coming by boat.

Throwdown Crab Cakes and More

At any given time, the Lobster Dock has up to several hundred pounds of live lobsters in their sheltered outdoor cold-water tanks. You can choose your lobster and watch (or not watch) as it's dropped into a netted bag and immersed in one of the steaming, gas-fired, seawater-filled outdoor cookers next to the tanks.

This is as fresh as lobster gets, and you're never far from the action, as lobsters are cooked throughout the day in the outdoor pots. The Weisses procure their lobsters from Atlantic Edge Lobster just down the road, and occasionally from Mill Cove Lobster Pound, also in Boothbay Harbor. Lobster dinners

The Lobster Dock beckons on a sunny summer day in Boothbay Harbor.

come with corn on the cob, a biscuit, and melted butter. The bugs range in size from 1¼ pounds to 3 pounds and more. Lobster rolls here come in both the hot-buttered and cold-mayo'ed varieties.

A few years ago, celebrity chef Bobby Flay featured Mitch's crab cakes on one of his *Throwdown! with Bobby Flay!* television segments. This is quite a high honor, to receive such recognition from a major Food Network personality. What makes Mitch's crab cakes so special? Aside from all the fresh crabmeat, he tops them with his special remoulade sauce and serves the cakes with a side of homemade summer salsa. Flay was suitably impressed, and crab cake sales at the Lobster Dock have been strong ever since.

Other tasty and unusual starters include a bowl of mussels mariniere, fried calamari with a fiery fra diavolo sauce on the side, and crunchy artichoke hearts that have been lightly deep-fried and topped with garlic, lemon, butter, and a sprinkling of Parmesan cheese. The milky, Maine-style clam chowder and the thick, creamy lobster stew, which is loaded with claw and knuckle meat, come in cup and bowl sizes and are not to be missed.

The deep fryers are busy here, cooking up lots of clams, scallops, Maine shrimp (the small, sweet variety), oysters, french fries, and thick-cut, beer-battered onion rings. You can get your deep-fried goodies à la carte by the pint or as part of a fried dinner that comes with coleslaw and a choice of potato.

If you prefer your lobster a bit more dressed up, try the baked, stuffed lobster, which is served as a special on many nights in the summertime. There's also a tasty lobster scampi combo served over pasta and offered as an occasional special.

A standard pasta offering on the menu, and perhaps Lobster Dock's signature dish, is the seafood fra diavolo. This seafood orgy consists of a whole lobster, scallops, shrimp, and mussels served over linguini and smothered in Mitch's spicy red sauce. A couple of generous slabs of garlic bread help sop up all that wonderful seafood-flavored sauce.

A couple more items of note: beef and wine. On weekends, Mitch serves generous cuts of prime rib that have been slow roasted and garlic infused. You have your choice between 12- and 16-ounce cuts. Any day of the week, you can have a grilled black angus New York strip steak, hand-cut on the premises.

What's good food without good wine? The Lobster Dock isn't a BYO establishment, but it has a short, excellent wine list at very reasonable prices. Also, for that special occasion, there's champagne, everything from a simple flute of the house bubbly to a bottle of Dom Perignon. (Don't forget—we're in Boothbay Harbor.)

The best time to come to the Lobster Dock is in the early evening in summertime to watch the sun set. With lobster on the table and wine in hand, you'll feel blessed to be in this part of the world at a time when it's looking its best.

A Picturesque Glimpse into the Lives of Lobstermen

When you dine at a lobster shack, you don't see all of the hard work that goes into bringing your bug from the bottom of the sea all the way to your plate. A recently published book, *The Lobstering Life*, sheds light on the rough and romantic life of lobster fishermen—one that goes mostly unseen by the rest of the world.

This beautiful, full-color photo book contains dozens of images showing lobstermen (and -women) hard at work on the docks, in their boats, and on the high seas—baiting, setting, checking, and emptying hundreds of traps each day in their Sisyphean quest to catch enough lobsters to earn a steady living.

Shot mostly in Maine and Massachusetts, *The Lobstering Life* is the work of photographers David Middleton and Brenda Berry, who spent months tagging along on lobster boats and hanging around the docks to learn as much as they could about the lobster trade. Their hard work and inquisitiveness pay dividends in the form of numerous images that vividly capture the world of lobstering.

Pick up a copy before embarking on your lobster shack odyssey, and you'll develop a heightened sense of respect and admiration for those who work so hard to bring the bounty of the sea to the shore (and shacks) every day.

Boothbay Lobster Wharf

97 Atlantic Avenue, Boothbay Harbor, ME

☎ 207-633-4900

🦞 www.boothbaylobsterwharf.com

Open late May to mid-October

Boothbay Lobster Wharf's lively, festive dining deck.

This place has its roots in the old Boothbay Lobstermen's Co-op, an association of local lobstermen who pooled their resources around a single wharf, shared expenses and revenues, and lived an all-for-one, one-for-all existence.

Unlike a number of other lobster cooperatives up and down the Maine coast, this one eventually went bust and disbanded, and it was put up for sale half a dozen years ago. While it was still a going concern, the co-op had built a beautiful wharf with a dockside cookhouse and an enclosed eating area, a couple of adjacent shops, and a huge, sunny deck where diners can enjoy boiled lobster fresh from the boats while overlooking Boothbay's gorgeous harbor.

New Owners, New Lease on Life

In 2006 the husband-and-wife team of Todd and Kim Simmons bought the Lobstermen's Co-op, renamed it the Boothbay Lobster Wharf, and carried on with many of the same fine traditions that made the co-op popular with tourists and locals.

Todd has been a lobsterman all his life, and he has a boat and manages a small fleet in his hometown of Port Clyde, an hour or so away by car in the direction of Penobscot Bay to the east. Wanting to diversify his lobster-fishing business, he purchased the co-op property primarily for its fine restaurant setup on the pretty harbor. In addition, he kept the lobster-fishing-services portion of the business alive, selling gas and bait to local Boothbay lobstermen and buying their catch when they returned to port.

All in all, it's a win-win for lobstermen and lovers of fresh seafood alike. Todd and Kim (who handles much of the back-office functions) have kept the wharf, with its seafood shack and other amenities, in tip-top shape, and legions of lobster lovers fill the sunny deck all summer long. There are some 20 umbrellaed tables on the deck outside, overlooking the harbor and the town across the way. And there's an enclosed, bright, airy indoor dining area with a dozen highly varnished picnic-style tables as well as a full-service bar that's stocked with beer, wine, and spirits. Throw in the lobster tanks and cookers on the deck, and you've got a formula for fun.

Tucking into a plate of boiled lobster on Boothbay's outdoor dining deck.

Part of the charm of this place is the 15 lobster boats that call Boothbay Lobster Wharf home. The boats come and go throughout the day, and it's particularly fun to watch them offloading their catch, usually in early to mid afternoon. You can observe the crates of lobsters as they're winched out of the boats, then wheeled into an adjacent building, where large cold-water tanks full of fresh seawater keep the lobsters in top shape. There's also a lobster-picking room, where fresh meat is picked for lobster rolls and for the Lobster Wharf's seafood market throughout the day.

Go for the Lobster

Boothbay Lobster Wharf's menu is broad and varied, with all sorts of deep-fried seafood, sandwiches, seafood rolls and wraps, burgers, chowders, and finger foods like cheese sticks and fried zucchini or mushrooms.

But what you want to go for here is the fresh-off-the-boat lobsters. Everything else on the menu pales by comparison. There's a separate lobster stand on the pier, and you're encouraged to select your own from the seawater tanks that sit right next to the outdoor cookers. If you wish, have them throw an ear or two of fresh corn into the netted cooking bag with your bug, then sit back and wait for your number to be called. There's a separate shack for virtually all the other food items, so feel free to go there as well and supplement your lobster dinner with some chowder or perhaps a salad.

As lobster shacks go, this place has one of the nicest decks you'll find anywhere. Since it was rebuilt so recently, it's in very good shape. There's live music, usually on weekends, and it's a great place to kick back and have a cold one or two, whether you're dining there or not. The indoor dining area has a wonderful second-floor banquet room of sorts with even better views of the harbor, thanks to its wrap-around sliding glass windows. See if you can get up there and sneak a peek.

Boothbay Lobster Wharf has probably the freshest lobster you'll find anywhere in town, so if it's lobster you seek while in Boothbay, this place should be right at the top of your list.

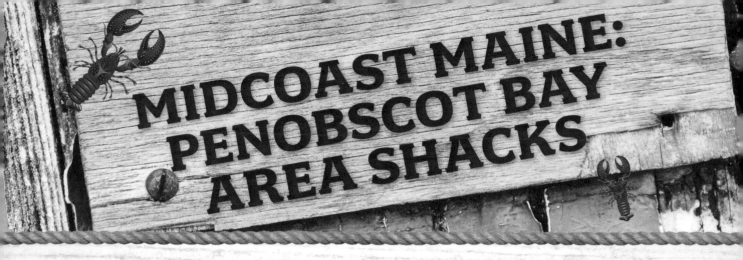

MIDCOAST MAINE: PENOBSCOT BAY AREA SHACKS

The eastern portion of Midcoast Maine has perhaps the highest concentration of lobster shacks that are joined at the hip to real, live lobster-fishing operations. Nowhere else will you find so many places to eat lobster while gazing off the end of the dock as lobster boats pull up and offload their catches. Some of Maine's oldest and best-known lobster shacks dot the shores of the Pemaquid Peninsula and Muscongus and Penobscot Bays. Lobster eating doesn't get much better or more honest than this.

From the Pemaquid Lobster Cooperative to Cod End to Waterman's Beach Lobster to Young's Lobster Pound, the list of authentic lobster shacks in this part of Maine is long. And the quaint fishing villages, many of them doubling as artist colonies in the summer, have lots to offer beyond lobster dinners.

Damariscotta is the best place to start your exploration of this part of the Maine coast. From there, you can descend the Pemaquid Peninsula, double back up toward Waldoboro, then east to Thomaston, then south again toward Port Clyde. Once you've made your way back up to Thomaston, cruise through Rockland, Rockport, and Camden, then wrap up your tour of this region in Belfast on the northern reaches of Penobscot Bay. Take your time in this part of Maine and savor the maritime life that has left an indelible imprint on every town and village in the region. And don't forget to have as many lobsters as you can!

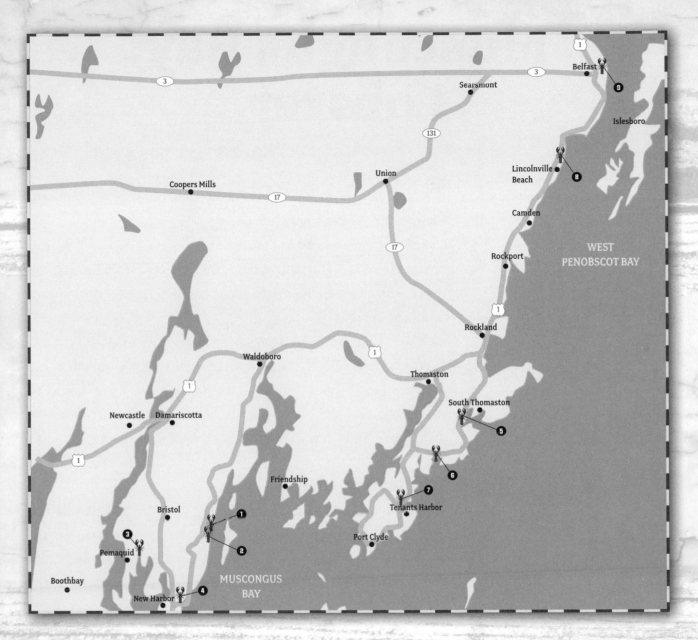

Muscongus Bay Lobster

✗ 28 Landing Road, Round Pond, ME

☎ 207-529-2251

🦞 www.mainefreshlobster.com

Open mid-May to mid-October

Round Pond is a small, picturesque cove off Muscongus Sound, some 10 miles southeast of Damariscotta. The cove provides shelter for a variety of commercial and pleasure craft—and it has a lively lobster pound or two on its shores, where fresh red guys are cooked up and served with all the trimmings on sun-splashed decks cooled by distant ocean breezes.

The most popular and best-known lobster shack on Round Pond is Muscongus Bay Lobster, a large, open-air eatery that's a spin-off of the Muscongus Bay Lobster Company. This place is a beehive of activity in the summertime, both at its open-air lobster pound and on its fishing dock, where lobster boats come and go throughout the day.

The Round Pond Renys

Muscongus Bay Lobster (named after the sound and bay that lie just beyond Round Pond cove) is owned and operated by the Reny family, who live in a house just up the hill from the Muscongus Bay dock. Dan Reny is the third generation to run the business, and Dan's wife, Andrea, recently gave up her teaching job to help out.

Dan's grandfather got things going back in the 1960s with a modest operation that grew slowly over the years. Dan's father and uncle ran Muscongus Bay for a number of years, but they tired of it as they neared retirement age. Dan, who had been studying aquaculture in college (oyster farming in particular), stepped up in 2000 to keep the business in the family, and he's been running Muscongus Bay Lobster ever since.

Dan Reny, owner of Muscongus Bay Lobster, in his cook shack.

The Deck Is Where It's At

The best thing about this place (other than the fresh boiled lobsters, of course) is the amazing deck that overlooks Round Pond and provides ample seating for up to a couple hundred diners at a time. It's a large, wooden structure with dozens of wooden picnic tables and benches spaced in such a way that it never feels crowded even when it is. Live music happens on Sundays, and it's a BYO operation, so feel free to bring your cooler down to the deck and enjoy some cold ones or a bottle of wine with your meal. It's a great place to spend a sunny afternoon, and there's plenty of good people-watching, what with the large crowds, especially on weekends.

No shirt? No shoes? No problem at Muscongus Bay Lobster's deck.

The cook shack is a decent-sized wooden structure featuring large windows on the front with wooden shutters that hook to the ceiling. Dan's plan is to expand the shack in order to increase the size of his kitchen so he can simultaneously expand his menu.

Handpicked Lobsters from the Dock

Each day, Dan buys hundreds of pounds of lobsters from the 10 boats that he services as a wholesaler from his dock, and he and his assistants handpick the lobsters they want for their cook shack. This guarantees the best lobsters from one of the best lobster-fishing areas around.

When you approach the welcoming order windows on the cook shack, one of the first things you'll notice are the cold-water tanks just on the other side of the counter that separates customers from the kitchen help. You pick your size—even your own lobster if you wish—and watch as it's plucked from the tank, dropped in a netted bag, and plunked into the steaming-hot-seawater boiling tank. Be sure to let them know if you'd like an ear of native corn with your bug. They'll pop one in the netted sack before putting it in the cooker. Muscongus gets its corn fresh almost daily in the summer from locally famous Spears Farms in nearby Northboro.

There's also a killer lobster roll on the menu: 4 ounces of fresh-picked lobster meat mixed with a bit of mayo and stuffed into a locally baked white or whole-wheat roll. There's also a crab roll, with 4 ounces of fresh-picked meat, and a shrimp roll that's filled with small, sweet shrimp harvested from the Gulf of Maine. All three rolls come with chips and a pickle.

Dan works with local diggers to get his clams for steaming and for serving raw on the half shell. In addition to raw clams, Muscongus sells tons (over 10,000 pounds per season) of locally farmed oysters. One of Dan's plans for the deck is to get an old dory, saw it in half, and make it into an oyster bar, separate from the cook shack. It'll be a very nice addition to an already splendid place for outdoor eating.

Part of the kitchen expansion calls for the addition of a grill for burgers, hot dogs, grilled cheese, and other items for those not inclined to eat seafood. But why bother? The number one reason to come here and eat (other than the gorgeous deck, the beautiful cove, and the music on Sundays) is Muscongus Bay's whole Maine lobsters that are as fresh as can be.

Round Pond Lobster

As you pull into the parking lot for Muscongus Bay Lobster, you'll pass by a small shack on your right with a simple, hand-painted sign that reads ROUND POND LOBSTER. This place, which sits somewhat precariously between the parking lot and the water's edge, is a shack in every sense of the word. No more than 20 feet deep by 30 feet wide, with room inside for a cold-water lobster tank, a couple of small cookers, and an old refrigerator or two, Round Pond Lobster looks more like a storage shed than a restaurant.

When Round Pond owner Buddy Poland was recently told that his tiny lobster shack is one of the more informal ones on the Maine coast, he replied in his thick, deadpan, Maine accent, "*Thee* most in*fah*mel!" He's probably right.

Round Pond Lobster is an offshoot of Buddy's lobster cooperative, where 10 boats fuel and bait up each day, motor out to their traps before dawn, and return with their catch, which is offloaded and sent down the food chain to restaurants, grocery stores, and other retailers interested in selling Maine's "other red meat."

Buddy saves some lobsters for cooking up in his shed,

and he sells them through the window next to the front door. The menu is quite simple: lobsters, steamers, corn on the cob, and potato chips; and there's soda out of a vending machine. (Round Pond is BYO, by the way, and diners are welcome to bring their own side dishes.)

Next to the shed is a dock with several wooden picnic tables on it and a winch at the dock's end for offloading crates of freshly trapped lobsters. That's the sum total of the operation, and Buddy likes it that way—uncomplicated, informal, and open for business only when he feels like it.

Despite the devil-may-care attitude of the place, Round Pond does a good amount of business in the peak of the summer, packing the deck with hungry diners and treating them to some truly fresh lobster. So if you're in the mood for no-frills seafood and a back-porch atmosphere, Round Pond Lobster won't disappoint. And the view of Round Pond, by the way, is superb. (Call 207-529-5725.)

Pemaquid Lobster Cooperative

Over on the other side of the Pemaquid Peninsula is the Pemaquid Lobster Cooperative, the longest continuously operated lobster cooperative in the state of Maine (according to its members). This place is a throwback to the days when lobsters were trapped and eaten locally in a rural setting reminiscent of an Andrew Wyeth painting.

⚒ 32 Co-op Road, Pemaquid, ME

☎ 207-677-2801

🦞 www.pemaquidlobstercoop.com

Open mid-May to mid-October

The co-op is in a weatherbeaten, open-air, shed-like structure with some sheltered tables inside and several picnic tables out in front. Wildflowers abound, and sweeping views of the broad Pemaquid River make you thankful that the area has retained its natural beauty. This is the place to come and experience a good, old-fashioned lobster boil the way they were done more than 50 years ago.

The Roots of the Cooperative

Back in 1947, after the end of World War II, a group of local Pemaquid Peninsula lobstermen threw their lots together and formed the Pemaquid Lobster Cooperative. The idea was to share expenses (dock, gas, bait) and revenues (lobster sales) in a mutually beneficial partnership. The co-op started with several lobstermen and steadily grew until, at its height about 20 years ago, there were about 30 co-op members.

That was around the same time the co-op decided to get into the restaurant business, to hedge their bets and to make a little extra money on some of the lobsters they caught. With a beautiful location and low overhead, they erected their shack, installed a lobster cooker and some tables, and set about serving up boiled bugs to the locals and to tourists who managed to find the place. Things went well, and they installed

Pemaquid Co-op's primitive, colorful sign beckons from the roadside on Route 130 near Pemaquid Harbor.

deep fryers and expanded their menu with deep-fried seafood about 10 years ago.

At the same time, their membership began to diminish, as many of the older lobstermen retired and only a few younger ones signed on to take their place. Today, there are about 13 members, yet they continue to fish year-round, filling in the winter months primarily with shrimping in the Gulf of Maine.

Is It Worth the Long Drive?

In a word, *yes*. This place isn't really easy to find, as it's down some long and winding, infrequently traveled roads, and it's tucked away down a dirt road leading to the co-op dock. But when it comes to eating lobster in its element, this is about as genuine as it gets.

Lobster comes in a surprising variety of forms, given the co-op's rural setting. The most popular lobster dish is the Shore Dinner, which consists of a 1¼-pound lobster, steamed clams, corn on the cob, coleslaw, dinner roll, and melted butter, all for around $20—one of the best lobster bargains you'll find anywhere. The Harbor Dinner is the same thing, minus the steamers and corn and about $5 less than the Shore Dinner.

The lobster roll is large and meaty, served cold on a split-top bun. Twin lobsters and "lazy lobster" are both available at market price, and a large lobster salad with greens and lots of lobster meat is a meal unto itself. There's also a wonderful homemade lobster stew, loaded with fresh-picked meat, that comes in both cup and bowl sizes.

Pemaquid Lobster Cooperative's outdoor tables offer a fine view of the harbor and co-op pier below.

The co-op makes a chowder of the day, depending on what comes in from local fishermen. Clams are dug locally, fresh haddock is always available, and there's always Maine shrimp from the co-op's own freezers. Deep-fried seafood baskets are popular. They come with fries and slaw and feature whole-belly clams, shrimp, scallops, and haddock. There are some good-sized grilled hamburgers, hot dogs, and a grilled chicken-breast sandwich.

You can bring your own beer and wine to the co-op, and soda is for sale and is dispensed from serve-yourself soda machines like the kind you see in fast-food places. Refills are free. There's only one flavor of ice cream—vanilla—but it tastes great on a slice of homemade pie, which is fresh-baked daily.

There's another reason to come here: the co-op accepts most major credit cards, which is a relative rarity among the more rustic lobster shacks along the New England coast. But the real reason to come to Pemaquid is to enjoy the fresh air, the view, and the glimpse at a real, down-on-the-docks lobster cooperative and the people who run it.

Shaw's Fish & Lobster Wharf

Several miles before reaching the tip of the Pemaquid Peninsula, where you'll find the world-famous Pemaquid Point lighthouse, you come upon a scenic cove named New Harbor. It's one of the last exclusively working harbors on the coast of Maine, filled with fishing and lobstering boats and bereft of the constantly increasing legions of pleasure craft found up and down the coast.

The cove's shores are lined with commercial fishing operations, and in the midst of these is a great lobster place named Shaw's Fish & Lobster Wharf. In addition to being a wonderful restaurant, Shaw's also serves as the debarkation point for boats taking people to and from Monhegan Island, a famous artists' retreat some 10 miles off the coast. So, there's a lot of activity around Shaw's wharf throughout the summer, and it's *the* place to go for lobster in the lower Pemaquid Peninsula area.

✖ 129 State Route 32, New Harbor, ME

☎ 207-677-2200

🦞 www.shawswharf.com

Open mid-May to mid-October

Two Levels of Fun

Pulling into Shaw's parking lot, you see the place a bit downhill, sitting right on the edge of the water. As you walk down and onto the wharf, Shaw's large commercial fishing dock is next door to your left, and to your right is a gift shop and ticket dispensary for the Hardy Cruise Boats to Monhegan Island. Inside the gift shop are a few large cold-water tanks filled with lobsters for take-away to cook at home or for enjoying in the restaurant upstairs (you can choose your own from these tanks, if you wish). There's also a fine raw bar at the end of the wharf on this first level, but we'll come back to that shortly.

An outside staircase leads to a splendid second-floor deck overlooking

A lobster boat offloading its fresh catch onto Shaw's pier.

New Harbor cove and all the fishing boats tied up and chugging in and out of the harbor. It's a gorgeous view—one that you can soak in while dining on Shaw's lobster and other goodies at one of the 15 picnic tables scattered around the deck. If it's lobster or other seafood that you seek, don't sit down yet, however; go through the doors into the restaurant proper, where you'll find a pine-paneled dining room and a large order counter across the room by the kitchen.

Singles, Doubles, and Triples

Boiled lobster tops the menu choices at Shaw's, and they serve up hundreds of them each week in the summertime. You're welcome to pick out your own "cooked to order" lobster weighing 1½ pounds or more from the tanks on the first floor, then come upstairs to claim it when it's ready. Or you may want to opt for one of the three standard lobster dinners on the menu.

First there's a single lobster dinner, which comes with a 1- to 1¼-pound boiled lobster, drawn butter, a small tossed salad with your choice of dressing, and a roll. Double your fun with two lobsters and the same side orders, or go for broke with the triple—three boiled bugs, salad, roll, and butter. Shaw's owner, Lloyd Mendelson, says the twin lobsters is the most popular dinner choice, but he also says they get quite a few orders for the triple.

Other lobster offerings at Shaw's include deep-fried lobster, served with potato or rice, coleslaw or salad, and a dinner roll and butter. Then there's

Shaw's popular Lobster Pie, which consists of a thick lobster bisque that's poured into a pie crust, then coated with seasoned cracker crumbs and baked firm. There are big chunks of fresh-picked lobster meat throughout the pie.

Shaw's lobster roll is the standard cold roll mixed with some mayo and served in a toasted, split-top bun. Lobster meat is picked fresh daily at Shaw's, and whatever isn't used is thrown away, as Mendelson is a firm believer in serving only the freshest of lobster from his dockside restaurant.

The overall menu is broad and expansive for a lobster shack, with lots of deep-fried seafood, at least half a dozen different broiled fish fillets, and a vast array of sandwiches. There's also a service bar next to the order counter where you can procure wine by the glass or bottle, and draft or bottled beer.

Dine on the Deck

Though the indoor dining room is warm and inviting, you'll want to grab a table on the deck, where the view is amazing and the sea breezes are as fresh as can be. Each table has a fine selection of condiments, including bottles of malt vinegar, and a roll of paper towels on a spool to keep things clean.

Shaw's wharf is home port for numerous lobster boats, and you can watch them unload in the early afternoon right beneath the second-floor deck. The pick of the catch goes straight into Shaw's cold-water tanks, so you're getting the best of the best when you order lobster here.

Back down on the first floor of the wharf, there's a raw bar that opens around 2 PM each day in-season, and it serves up fresh, locally harvested Pemaquid oysters. Order up a half dozen or more, along with a glass of beer or wine, sit back, and watch the boat traffic come and go before you. Lloyd claims that the raw bar was built virtually for free by a film production company in the late 1990s, when Shaw's was used as one of the locations for the Kevin Costner film *Message in a Bottle*.

Though the lights, cameras, and action may be gone for now, this place still plays a starring role in the lobster scene on Pemaquid Peninsula, and spending an afternoon or evening on Shaw's deck or at its raw bar is an experience not to be missed when touring this part of the Maine coast.

From Shaw's second-floor deck you can see straight out to the Gulf of Maine.

Waterman's Beach Lobster

343 Waterman's Beach Road, South Thomaston, ME

☎ 207-596-7819

🦞 www.watermansbeachlobster.com

Open mid-June to late September

If you happen to be in the Thomaston/Rockland area, and you're in the mood for some authentic lobster in the rough, you're in luck. Just head south on Route 131 from Thomaston or Route 173 from Rockland, and you're several minutes to half an hour from three of the best lobster shacks anywhere. The first one you'll want to seek out is Waterman's Beach Lobster, which is in a quiet part of South Thomaston, tucked away on the shores of island-dotted Muscle Ridge Channel.

A Quarter of a Century and Counting

Waterman's Beach Lobster celebrated its 25th year in business in 2011, and it's been quite a run for this modest stand perched in front of its namesake beach. The place was founded by Anne Cousens in 1986 as an offshoot of the fishing pier that juts out into the water in front of the shack. Cousens lived across the street from the pier, and she opened the shack so that lobsters coming off the boats could be cooked and served on the spot in a relaxed and beautiful setting.

The extended Cousens clan lives in a number of the houses along the road running past Waterman's Beach, and many family members have worked at the shack over the years. Anne's daughter, Lorri, and Lorri's cousin Sandy Manahan have worked at Waterman's Beach since they were teenagers. When Anne decided to retire in 2001, she sold the business to Lorri and Sandy, who remain the owners to this day.

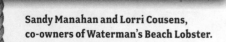

Sandy Manahan and Lorri Cousens, co-owners of Waterman's Beach Lobster.

An Award-Winning Eatery

The shack was a hit from the beginning, garnering praise locally and even nationally in food and travel magazines. In 2001, the same year Anne retired, Waterman's Beach Lobster was honored with the coveted James Beard Foundation's America's Regional Classics award for excellence in regional cuisine. At first, the modest owners of the stand didn't know what to make of it, but when foodies nationwide began to show up for some lobster in the rough, they realized the influence that the award carried. They now proudly display the James Beard plaque on the outside wall of their shack, right by the order window, for all to see.

Waterman's Beach Lobster hasn't rested on its laurels. It's still a hardworking place staffed almost entirely by Cousens family members and their significant others. The place hums during its short summer season, yet in most ways it's still the simple, unpretentious place that it was when it first opened.

Low-Tech Kitchen, High-Quality Food

The kitchen at Waterman's Beach sort of resembles the type of setup you might expect to find at a small, woodsy retreat center or a summer camp. It's a tight space, somewhat crowded with a cold-water tank for lobsters, a couple of small countertops, some plug-in appliances, and a screened-in, back-porch-type cooking area with a few primitive gas burners and a number of metal pots with lids for steaming lobsters, clams, and corn. The food they produce in this somewhat cramped space, however, is consistently outstanding; and though the Waterman's Beach menu is quite simple, what they do, they do very well.

Good, honest, down-home cooking is a hallmark of Waterman's Beach Lobster.

Lobster, of course, is the big draw. The bugs are steamed one or two at a time in the stovetop pots, and they come out firm and succulent and tasting of the nearby sea. You can get a 1-, 1½-, or 2-pound lobster dinner, which comes with steamed corn on the cob and sides of coleslaw, potato chips, and a slice of homemade bread. A 1- or 2-pound bag of steamers makes for a good appetizer or side dish, if you're really hungry.

The other main food group on the menu is the seafood rolls and melts. The lobster roll features cold lobster meat lightly tossed in mayo, and the crab roll receives similar treatment. Lorri and Sandy toast the kaiser-like buns on a small, plug-in griddle. There's also a crab melt and a tuna melt, nicely prepared and topped with cheese. The crab sandwiches are particularly popular here.

For years, Anne Cousens baked pies and sold them by the slice. Blueberry, apple, raspberry, pecan, lemon sponge, chocolate cream, and rhubarb are the standard offerings. A family friend took over baking duties when Anne retired, and the fine tradition of home-baked pies continues.

Waterman's Beach gets its ice cream from the locally famous Round Top Ice Cream stand in Damariscotta. There are 10 fine flavors of hard-packed ice cream to choose from in a cone or a dish or, best yet, over a big slice of home-baked pie.

Eatin' on the Beach

You've got three choices for where to enjoy your repast, and all of them are great options. First, there's the back deck, a covered, open-air porch with picnic-table seating for fifty on the side and back of the building. Sitting here, you can't help but notice the collection of empty wine bottles lining the railing

that wraps around three sides of the porch. Waterman's Beach is BYO for beer and wine, and customers love to display their drained bottles on the rail.

The second option is an open-air front porch that overlooks the small beach and the pier. There are several smaller, round tables suitable for parties of two to four diners on this porch. Finally, there are a whole bunch of picnic tables lined up outdoors in front of the shack, right on the edge of the beach.

Next to Waterman's Beach is an open, seaside field that's great for letting the kids run wild for a while or for a little Frisbee or ball toss while waiting for your food to be ready. All in all, this seaside eatery delivers in just about every way you can imagine, and you can't help but think that James Beard definitely got it right on this one.

Fresh-baked pies are delivered to Waterman's Beach Lobster nearly every day in summertime.

Miller's Lobster Company

They say simple things are often the best, and that would certainly be true in the case of Miller's Lobster Company, a small lobster wharf and eatery in Spruce Head, some 10 rural miles south of Thomaston on Wheeler's Bay. Miller's may have the most simple and spare menu of any lobster shack in Maine and one of the shortest seasons of operation, open only between Father's Day and Labor Day. Yet it's consistently on the short list of favorite lobster shacks for food and travel writers of all stripes, and its reputation is legendary among lobster aficionados.

83 Eagle Quarry Road, Spruce Head, ME

☎ 207-594-7406

🦞 www.millerslobster.com

Open mid-June to early September

The Lobstering Millers

Back in the 1970s, Luther Miller, a lobsterman operating from a small wharf in Spruce Head, set up some cold-water tanks on his dock and started selling live lobsters to locals and tourists. In 1977 Miller diversified further and bought a truck to haul lobsters from the wharf directly to various wholesalers and retailers around New England.

Shortly after that, Miller and one of his sons, Steve, installed a cooker and a few picnic tables on the dock and began serving hot boiled lobsters to customers in their beautiful Wheeler's Bay setting. In the early 1980s they built a long, narrow, open-air pavilion with a roof over it next to their cook shack and installed a bunch of picnic tables to give diners a place to sit and enjoy their lobsters in inclement weather. More open-air picnic tables were put out by the end of the wharf, where the view of the bay is best. The setup has remained pretty much the same since then, with some 25 tables, the pavilion, and a small cook shack, all painted a distinctive rustic red with white trim.

Miller's cook shack and outdoor dining pavilion.

Miller's Today

Luther and Steve Miller retired from the business in the 1990s, and Miller's is now run by Steve's brother, Mark, Mark's wife, Gail, and their daughter, Rachel. Mark is a lobsterman with his own boat, and the Millers have nine other boats that work exclusively for Miller's in the summertime. So there's always plenty of activity on the wharf, with lobster boats coming and going and catches being offloaded straight onto the dock. It's quite an education to watch the lobstermen go about their work, and it's definite reassurance that the lobster you'll have at Miller's is off-the-boat fresh.

Gail Miller, co-owner of Miller's Lobster Company.

The Maine Lobster Festival

Each year during the first week of August, the town of Rockland plays host to the Maine Lobster Festival. It's the largest get-together celebrating Maine's most famous and beloved crustacean.

There's a parade, a sea-goddess coronation, lobster-crate races, a seafood cooking contest, live entertainment, and lots and lots of freshly cooked lobster, which you can enjoy under the main eating tent overlooking beautiful Penobscot Bay. The festival has what's billed to be the world's largest lobster cooker, and it cranks out more than 20,000 pounds of cooked bugs at each year's get-together.

For details, visit the festival website at www.maine lobsterfestival.com.

Miller's menu is brief and to the point: Lobster dinners are available with bugs of various sizes between 1 and 3 pounds. Each dinner comes with drawn butter and potato chips, and your choice of potato salad, corn on the cob, or coleslaw. Steamed clams and mussels are also available à la carte, as are fresh-picked lobster rolls, crabmeat rolls, and Maine shrimp rolls, all served on toasted buns.

The only non-seafood entrée on the menu is a hot dog that comes with a bag of chips. Then there are various types of home-baked pies, served by the slice, for dessert. Beer, wine, and soft drinks are available. And that's it. You're welcome to bring your own side dishes to round out your lunch or dinner—it's okay with the Millers.

The menu here isn't extensive or varied, but it doesn't have to be, because lobster is what this place is all about.

Cod End

Going to Cod End is like stepping back in time, when fishing shacks and docks (and boats, for that matter) were made of rough-hewn wood, and fishermen lived down by the water in tight-knit communities of like-minded people, all working to harvest the bounty of the sea. The village of Tenants Harbor is just such a place, with a small but scrappy fishing fleet and the timeless feel of a fishing village that hasn't changed much in decades.

Cod End is a food shack, a seafood market, and a point of debarkation for numerous lobster boats based in Tenants Harbor. The Miller family has owned and run this place since the early 1970s, and they have a sterling reputation for selling and cooking some of the best and most innovative seafood in the Penobscot Bay region.

✕ 12 Commercial Street, Tenants Harbor, ME

☎ 207-372-6782

🦞 www.codend.com

Open mid-June to mid-September

The Migration from Cape Porpoise

A little over 40 years ago, Red Miller, his wife, Anne, and their children lived in the Cape Porpoise section of Kennebunkport, where the couple taught in the local schools and Red lobstered in the summertime. Seeking a better life (and better lobstering) farther up the coast, they pulled up stakes and searched for a new home, eventually settling in Tenants Harbor, where they set up a shack and a dock on the scenic, sheltered harbor. They continued with their teaching careers, and Red eventually brought his lobster boat up the coast to fish and set traps in the summer with his sons.

Ann thought it might be a good idea to open a seafood market and also serve hot food at the shack, so she started boiling up lobsters and

Cod End's Shore Dinner. Note the large stone, which is used for cracking the shells.

baking pies for the locals and the few tourists who frequented the area at that time. It wasn't long before the newly named Cod End fish market and eatery developed a word-of-mouth following, and it's been open every summer since. The seafood market is known for vending the freshest of fish from the local boats in Tenants Harbor and Port Clyde to the south, and they only sell what's caught locally that day.

Cod End's rustic deck is a great place to spend a summer evening.

Red and Ann both passed away in recent years. Their sons and one daughter still fish the local waters, and the Millers' other daughter, Susan, has assumed command of Cod End's seafood market and eatery, carrying on in her mother's fine tradition of serving up fresh-cooked lobsters and an array of creatively prepared seafood. Cod End is one of the most genuine places you'll find along the coast of Maine, and it's worth a special trip just to check it out and to enjoy a meal on the wide-planked deck.

A Simple Menu and Excellent Specials

Cod End keeps its regular cookhouse menu quite simple, with lobsters, lobster rolls, a limited number of deep-fried plates and side orders, and some basic sandwiches. The lobsters are almost always hard-shell and come as part of a dinner or as a shore dinner, which features native corn on the cob, a pound of steamers, a fluffy dinner roll, and coleslaw. For any cooked lobster that you order, you're given a stone the size of a baseball to crack the claws and knuckles—a nice touch that adds to the earthy feel of the place.

The lobster roll is a big seller. It's a cold roll with lots of meat. Between the lobsters, lobster rolls, and the thick, meaty lobster stew, Cod End goes through a couple hundred pounds of lobster on a typical summer day.

The real treat here is often the daily specials that come out of the cookhouse. Susan's nieces Stephany and Darci are innovative cooks trained in the culinary arts, and they come up with all sorts of unique seafood dishes, such as fish tacos, seafood-stuffed haddock au gratin, seafood ravioli with wild mushrooms, grilled swordfish with peach salsa, and much more. You can also go into the fish market, pick out a piece of fish, and the cooks at Cod End will cook it up for you.

A lot of summer people order carryout at Cod End and take their food with them to their nearby homes or rentals. But an afternoon or evening on the outdoor deck or the indoor rough-hewn wooden tables is highly recommended. Cod End is a BYO establishment, and the atmosphere is very casual.

Don't let this place slip out of your net if you happen to be in the Penobscot Bay region of coastal Maine. Cod End is a real find and about as genuine as a lobster shack experience can get.

McLaughlin's Lobster Shack

The tiny hamlet of Lincolnville Beach, Maine, sits just up the road from tony Camden and within eyesight of the exclusive isle of Isleboro, a couple of miles offshore in the middle of Penobscot Bay. It's a small enclave on Route 1 with a small, crescent-shaped beach, a large, full-service seafood restaurant—and McLaughlin's Lobster Shack!

US Route 1, Lincolnville Beach, ME

207-789-5205

www.thelobshack.com

Open early April to late November

From Takeout Annex to Lobster Shack

McLaughlin's started out in 1980 as a takeout annex for the adjacent Lobster Pound restaurant. Housed in a simple, one-story wood-frame building, the annex served its purpose well for 16 years, with deep fryers, a lobster cooker, and a grill churning out seafood and other snacks for people on the go.

The Lobster Pound was founded by the McLaughlin family, and in 1996, son Rick McLaughlin decided to give the annex its own name and identity. Thus was McLaughlin's Lobster Shack born. McLaughlin's has been doing its own thing for over 15 years now, serving boiled lobsters, deep-fried seafood, and a variety of sandwiches to locals, tourists passing through, and people coming and going on the nearby Islesboro ferry.

Originally just a shack with an order counter and some picnic tables outside, Rick added an indoor dining room in 1991 and installed a woodstove and a gas fireplace to give the room a warm, cozy feel on chilly days. In summertime, most customers still dine outdoors at the numerous picnic tables and on the small patio in back. But the indoor space gets crowded in spring and fall, when there's a definite downward shift in temperature.

The order counter at McLaughlin's Lobster Shack.

Lobster Dinners Galore

There are a variety of lobster dinners at McLaughlin's, the most popular of which is the Maine Lobster Dinner. It features a whole boiled lobster, between 1 and 1¾ pounds, accompanied by corn on the cob, french fries or rice, homemade cornbread, and melted butter. The next step up is the New England Shore Dinner, with the same choices of lobster size and with sides of steamers, sweet corn, fish chowder, fries or rice, and cornbread. Either of these dinner combo plates should be plenty more than enough for even the most famished diner.

There's also McLaughlin's Lazy Lobster dinner,

A bucket of fresh-cooked bugs for meat picking at McLaughlin's.

with handpicked lobster meat bathed in butter. It, too, comes with fries or rice, corn on the cob, and cornbread. And the most popular item on the menu (as it is at so many lobster shacks) is the lobster roll, served cold, with the equivalent of meat from a 1-pound lobster, lightly tossed in mayo and served on a buttered, toasted bun.

McLaughlin's keeps its lobsters in fresh seawater drawn straight from Penobscot Bay, and it uses the same water source for its busy lobster cooker. Rick boasts that virtually all his lobsters come from a boat named the *Fundy Spray*, which is moored about 50 yards offshore in back of the shack. The lobsterman delivers fresh bugs daily in season, and if you time it right, you might even see them being delivered to McLaughlin's tanks.

There are plenty of deep-fried platters, burgers, and other sandwiches to enjoy here, but in such a beautiful setting on Penobscot Bay, with fresh lobsters so close by, it'd be a shame to have anything else.

HADDOCK AND MAINE SHRIMP WITH LEMON CRUMBS

Rick McLaughlin offers this tasty recipe for a seafood dish that's good any time of the year.

INGREDIENTS

4	tablespoons butter
½	pound haddock fillets
¼	pound Maine shrimp
2	tablespoons butter
	Cornbread crumbs
	Juice of ¼ lemon

Preheat oven to 400°F. Melt 4 tablespoons butter in a shallow baking dish. Place the haddock and shrimp in the dish with the melted butter. Cover with aluminum foil and bake for 15 minutes. Remove from oven. Sprinkle cornbread crumbs over the top of the seafood, followed by the lemon juice, then top with 2 tablespoons butter. Return baking dish to oven, and cook uncovered 3 to 5 minutes or just long enough to brown the top. Serves 1–2.

Young's Lobster Pound

Most lobster shacks have a small, intimate, shingled-shanty look and feel to them, redolent of old-time New England maritime charm. Such is not the case with Young's Lobster Pound of East Belfast, Maine. This venerable lobster-in-the-rough establishment is housed in a two-story, red-and-white steel-sided warehouse sitting on the docks of East Belfast, Maine. But what it may seem to lack in charm on the outside it more than makes up for with its great boiled lobster and other seafood fare within (and for the great view out back).

✕ 2 Fairview Street, East Belfast, ME

☎ 207-338-1160

Open year-round

Wall-to-Wall Lobsters

The first thing you notice when you step into Young's is the astounding number of aquamarine-colored, cold-water tanks stacked three-high and stretching some 100 feet down both sides of the interior of the building. This has to be one of the largest holding pens for any lobster operation anywhere. Young's has the capacity to hold up to 30,000 pounds of live lobsters at any time, most of which are earmarked for Young's wholesale business; but plenty of bugs still make their way into the two tanks by the order counter for dining on the spot or for carryout to cook at home.

With a broad center staircase about halfway back through the building, Young's interior resembles the hold of a car ferry. Substitute the lobster tanks for automobiles, and you get the picture. The floor is made from wide-planked, well-worn, highly sturdy timber, giving the place an earthier feel inside than that projected by the metal exterior. Before wandering back through the maze of tanks and lobster crates, take note of the order counter to one side by the front door, size up the menu, and

Young's two levels of back decks, which overlook Belfast Bay.

place your order for lobster or whatever strikes your fancy before seeking out a table.

Boiled, Steamed, Grilled, or Chowdered

Young's doesn't do the deep-fry thing. Every item on the menu is boiled (lobsters), steamed (clams and mussels and crab and shrimp), grilled (fish fillets and scallops), or cooked on the stovetop (chowders and stews). Lobster should be your main focus here—and not just because you're surrounded by thousands of them.

The lobster dinners come in a variety of types and sizes, the most popular being the straight-up 1- to 1¼-pound lobster with drawn butter and potato chips. You may add on some steamers, or opt for the Shore Dinner, which comes with a 1½-pound lobster, steamers, a choice of corn or coleslaw, and your pick of either a chowder or seafood stew. Lobster and crabmeat are picked throughout the day in a small annex building, so the cold lobster and crab rolls are as fresh as can be.

Among the chowders and stews, you may choose from clam chowder, fish chowder, lobster stew, or crab stew. All are made fresh daily in large cauldrons in the kitchen annex. The grill features fresh fish

---

The Lobstering Life, Chronicled

If all this talk of lobsters and lobstering has made you curious about what it might be like to lead the life of a lobster fisherman, check out Linda Greenlaw's *The Lobster Chronicles*. It's a warm, funny, moving, and incisive memoir that takes a look at life in the small, insular lobster-fishing community on Isle au Haut, Maine.

Greenlaw grew up on Isle au Haut, and after four years of college and seventeen more captaining a commercial swordfishing boat, she decided to return to her home island, where her parents still lived, to reacquaint herself with her roots and try her hand at lobstering. The essay-like chapters in the book explore the colorful, often comical, characters and relationships of the Islanders, and the book takes a keen-eyed look at the joys and despair of baiting, setting, and hauling traps in the eternally beguiling world of lobstering.

The interior of Young's, with coldwater tanks capable of holding up to 30,000 pounds of live lobsters.

fillets, such as swordfish, halibut, and haddock, all locally caught. There's not much on the menu that isn't from the sea; but if you don't want seafood for whatever reason, there's a hot dog plate that comes with coleslaw, chips, and a pickle.

Stairway to (Lobster) Heaven

The intriguing center staircase leads to a large second-floor dining area with seating for at least a couple hundred people. And there is a sliding glass door at the back that leads to a balcony of sorts, which is where you want to be once you've got your food and you're ready to eat.

The view from the back of Young's is one of the best of any lobster shack anywhere. For starters, you're about 25 feet above water level, so you have a heightened perspective over all that stretches out before you. Just off the end of the wharf is the salty water of Belfast Bay. On the opposite bank is the charming waterfront district of Belfast, with shops and restaurants, a marina, and more.

Looking to the left and out to sea is the showstopper: a gorgeous view of nearby Penobscot Bay and, in the distance, Isleboro. It's a mesmerizing sight that's best enjoyed from the second floor, which has a couple of highly coveted picnic tables and Adirondack-type chairs.

If the second-floor balcony is full, descend the outer staircase to the broad concrete-floored deck at the end of the wharf, where there is a sea of picnic tables awaiting you right by the water. It's this

Captain Seaweed, a whimsical sculptured bear, greets you at the front entrance to Young's Lobster Pound.

backyard of sorts that may be the best thing about Young's, and you'd never even know it's there from just looking at the front of the building.

There is one redeeming factor about the front of Young's, however. Captain Seaweed, a whimsical wooden sculpture of a bear in a fisherman's rain slicker and holding a lobster by the back, greets you as you step into Young's. As doormen go, you couldn't do much better—plus you don't have to tip him. This is, after all, a lobster shack!

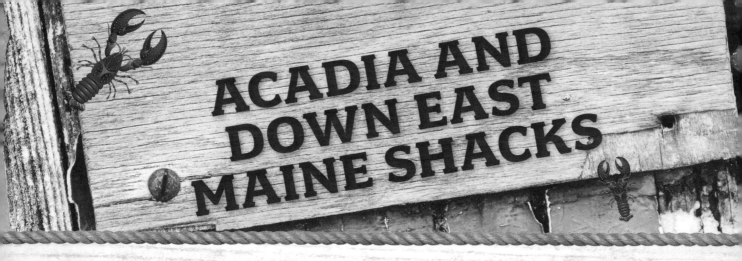

ACADIA AND DOWN EAST MAINE SHACKS

Acadia is the pot of gold at the end of the Maine-coast rainbow. Every summer, this scenic part of the Pine Tree State draws millions of visitors, who come primarily to enjoy the beauty and serenity of Acadia National Park on Mount Desert Island and to do the tourist thing in Bar Harbor.

There are a number of fine lobster shacks in Acadia and Down East Maine. Millions of pounds of lobster come out of the local waters every year, so you can count on getting really fresh, caught-that-day lobsters throughout the summer season. From Thurston's Lobster in the tiny town of Bernard to Stewman's in busy, bustling Bar Harbor to Trenton Bridge Lobster Pound just across the causeway on the mainland, there's a variety of lobster-shack experiences to choose from.

Several lobster shacks in this part of Maine use outdoor, wood-fired lobster cookers, with little tin chimneys poking straight up into the air. It's a pleasant sight, and the faint smell of wood smoke certainly adds to the atmosphere of these places, which claim that their cookers produce the best-tasting lobsters anywhere.

If you head east from Acadia on the Down East Highway, you'll find a couple of places that sell off-the-boat-fresh lobster. From the carnival-like Ruth and Wimpy's in Hancock all the way to small and simple Quoddy Bay Lobster in Eastport on the Canadian border, there is some fine lobster to be had in coastal Maine's final frontier. Enjoy!

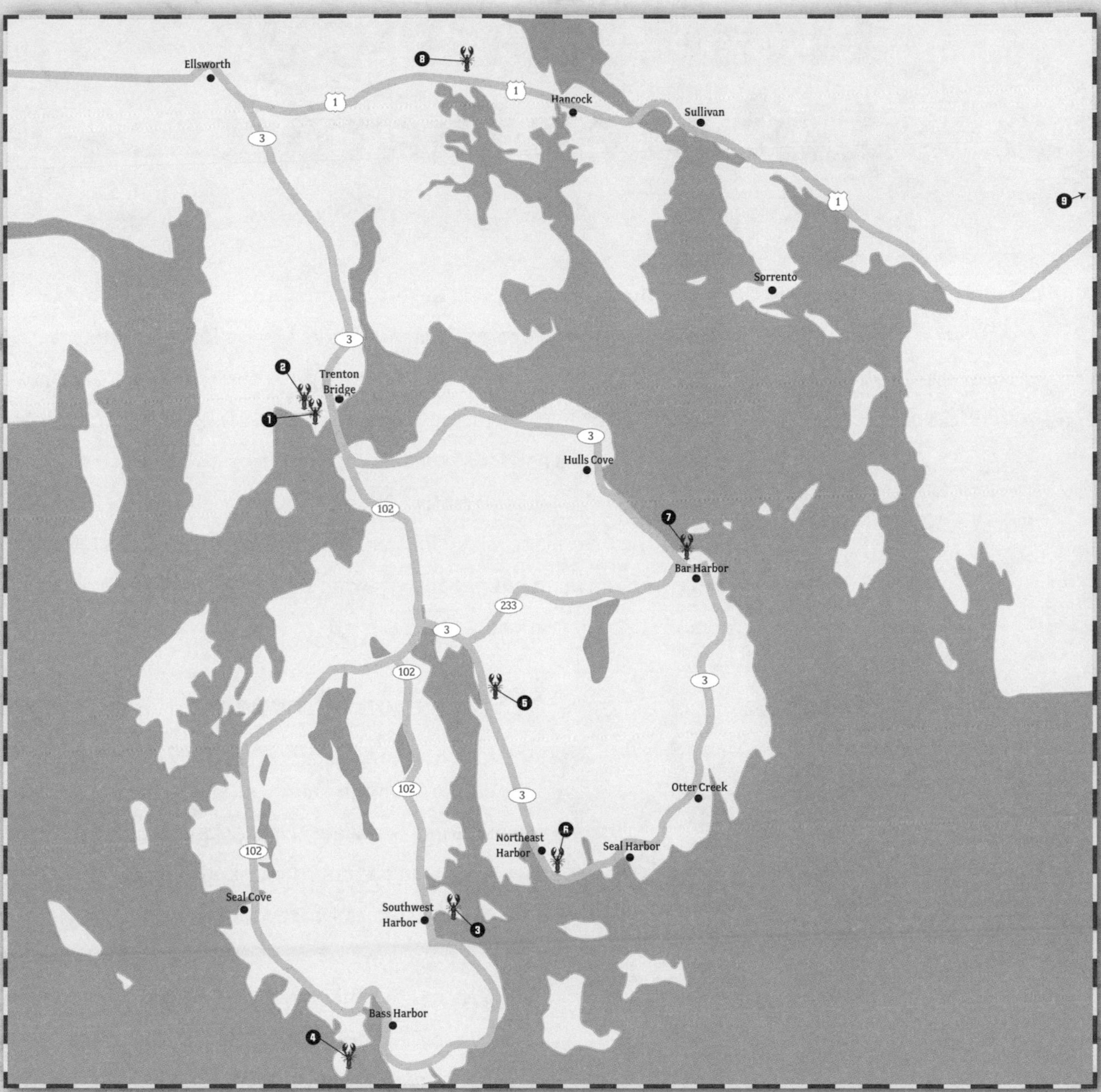

Map labels:
- Ellsworth
- Hancock
- Sullivan
- Sorrento
- Trenton Bridge
- Hulls Cove
- Bar Harbor
- Otter Creek
- Northeast Harbor
- Seal Harbor
- Seal Cove
- Southwest Harbor
- Bass Harbor

Route markers: 1, 3, 102, 233

Trenton Bridge Lobster Pound

✗ 1237 Bar Harbor Road, Trenton, ME

☎ 207-667-2977

🦞 www.trentonbridgelobster.com

Open late May to mid-October

On the right-hand side of southbound Route 3 in Trenton, Maine, just before the bridge to Thompson and Mount Desert Islands, you'll notice half a dozen short metal chimneys by the road, spewing smoke into the air from six primitive-looking open-air cookers. Just behind this roadside setup is a whitewashed building bearing a sign on the roof that reads LOBSTERS. This is Trenton Bridge Lobster Pound, one of two fine establishments that cook up lobsters roadside on this stretch of Route 3, serving them up to hungry passersby on their way to and from Bar Harbor and Acadia National Park.

A Succession of Owners

For all practical purposes, Trenton Bridge Lobster as we know it today got started in 1956, when George and Gertrude "Gert" Gascon purchased the Ogden Lobster Pound next to the bridge spanning the Mount Desert Narrows in Trenton. Through a succession of owners over the next 40 years, all of them related but having different last names as the business passed down along the maternal side of the family, Trenton Bridge Lobster Pound has become an institution in Acadia.

Current owners Anthony and Josette Pettegrow and their son, Warren, are the third and fourth generations of the Trenton Bridge Lobster clan to own and manage the place. The biggest area of growth

Trenton Bridge's wood-stoked outdoor lobster cookers must be tended frequently throughout the day.

Diners enjoy their lobsters beneath the awning on one side of Trenton Bridge Lobster's roadside stand.

for Trenton Bridge in recent years has been the wholesaling and overnight-delivery businesses, but the seasonal lobster shack is still their pride and joy. Each spring, they fire up the outdoor cookers, set up the dining tent, and open their shuttered front doors with bright-red lobsters painted on them to welcome lobster-loving crowds from Memorial Day to Columbus Day.

It's the Wood That Makes It Good

The Pettegrows and their cooks swear that the combination of wood-fueled heat and seawater gives their lobsters, steamers, and crabs a distinctive flavor like no other. With smoke billowing from the chimneys,

seawater roiling and boiling within, and netted lobsters, corn, and shellfish being dunked into and pulled from the cookers throughout the day, it certainly is a fun spectacle to watch, even if it may be hard to grasp how wood affects the flavor of seafood that's immersed in sealed, cast-iron cauldrons.

Regardless, Trenton Bridge Lobster serves up some highly tasty bugs in sizes from a pound on up. You can pick out your lobster inside the shack while you place your order or simply specify a weight and they'll take it from there.

The menu is brief and simple: boiled lobsters, steamed clams, lobster rolls, crabmeat rolls, clam chowder, lobster stew, lobster or crab cocktail,

coleslaw, potato salad, and blueberry pie or cake. There are occasional specials, which you'll find listed on the blackboard just behind the order counter inside. Trenton Bridge is BYO, so feel free to bring your own beer or wine to enjoy with your meal either in the smallish indoor dining room or outside on the side of the building underneath the seasonal tent.

Whether you're coming from or going to Mount Desert Island, Trenton Bridge Lobster Pound is a must-stop kind of place to have a lobster and check out the crazy-looking cookers that add lots of character (and maybe some special flavor) to your lobster lunch or dinner.

Trenton Bridge's wood-fired roadside lobster cookers are a sight to behold.

TRENTON BRIDGE'S LOBSTER QUICHE

When you're at Trenton Bridge, you should definitely have their whole lobster, boiled outdoors in one of their wood-fed-fire pots. But when you're back home, give their lobster quiche a try. It's simple to make, and it's a warm and comforting dish, especially on a cold winter night.

INGREDIENTS

½ cup grated cheddar cheese	¾ teaspoon salt
½ cup grated Swiss cheese	1 tablespoon minced onion
½ pound lobster meat, cut into bite-size pieces	½ teaspoon dry mustard
4 large eggs	2 tablespoons flour
3 cups milk	

Line a large pie plate with the grated cheeses. Spread the lobster meat over the cheeses. Beat the eggs, milk, salt, onion, mustard, and flour together. Pour the mixture over the lobster and cheeses. Bake 10 minutes at 400°F, then 40 minutes at 350°. Serves 4–6.

Lunt's Gateway Lobster Pound

The other big lobster magnet in Trenton is Lunt's Gateway Lobster Pound, just up the road ¼ mile or so from Trenton Bridge Lobster and across the street from Bar Harbor airport. Lunt's is also a wood-fired-cooker operation, with several outdoor cookers and chimneys by the roadside and a large stack of firewood at the ready.

<X> 1133 Bar Harbor Road, Trenton, ME

☎ 207-667-2620

🦞 www.luntsgatewaylobster.com

Open mid-May to mid-October

The Marriage of Lunt's and Gateway

Lunt's Gateway is the creation of Dick and Joyce Harding, who have been on the Trenton restaurant scene in one form or another since 1970. They started with a snack stand that eventually morphed into a full-service restaurant called Gateway's right next to the airport on Route 3. Across the street there was a place called Lunt's Lobster Pound, which the Hardings bought in 1983. Dick started running Lunt's while Joyce held down the fort at Gateway.

Come 2007, the airport laid claim to the land where Gateway's sat in order to increase the size of its landing strips. They bought out the Hardings, who took their proceeds from the sale and consolidated their food operation across the street at Lunt's to form Lunt's Gateway Lobster Pound.

All of the Hardings' children have worked at Lunt's Gateway at one time or other, and the childrens' children are now populating the summer workforce. It's truly a family operation.

Fresh lobsters and corn about to get dunked into one of Lunt's outdoor, wood-fired, roadside cookers.

Deep-Fried Food and Indoor Dining

What separates Lunt's Gateway from Trenton Bridge down the road is the broader menu at LG and the larger amount of indoor, air-conditioned seating. In some ways, it's a matter of preference: for a more rustic and authentic lobster-shack experience, go to Trenton Bridge; for a wider variety of food choices and more indoor seating, head for Lunt's Gateway.

The menu at Lunt's Gateway features deep-fried seafood baskets, sirloin steak, barbecued ribs, burgers, hot dogs, grilled cheese, french fries, mozzarella sticks, fried mushrooms, Buffalo wings, and potato skins. Some of these items are only available in the full-service dining room.

Then there's the lobster. The standard lobster dinner comes with coleslaw, french fries, and a dinner roll. You can also order larger lobsters à la carte and throw in some steamed clams or mussels for a

Lunt's does an interesting combination with its indoor dining room and gift shop.

tasty side dish. Lunt's Gateway's outdoor cookers are a lively scene, with workers dunking and retrieving netted bags of lobsters and corn throughout the day and lots of tourists and diners snapping pictures of the proceedings. For dessert, there are home-baked pies and ice cream to go along with them. Beer and wine are available for purchase in the dining room.

Interesting Spots for Dining

Lunt's Gateway has a few different places to dine, and you can take your pick, depending on your preferences. First, there's the interior dining room, which actually shares space with the gift shop. Right next to your table, there may be a display of stuffed animals, key chains, T-shirts, or coffee mugs. It's a nice, informal atmosphere as conducive to shopping as it is to dining.

On the back of the building is a sunny, screened-in porch. This is ideal both for sunny days and days when rain or cold breezes discourage outdoor dining. And right outside the back porch is a beautifully landscaped garden-type area with lots of perennials, a lush green lawn, a gazebo, some Adirondack chairs, and several picnic tables tucked comfortably next to the woods toward the back of the property.

Like Trenton Bridge Lobster, this is a must-stop when coming from or going to Acadia or Bar Harbor, to enjoy a wood-fire-cooked lobster. Plus, it has a little indoor air-conditioned comfort if you need it and a pretty garden in back that makes you feel miles away from the tourist traffic zipping by out front.

Captain's Galley at Beal's Lobster Pier

"The Captain's Galley at Beal's Lobster Pier" is quite a mouthful. It's also a nice seafood shack (Captain's Galley) on an old working wharf (Beal's Lobster Pier) near the edge of the harbor next to the Coast Guard station in the town of Southwest Harbor, Maine.

As you catch your first glimpse of the place from Clark Point Road, you see that the front one-third of the massive building is a shingled shack and the back two-thirds houses the commercial fishing operation that has thrived in this spot for more than 75 years. The lobsters clearly don't have to travel very far before ending up in the cold-water tanks of the lobster shack's order area.

182 Clark Point Road, Southwest Harbor, ME

www.bealslobsterpier.net

Open late May to mid-October

Three Generations of Beals (and One of Madeiras)

The Captain's Galley is currently leased by Suzanne and Pete Madeira. Suzanne, whose maiden name is Beal, is the granddaughter of the founder of Beal's Lobster Pier, and once upon a time Pete managed the pier for 16 years, after his discharge from the adjacent Coast Guard station. Beal's is where they met.

The lobster pier has been around since the 1930s, but the restaurant didn't really get started until 1969, when Suzanne and her sister-in-law began selling lobster rolls on the dock. Suzanne's father decided to open a restaurant in the early 1980s, but by that time, Suzanne and Peter had taken off to start a family and pursue other careers. Come 2005, the Madeiras showed back up at the place and leased the Captain's Galley, and they've been running it ever since.

Hundreds of pounds of fresh lobster are offloaded onto Beal's dock every day.

The Lay of the Land

Beal's is a fun place at which to dine and an interesting place to explore once you've eaten. As you approach the welcoming double front doors of the shack (nearly always wide open in summertime), you'll notice a bunch of outdoor tables along the side of the building, some with umbrellas and laminated nautical maps. When you enter, you'll find a helpful order menu above the counter, which is located next to a couple of large cold-water tanks. If you wish, you can select your lobster directly from these tanks.

There are two lines: one for steamed food (lobsters, clams, mussels, and corn on the cob) is to the left by the lobster tanks, and the other is for deep-fried, grilled, and all other comestibles. Be sure you're in the right line for what you want.

Lobsters and lobster rolls are highly recommended here. Once your bug is steamed, the youthful kitchen staff will crack and split the shell with a knife in full sight right behind the counter and hand it over to you on a tray with a cup of melted butter. The wait time between placing your order and when your number is called is typically 15 minutes or so. Plan to spend some time waiting in line on busy summer days and nights before you reach the order counters. Drinks are available at a separate window on the side of the building, and they have beer and wine in addition to soft drinks, so you can scout out a table and enjoy a beverage while you wait for your food.

In addition to the dozen or so open-air tables along the side of the shack, there are a bunch of sheltered picnic tables a little farther down the pier that offer shade, protection from rain, and great views of the harbor.

The best of the rest of the menu includes the fried-seafood combo basket, which comes laden with deep-fried clams, scallops, shrimp, and haddock and includes fries and coleslaw. Then there's an intriguing crab-corn bisque made with fresh crab meat. Burgers, grilled cheese, and hot dogs are available for those shying away from the seafood items.

Check Out the Wharf

You're welcome to wander out to the end of the wharf, where you'll pass Beal's indoor seafood-processing areas then out to the offloading areas for boats, where you can take an up-close look at the lobster crates being hoisted ashore.

Sunsets can be lovely at the Captain's Galley, so try and time your evening meal with the setting sun. It's best enjoyed with a fresh-cracked lobster and perhaps a bottle of wine, allowing you to toast your good fortune at finding this authentic, somewhat hidden place on scenic Southwest Harbor.

Captain's Galley Beal's sunny, relaxing deck next to the harbor.

Thurston's Lobster Pound

There are two shifts of activity at Thurston's Lobster Pound during the busy season between Memorial Day and Columbus Day. The first shift begins around dawn, as lobstermen's pickup trucks fill Thurston's parking lot and driveway. The lobstermen then take to their boats with fresh bait and traps from Thurston's large dock, and they depart for a day of work on the water.

By early afternoon, the fishermen return and the pickups slowly begin to disappear from the parking lot. They're replaced almost instantly by SUVs, minivans, and sedans, as customers start showing up for lunch on the water. Co-owner Sharon Gilley says it makes for an interesting mix of cultures, as the lobstermen and the customers criss-cross in the parking lot and down by the dock. By evening, it's all hungry customers, eager to enjoy a lobster dinner overlooking scenic Bass Harbor.

✕ 1 Thurston Road, Bernard, ME

☎ 207-244-7600

🦞 www.thurstonslobster.com

Open late May to mid-October

The Belle of Bernard, Maine

Thurston's holds a lofty place in the lobster world on Mount Desert Island and Acadia. It's perhaps the best-known and most popular dine-in-the-rough lobster shack in the region, with two levels of screened-in deck dining and a busy, friendly order counter just inside the entrance to the shack's upper level.

You'll find Thurston's just about as far from the Route 3 approach to Mount Desert Island as you can get. It's down a winding, narrow road in the tiny

Thurston's is two floors of lobster fun on Bass Harbor in Bernard, Maine.

Bathed in golden light, Thurston's second-floor deck has a great view of the harbor.

hamlet of Bernard, across a small bay from the town of Bass Harbor on the southwest corner of the island. Under good traffic conditions, it only takes about half an hour to get there once you're on Mount Desert, and you're rewarded with a shack on a harbor that's far less crazy and congested than Bar Harbor on the other side of the island. So, by most measures, going to Thurston's is certainly worth the extra mileage it takes to get there.

The New Kid on the Block

Thurston's first opened in 1993, which makes it one of the newer lobster shacks in Acadia. It was started by Michael and Elizabeth Radcliffe, and in 2005 Michael and Sharon Gilley became the new owners.

The shack started small and grew rapidly, with several additions and upgrades tacked on over the

Acadia's Island Explorer Bus Service

There's a wonderful way to get around Mount Desert Island—it's free, it's easy on the local environment, and it helps reduce traffic congestion island-wide during the busy summer tourist season.

Island Explorer buses run eight routes around the island and Acadia National Park, linking points of interest, hiking trails, beaches, restaurants, hotels, campgrounds, shops, and more. You simply park your car at any of the designated stops on the island, board the bus, sit back, relax, and enjoy the ride.

The buses are fueled by clean-burning propane, and

you can get off and reboard at any of the designated stops while the buses are running. Most routes run every 30 to 60 minutes between 8 AM and 10 PM. LL Bean is a major sponsor of this initiative to reduce congestion and pollution in and around the national park, and to date more than 4 million people have used the system.

So give yourself a break, get out from behind the wheel, and let someone else do the driving while you take in the magnificent attractions and scenery of Acadia. For information on routes, schedules, parking, and more, visit www.exploreacadia.com.

years. The building is a pretty sight from the road: two stories of wooden decks extending 75 feet or so out into the harbor on wooden pilings. Each level is screened in and roofed with bright, yellow awnings, which cast a warm glow when you enter the dining areas during daytime.

Lobster Fresh Off the Boat

If you happen to be having an early lunch on one of Thurston's decks, there's a good chance you'll see lobster boats offloading their fresh catches onto Thurston's adjacent wharf. It doesn't take long before some of those freshly caught bugs make their way into Thurston's cold-water tanks at the restaurant, meaning your lobster will be off-the-boat fresh any time of day.

Lobster is the big draw here, as exemplified by the large gas-fired outdoor cooker smack-dab in front of the eatery. Order your lobster à la carte or as part of what they call a "plain dinner," which includes corn on the cob, coleslaw, a roll, and blueberry cake for dessert. Other lobster dinners throw in a pound of steamed clams or mussels along with all the other fixings. There's also a very respectable cold lobster roll, which of course has fresh meat picked daily in Thurston's expansive kitchen.

Other offerings include clam chowder, lobster stew, a crab roll, crabcake sandwiches, burgers, hot dogs, grilled cheese, grilled chicken topped with tasty Boursin cheese, PB&Js—and for any vegetarians in your party, grilled Boca burgers.

A vintage pickup truck bearing this whimsical license plate is a permanent fixture in Thurston's parking lot.

Blueberry Mania

Desserts are all homemade and favor blueberries, with blueberry pie, blueberry cake, blueberry crisp, blueberry ice cream, and cheesecake with a blueberry topping on offer. Sodas and juices are available, and Thurston's also serves a variety of beers on draft or in the bottle and wine by the bottle or glass.

This is a great place to come with the family for some excellent lobster and screened-in-porch dining far from the crowds of Bar Harbor and the other congested parts of the island. Thurston's can get busy and congested during peak dining hours in the summer, but they're expert at handling the increasing number of people who make the long drive to the scenic end of the island to seek them out. If you're looking for a quiet, peaceful lobster dinner in a lovely setting, you'll find it here.

Abel's Lobster Pound

Route 198, Mt. Desert, ME

☎ 207-276-5827

Open late June to early September

Abel's is about as elegant a lobster shack as you'll find anywhere. This beautiful eatery is nestled into an evergreen-covered hillside overlooking Somes Sound, a fjord-like body of water that juts deep into Mount Desert Island. There are yachts and other large pleasure craft moored just offshore from Abel's, and from the picnic tables scattered around the pine-shaded grounds, the watery view is serene.

Abel's is housed in a stone-and-shingled two-story building that resembles a small-scale national park lodge. There's indoor seating in the rustic dining room overlooking the grounds below and a small bar area between the front door and the entrance to the kitchen.

But the real place to be is outside at the picnic tables, each one sanded and repainted annually with a deep-green, high-gloss, military-grade paint. Also to be found in this backyard of sorts is a large, wood-fired outdoor lobster cooker and cold-water lobster tanks. After the sun goes down, the grounds are lit with tiki torches, and each table has an old-fashioned, bright-red kerosene lantern to add a warm glow to the setting.

Serving Lobsters Since 1938

Abel's Lobster Pound is one of the oldest ones on Mount Desert Island. Current owner Ted Stanley's father worked at Abel's as a child in the 1940s. Stanley Père became Abel's owner and eventually passed the pound on to Ted and Ted's wife, Shae. Over the years, the place hasn't changed a lot, and Abel's has a fiercely loyal following of well-heeled customers, many of them from big-name families in America, who insist

Abel's Lobster Pound looks like a miniature national park lodge.

that the Stanleys keep things just like they are: simple, understated, quiet, and low-key. The Stanleys are more than happy to oblige.

Great Food from Within and Without

The wood-fired outdoor lobster cooker and cold-water tanks sit underneath a small, open-air, roofed building and is manned by one of Ted's cousins along with one or two youthful helpers. You may select your own lobster from the tanks, if you wish, and watch the staff drop it into a net and lower it into the cooker.

Boiled lobster dinners come in small, medium, and large sizes, with lobsters running between $1\frac{1}{8}$, $1\frac{1}{4}$, and $1\frac{1}{2}$ pounds, respectively. Included in the dinners are drawn butter for the lobster, homemade rolls, and a choice of french fries or baked potato. A quart of steamed clams may be added to the small or large lobster dinners for an additional charge. A twin lobster dinner is also available, as are select lobsters larger than $1\frac{1}{2}$ pounds, upon request.

In Abel's spotless, old-fashioned indoor kitchen, several more lobster dishes are prepared by Ted and his expert cook staff. There's a lobster sauté (aka lazy man's lobster), lobster Newburg, a lobster salad, lobster Caesar, and lobster in an alfredo sauce. For those who don't want to partake of lobster, there a rib-eye steak, a grilled chicken breast, and prime rib.

The kitchen's lunch menu features a very tasty lobster roll that's extremely light and creamy and served on a round bun with lettuce and a sweet dill pickle and potato chips on the side. Other sandwich

A netted lobster being dropped into Abel's wood-fired outdoor lobster cooker.

choices are the grilled chicken and grilled chicken Caesar sandwiches, each served with pickle and chips.

For openers, you may want to try a cup of Abel's hearty lobster stew, which is chock-full of fresh lobster meat in a creamy broth. Homemade desserts include apple pie, blueberry pie, bread pudding, and a brownie sundae. The full-service bar inside will provide any beer, wine, or mixed drink you may desire.

The prices are fairly steep at Abel's, but you get an incredible meal, an unforgettable setting, and a chance to see some amazing boats and wildlife (including the occasional bald eagle) while you dine on the shores of Somes Sound. Save this place for a special celebration or for your last day of vacation. It'll definitely be one of the highlights of any trip you make to Mount Desert Island and Acadia National Park.

Docksider Restaurant

14 Sea Street, Northeast Harbor, ME

☎ 207-276-3965

Open late May to mid-October

Just off the main street and up the hill from the marina in Northeast Harbor (which is actually in the southern portion of Mount Desert Island), you'll find a quaint little eatery in a white frame building with bright-red trim and a patio with tables and umbrellas alongside. The Docksider Restaurant has been a casual dining fixture in this charming little town for more than 30 years, and it serves up lots of locally caught lobster along with a variety of other seafood, sandwiches, and dinners—and some excellent ice cream for dessert or just for take-away from their outdoor order window.

A Seasonal Stalwart

Judging from the Docksider's warm, varnished-wood interior dining room, you might think this place is open year-round, but it adheres closely to its Memorial-Day-to-Columbus-Day schedule. Current owner Teresa Clark says the miniscule number of year-round residents and Northeast Harbor's relative remoteness from the rest of the civilized world make being open all year a virtual impossibility. Plus, they'd probably have to retrofit the building with insulation, which might compromise the shack-like charm the place currently has.

Clark started working as a waitress at Docksider's in the late 1980s, and she eventually bought the place in 2002. She and her hardworking staff, which includes several of her relatives, go at it seven days a week during the open season, never stopping to rest until the autumn winds blow and it's time to shut down.

The Docksider's patio area is a great place to eat lobster and ice cream in shady comfort.

Indoors or Out?

You have your choice at Docksider's, and what you want to order may help you decide. The outdoor patio is ideal for messy meals and snacks, like lobster, steamers, and ice cream. The atmosphere is very casual, and you're separated from the street by a thin wall of see-through latticed woodwork. Lots of summer people use the outdoor carryout window to order bunches of cooked lobsters to take home and eat. It's very convenient and hassle-free. The patio is also a good spot if you have rambunctious youngsters in tow.

Should you wish to have some beer or wine with your meal, you'll have to head inside, because Docksider's doesn't serve alcohol on the patio. Teresa says she wants to keep things low key and doesn't want the outdoor seating area to turn into a rowdy nightspot.

Indoors is a good place for Docksider's fine comfort foods, such as their chowders and stews, the fried-seafood baskets, the baby back ribs, and the large salads, many of which are topped with fresh seafood.

What's Good to Eat?

All the seafood at Docksider's is locally sourced and super fresh. The lobster roll is a lunchtime standout, with fresh-picked meat in a toasted split-top bun. Another good choice is the fried haddock sandwich. The fillet is light and flaky, and the homemade tartar sauce is in a handy squeeze-bottle container on each table. There are plenty of grilled items, like burgers and hot dogs and chicken sandwiches and subs for non-seafood folks.

Dinner's best choices are the tricked-out lobster and steamed clam dinners. The Islander comes with a cup of Docksider's milky, Maine-style clam chowder, a whole lobster, a side order of your choosing, blueberry pie, and coffee. The Downeaster opens with a cup of chowder, followed by steamed mussels or fried shrimp, then a lobster with a side. The Shore Dinner features chowder, steamers, lobster, and your choice of potato or salad. All are affordably priced and quite

The Docksider's warm and cozy inside dining room.

The Love Life of Lobsters, Revealed

The undersea life of *Homarus americanus*, the common American lobster, has until recently been shrouded in mystery. Writer Trevor Corson's delightful book, *The Secret Life of Lobsters*, which was published in 2004, tells the story of lobster research undertaken in the past quarter century by a group of creative and unorthodox scientists in tandem with the sometimes cooperative lobster fishermen of Little Cranberry Island off Mount Desert Island. Between the scientists, the lobstermen, and the lobsters, you may at times think you're reading a Russian novel that's full of love, war, intrigue, vast migrations, and complicated relationships.

Written in an entertaining and engaging narrative style, Corson delves into the amorous ways of the normally private and evasive red crustacean. You'll learn about the lobster's amazing courtship and mating rituals, which make the antics on TV's *Jersey Shore* seem like child's play. Then there are chapters devoted to such subjects as molting, fighting, surviving, sensing the underwater world through amazing antennae, and moving around on the ocean floor, sometimes covering hundreds of miles at a time.

This book will explain more than you probably ever wanted to know about lobsters and lobstering, but it's a great read full of surprises and revelations around nearly every corner. And it won't spoil your appetite for Maine's favorite red meat.

a bargain for this part of Mount Desert Island.

A number of seafood dinners come from the deep fryers, such as Maine shrimp, clams, scallops, and haddock, or all of the above in a seafood combo platter. Each dinner comes with a couple of side orders, one of which, interestingly, is pickled beets. There are a couple of baked fish dinners in the form of salmon and haddock, and both come with a couple of side orders of your choosing.

Kids have their own menu of items to choose from, many of which fall significantly short of gourmet status (which is fine with most kids, anyway). There's a kids'-sized fish & chips plate, chicken fingers, PB & J, hot dogs, grilled cheese, and for the truly adventurous, linguine with marinara sauce. Youngsters may, of course, order from the regular menu if they want something more substantial or exotic.

The Docksider is a great place for families, with its informal atmosphere and its outdoor dining—and because it has some killer ice cream from the Sugar Maple Creamery of Maine and Massachusetts, which uses organic milk from Maine dairy farmers. Be sure to grab a cup or a cone, then go and walk off your meal down by the harbor or back up on Main Street. And be sure to get there in season because you won't want to miss this little gem in the scenic southwestern corner of Acadia.

Stewman's Downtown Lobster

Bar Harbor in the summer months can be your dream come true—or a true nightmare. The place is packed with tourists, and getting around is a major challenge, let alone finding any peace and quiet in this bustling part of Mount Desert Island.

If you like crowds and gift shops and souvenir stands hawking T-shirts, coffee mugs, and lobster paraphernalia, then you'll feel right at home. But if you'd prefer to relax and enjoy a lobster and some steamers or other seafood and perhaps a beer or two out in the fresh air on a dock, there's only one place that fits the bill.

Though there are no real, true dine-in-the-rough lobster shacks in Bar Harbor anymore (most have grown into full-blown restaurants), the one place you can go for steamed lobster in a fun, outdoor, harborside setting is Stewman's on West Street, just a block or two from all the hubbub on Bar Harbor's main thoroughfare.

Two Levels of Fun

Stewman's Downtown, as this location is known (there's another Stewman's in Bar Harbor's Holiday Inn Regency), is a big, bustling, two-level pier with a variety of things going on. Most of the action takes place out on the open-air pier, where there are numerous tables overlooking the harbor, especially near the adjacent ferry port. You may grab a table on the ground-floor level or take the outside staircase

✕ 35 West Street, Bar Harbor, ME

☎ 207-288-0346

🦞 www.stewmans.com

Open early June to early October

Stewman's dockside cook shack, where lobsters and other steamed and raw seafood are prepared.

to the upper level, where more tables and umbrellas await.

In addition to all the seating, there are a couple of bars, one on each level, where you may belly up at a barstool or simply order a drink to enjoy out on the deck. Stewman's is a full-service lobster pound, so you won't have to wait in line to order your food or fetch it when it's ready, and servers will also take any and all drink orders at your table.

A Full Lobster Menu and Then Some

Stewman's is known for its lobster, and there are some great dishes to choose from. First, there's the Lobster Boat Cobb, a large Cobb salad with greens, tomato, black olives, hard-boiled egg, crumbled bacon, avocado slices, and a bleu cheese vinaigrette dressing. Then there's Stewman's lobster roll, which consists of fresh-picked lobster meat and a bit of mayo packed into a toasted split-top bun. If whole lobster is

Stewman's two levels of sun-splashed decks make a great spot for dining al fresco in Bar Harbor.

your desire, you may order one by the pound (feel free to pick out your own from the tanks by the outdoor cook shack); lobsters here are steamed in a kettle of seawater and served in an oval roasting pan with drawn butter and lemon.

The lobster meal of choice is what Stewman's calls the "Down East Lobster Experience." It's essentially a shore dinner that consists of a 1¼-pound bug, steamed local clams, corn on the cob, steamed red bliss potatoes, and a slice of Maine blueberry pie.

Stewman's expert cook staff will crack your lobster before serving it to you.

The rest of the menu might be described as fancy/basic, with items like stone crab claws for an appetizer, a couple of very tasty seafood dips, deep-fried seafood baskets, innovative salads with grilled meats on top, strip steak, grilled salmon, and several unusual and innovative sandwiches.

Stewman's Downtown brings together much of what Bar Harbor is known for: large crowds, good seafood, and a lively atmosphere. And it's the best place to enjoy lobster on a pier over the water.

The President Ate Here!

In July 2010, the First Family took a summer vacation to Mount Desert Island and Acadia National Park, where they visited the Bass Harbor Head Light, hiked some trails in the park, and dined out at local restaurants. The Obamas seemed to know that, if you visit the Maine coast in the summertime, you have to have lobster. So, their advance crew scoped out lobster places in Bar Harbor where the Obamas were staying, and they decided on Stewman's Downtown for dinner one night.

Stewman's manager was given just 20 minutes' notice of the president's arrival, so there was no time to make any huge efforts to spiff the place up. The Obamas arrived by boat, stepped on to the pier, and took seats at an outdoor table. Their waiter had been working at Stewman's

for less than a week, and needless to say, he couldn't believe who had just been seated in his station.

The Obamas immediately put him at ease, with Barack and Michelle ordering lobsters and the girls a shrimp basket. The cook who handled the Obamas' lobster order felt a little intimidated by the 20 or so people watching him cook and crack the bugs, but he carried out his presidential culinary duties with distinction.

The First Family thoroughly enjoyed their repast on the pier; Barack posed with Stewman's entire staff for a photo; and it's said he left a generous tip when he paid with his personal credit card. As quickly as they arrived, the Obamas were soon gone. How's that for 15 minutes or so of lobster fame?

Ruth and Wimpy's Restaurant

792 US Highway 1, Hancock, ME

207-422-3723

www.ruthandwimpys.com

Open early April to mid-December

If you're on the Down East Highway (Route 1) heading east from Acadia to Maine's coastal frontier, there are two stop-offs to make in the town of Hancock. The first is Ray Murphy's live chainsaw-art show, which is held nightly in-season at Murphy's warehouse/theater on Route 1. The other is Ruth and Wimpy's Restaurant, a marvelous lobster eatery and diner just down the road from Chainsaw Ray's place.

Meet the Wilburs

Ruth and Wimpy Wilbur bought their eponymous restaurant in 1990, after Wimpy retired from a 20-year career in long-haul trucking. Just like the restaurant's previous owner, they kept serving fresh lobster, and in short order, they embarked on an aggressive expansion of the menu that continues to this day. Out of their somewhat modest yet always busy kitchen come more than 100 different dishes, and over 30 of those contain lobster in some form or another.

Wimpy, whose real name is Thurston (no wonder he prefers the Popeye-character nickname), is a big-time collector, and inside Ruth and Wimpy's dining room are hundreds of different kinds of beer bottles, dozens of die-cast model cars, and a blizzard of signs with funny sayings on them plastered to the ceiling. Needless to say, kids love eating here, and the staff always invites the young ones to check out the restaurant's outdoor lobster tanks. Ruth is a native of Hancock, and Wimpy hails from nearby Waltham, so they're no strangers to the area or to the lobster business.

Ruth and Wimpy Wilbur.

Some fresh-cooked bugs emerging from the wood-fired outdoor cooker.

Thirty Ways to Have Your Lobster

Ruth says that at any given time, there are at least 30 different lobster dishes available at Ruth and Wimpy's. They love to come up with new ways to serve lobster, and it shows in the variety of offerings. Start with the outdoor lobster cookers, where whole lobsters are boiled to perfection and sold as part of a variety of dinners that also feature steamed clams, mussels, corn on the cob, salad bar, twin lobsters, lazy man's lobster, and lobster tails.

There are a number of pasta dishes on the menu that feature lobster, the most popular of which is the lobster and jumbo shrimp linguini. Other pasta

LOBSTER AND JUMBO SHRIMP LINGUINE

Ruth and Wimpy Wilbur say this is one of the most popular lobster dishes on their extensive menu of lobster offerings.

INGREDIENTS

1	pound linguine or fettuccine
4	tablespoons butter
4	teaspoons fresh-chopped garlic
12	fresh-picked lobster claws
12	cooked, deveined jumbo butterfly shrimp
4	cups white sauce (flour-thickened milk)
¼	cup white wine
	salt and pepper to taste
4	teaspoons shaved cheddar cheese

Cook linguine or fettuccine in a pot of boiling water. At the same time, melt butter in a large skillet. Briefly sauté garlic in butter, then add and sauté lobster-claw meat and jumbo shrimp. Blend in white sauce and white wine, and simmer until bubbling. Season with salt and pepper. Add shaved cheddar cheese, then serve over cooked linguine or fettuccine. Makes 4–5 servings.

dishes to consider include seafood fettucini, seafood marinara, and Lobster Newfredo. One of the house specialties is the Lobster Newburg, featuring sautéed lobster in a rich Newburg sauce; another is the sinfully rich sautéed lobster claw dinner. The house specials come with a potato and choice of vegetable or a trip to the salad bar.

Ruth and Wimpy's cold lobster roll and warm, creamy lobster bisque and lobster stew are not to be overlooked. The roll is served cold with just a touch

Home of Wilbur the Lobster

The first thing you notice as you come upon Ruth and Wimpy's is the 11-foot-long red fiberglass lobster sculpture in front of the place. This is Wilbur, who presides over Ruth and Wimpy's parking lot and lets you know that there's plenty of good lobster to be had inside.

The work of Maine artist Joe Rizzo, Wilbur has been pulling in curious travelers and diners off the highway for some 20 years. Several well-heeled people (including actress Kirstie Alley) have attempted to buy Wilbur, but owners Ruth and Wimpy Wilbur (yes, that's where the lobster gets its name) steadfastly refuse to sell. At one time, Wilbur made it into the Roadway Express Trucking Company wall calendar as one of the twelve most interesting roadside attractions in America. Wilbur was Mr. April.

of mayo and nothing else, and the bisque and stew are both chock-full of lobster meat and come in cup and bowl sizes. Ruth says they pick all their lobster meat daily out by the cook shack, and on a busy summer day, they'll pick upwards of 150 pounds for rolls, bisques, stews, and salads. Most of their lobster comes from Sorrento Lobster, Inc.'s massive lobster pound in the nearby town of Sorrento.

If lobster isn't your thing, then check out the diner side of the menu at Ruth and Wimpy's. The renowned Wimpy Burger is outstanding (and well it should be, given the cartoon Wimpy's predilection for hamburgers). This big burger comes dressed in cheese, onions, mushrooms, and bacon. There are another half dozen or so burger offerings, with various toppings from fried eggs to mashed potatoes to jalapeno peppers. There are also plenty of deep-fried seafood offerings, as well as steaks, salads, and foot-long sub sandwiches.

There are lots of other things to love about Ruth and Wimpy's, like the fresh-baked-daily dinner rolls, the chowders and bisques served in white china coffee cups, the outdoor deck/patio next to the lobster cookers, and the antique Cadillac that Wimpy has permanently parked right by the front door. This place is a lot of fun, and for the sheer variety of lobster dishes on the menu, it has few peers.

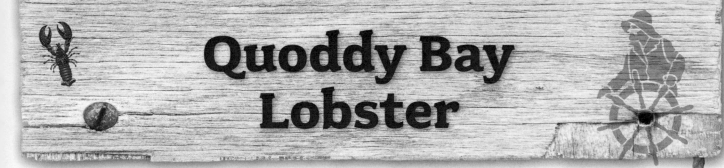

Quoddy Bay Lobster

This place is as far as you can go on the lobster-shack trail without leaving New England—or the country, for that matter. Though a relative newcomer to the shack scene, Quoddy Bay Lobster is a welcome addition, with its roots firmly in the lobster-fishing business, its quaint, dine-in-the-rough setup next to its fishing pier, and its unique, bird's-eye view of Canada just a mile or so across narrow Passamaquoddy Bay, which separates the two great nations.

⚒ 7 Sea Street, Eastport, ME

☎ 207-853-6640

Open mid-May to mid-October

A True Family Operation

Quoddy Bay Lobster was founded in 2007 by the husband-and-wife team of Brent and Sara Griffin. Both have deep roots in the Eastport area and in the fishing community that infuses the culture of extreme Down East Maine. Sarah's father fished for years off nearby Campobello Island, famous as the onetime summer home of President Franklin Delano Roosevelt. Brent's family has been lobstering the local waters for decades, and Brent took up the trade in Eastport in 1997.

After the Griffins wed and had a couple of children, Sara, who graduated from the University of Maine in 2002, was eager to get back to work. She and Brent came up with the idea of setting up a seafood market and takeout counter that would serve fresh lobster and chowders to locals and tourists in the summertime. When they opened Quoddy Bay Lobster five years ago, there were two full-time employees: Sara and her mother-in-law, Shelly, who worked at the takeout shack five days a week.

In addition, Brent's grandmother occasionally picks rock crab meat out of her home for Quoddy Bay Lobster. She gets the crustaceans from

Brent and Sara Griffin, owners of Quoddy Bay Lobster. (That strip of land in the background is Canada.)

Brent, who catches them in his traps. Various family members babysit Brent and Sara's children while they catch and sell their lobsters and other seafood.

Two Festive Times

In the intervening years, Quoddy Bay has hired several other employees, some of them family members, others from Eastport and surrounding towns. Sara is the driving force behind the eatery, constantly working at the order counter, cooking in the kitchen, and generally making sure that everything runs smoothly. Her enthusiasm for the business is infectious, and she's made many friends with the local customers and the summer people who come from around the United States and Canada to spend time in this quiet and remote corner of America.

Quoddy Bay does a good, steady business throughout the season, but there are two times of the year when things really get hopping. The first is the Fourth of July, when the Griffins rent a large tent and set it up next to their parking lot to handle the influx of lobster diners who seem to come out of the woodwork here for the holiday.

The other big bump comes in mid-September, when Eastport holds its Pirate Festival. Residents dress up in pirate garb and participate in parades, reenactments of pirate activities like sword fighting, and watch lobster-boat races from the town's waterfront. Being the only real lobster-in-the-rough place in town, Quoddy Bay Lobster has a captive audience for the three-day event. Come mid-October, it's time to close up for the season and wait for the return of the tourists (and the lobsters) next spring.

An Old Cannery Town

The town of Eastport is actually on Moose Island and is connected to the mainland by a causeway-type bridge. For years it thrived as a center for the sardine industry, and at its peak, there were some 35 canneries in town. As the sardine numbers dwindled in the local waters several decades ago, the canneries began shutting down, and the town slid into

Three friends share lunch in front of Quoddy Bay Lobster.

economic decline. (There are a couple of shuttered brick canneries adjacent to Quoddy Bay Lobster, just screaming for some developer to turn them into useful space once again.)

Around 2000, things started to pick up as Eastport began remaking itself into an artist's community of sorts. There's a quaint downtown area with shops and restaurants in vintage brick buildings, and local residents are once again upbeat about the town's prospects.

Smoked Lobster Pâté by the Bay

The Griffins take some of their fresh lobster meat, put it in a smoker, then whip it into a pâté that they serve with crackers as an appetizer or as part of a very tasty smoked lobster wrap. There's also a smoked salmon pâté and crab cakes as alternative openers to your meal.

Quoddy Bay gets its fish from across the border in Canada. It's brought in by truck nearly every day, and it's sold in the market and used in many of Quoddy Bay's tasty dishes, such as the seafood and fish chowders, the pan-seared haddock sandwich, and the smoked salmon pâté and wrap.

Lobster is, of course, the big draw here, and Brent's daily catch is stored in cold seawater tanks in a building right next to the seafood market. The Griffins steam their lobsters, and their lobster roll is locally renowned for its 4 ounces of fresh meat with no mayo or anything else added to it, unless upon request. There's also a simple, healthy lobster salad,

Quoddy Bay Lobster's in-the-rough dining area is right by the docks with a splendid view of the bay beyond.

with lobster meat sprinkled liberally over a bed of fresh lettuce and sliced tomatoes. Crabmeat is also very popular here and may be had in a crab roll or on top of a salad.

When it comes time to eat, go outside to the picnic tables strung out along the waterfront, overlooking the dock and the bay and Canada across the way. The Griffins plan to expand their pier and to put some tables on it when it's completed. But for now, there's plenty to see and do in this charming little lobster stand way out on the very tip of New England and America.

Index

The following is an alphabetical listing of all the lobster shacks in the book.

Shaw's second-floor dining deck offers a great view of New Harbor's fishing fleet.

Lobster Shacks by Type

Every lobster shack has its own unique qualities and characteristics. If you're looking for a certain type of experience while you're out exploring New England's lobster shacks, the following list may prove helpful in zeroing in on the establishments that best fit your needs and desires.

Family Shacks

Most lobster shacks are family-friendly operations, but there are a handful that are particularly appropriate for the entire clan.

Abbott's Lobster in the Rough, Noank, CT 33

Arnold's Lobster and Clam Bar, Eastham, MA 63

Ken's Place, Scarborough, ME 128

Lenny and Joe's Fish Tale, Madison, CT 25

The Lobster Pot, East Wareham, MA 52

Lobster Shack Two Lights, Cape Elizabeth, ME 135

Lunt's Gateway Lobster Pound, Trenton Bridge, ME 195

Ruth and Wimpy's Restaurant, Hancock, ME 210

Seafood Sam's, Sandwich and Falmouth, MA 56

Sprague's Lobster, Wiscasset, ME 158

Waterman's Beach Lobster, South Thomaston, ME 178

Woodman's of Essex, Essex, MA 91

Party Shacks

These places tend to rock out a little more, and the alcohol flows more freely, especially at nighttime.

Barnacle Billy's, Ogunquit, ME 114

Boothbay Lobster Wharf, Boothbay Harbor, ME 166

The Lobster Dock, Boothbay Harbor, ME 161

The Lobster Pot, Provincetown, MA 73

Petey's Summertime Seafood and Bar, Rye Beach, NH 105

The Place, Guilford, CT 20

Portland Lobster Company, Portland, ME 138

Ray's Seafood, Rye Beach, NH 102

Shaw's Fish & Lobster Wharf, New Harbor, ME 175

Stewman's Downtown Lobster, Bar Harbor, ME 207

Funky Shacks

These lobster shacks are a little more offbeat and unusual than many of their counterparts. Check 'em out if you like your eateries a little more on the wild side of things in terms of décor and atmosphere.

Blount Clam Shack, Warren, RI 45

The Clam Shack, Kennebunkport, ME 118

Cod End, Tenants Harbor, ME 183

Gurnet Trading Company, Brunswick, ME 147

The Place, Guilford, CT 20

Red's Eats, Wiscasset, ME 157

Round Pond Lobster, Round Pond, ME 172

Roy Moore Lobster Company, Rockport, MA 82

Ruth and Wimpy's Restaurant, Hancock, ME 210

Trenton Bridge Lobster Pound, Trenton Bridge, ME 192

Romantic Shacks

If you're looking for a quiet place in a nice setting to enjoy some lobster with the one you love, try these shacks, which are great for dates or a night away from the kids.

Abel's Lobster Pound, Mt. Desert, ME 202

Aunt Carrie's, Narragansett, RI 42

Five Islands Lobster Company, Georgetown, ME 153

The Friendly Fisherman, North Eastham, MA 67

JT's Seafood, Brewster, MA 59

Lobster Landing, Clinton, CT 29

The Lobster Pool, Rockport, MA 85

Nunan's Lobster Hut, Kennebunkport, ME 125

Thurston's Lobster Pound, Bernard, ME 199

Waterman's Beach Lobster, South Thomaston, ME 178

Dock or Deck Dining

One of the great things about going to a lobster shack is getting the chance to sit on a deck or right on the dock and watch the lobster boats come and go while you enjoy your meal. Here are some good choices for dining on the dock or on a deck.

Abbott's Lobster in the Rough, Noank, CT 33

Bayley's Lobster Pound, Scarborough, ME 131

Boothbay Lobster Wharf, Boothbay Harbor, ME 166

Cape Pier Chowder House, Cape Porpoise, ME 122

Captain's Galley at Beal's Lobster Pier, Southwest Harbor, ME 197

Champlin's Restaurant, Galilee, RI 38

Chauncey Creek Lobster Pier, Kittery Point, ME 110

Cod End, Tenants Harbor, ME 183

Five Islands Lobster Company, Georgetown, ME 153

Guilford Lobster Pound, Guilford, CT 17

Harraseeket Lunch & Lobster, South Freeport, ME 144

The Lobster Dock, Boothbay Harbor, ME 161

Mac's Seafood, Wellfleet, MA 70

Miller's Lobster Company, Spruce Head, ME 181

Morse's at Holbrook Wharf Lobster, Harpswell, ME 151

Muscongus Bay Lobster, Round Pond, ME 170

Pemaquid Lobster Cooperative, Pemaquid, ME 173

Portland Lobster Company, Portland, ME 138

Quoddy Bay Lobster, Eastport, ME 213

Round Pond Lobster, Round Pond, ME 172

Shaw's Fish & Lobster Wharf, New Harbor, ME 175

Sprague's Lobster, Wiscasset, ME 158

Stewman's Downtown Lobster, Bar Harbor, ME 207

Thurston's Lobster Pound, Bernard, ME 199

Young's Lobster Pound, East Belfast, ME 187

Shacks with Great Architecture and Design

Lobster shacks are often cited for their unique, iconoclastic architecture and interior designs. These shacks are worth a peek, even if you don't have the time to stop and eat.

Abel's Lobster Pound, Mt. Desert, ME 202

Barnacle Billy's, Ogunquit, ME 114

Blount Clam Shack, Warren, RI 45

The Clam Shack, Kennebunkport, ME 118

Cod End, Tenants Harbor, ME 183

Five Islands Lobster Company, Georgetown, ME 153

Gurnet Trading Company, Brunswick, ME 147

Lobster Landing, Clinton, CT 29

The Lobster Pot, Provincetown, MA 73

The Lobster Shack, Branford, CT 14

Nunan's Lobster Hut, Kennebunkport, ME 125

Red's Eats, Wiscasset, ME 157

Roy Moore Lobster Company, Rockport, MA 82

Ruth and Wimpy's Restaurant, Hancock, ME 210

Shacks with Unusual Menus

There's often more to lobster shacks than lobster, steamers, and corn on the cob. These shacks sport menus that dress up their offerings with some tasty and unusual menu items and specials.

Anthony's Seafood, Middletown, RI 46

Cod End, Tenants Harbor, ME 183

JT Farnham's, Essex, MA 88

JT's Seafood, Brewster, MA 59

The Lobster Dock, Boothbay Harbor, ME 161

The Lobster Pot, Provincetown, MA 73

Mac's Seafood, Wellfleet, MA 70

The Place, Guilford, CT 20

Portland Lobster Company, Portland, ME 138

Ruth and Wimpy's Restaurant, Hancock, ME 210

Rye Harbor Lobster Pound, Rye Harbor, NH 101

Woodman's of Essex, Essex, MA 91

One fresh-boiled lobster, ready to go!

Acknowledgments

As I researched and wrote this guide to the best lobster shacks in New England, I had plenty of help and support along the way. I'd like to gratefully acknowledge the following for their assistance:

- The lobster shack owners, managers, and employees, who opened your doors to me and were unfailingly patient and helpful as I gathered information, sampled food, took photographs, and asked hundreds of questions.
- Fred Liebling, my lifelong friend, who has a house in Maine, where I stayed for extended periods of time throughout the summer while doing research. Your hospitality and your lively and engaging company lifted my spirits as I endeavored to write up every lobster shack I could find in the Pine Tree State.
- Kermit Hummel, editorial director of Countryman Press, who championed the book to his publishing committee and whose primary instruction to me consisted of three words: "Make it fun." I hope I've succeeded in doing so.
- Countryman editor Caitlin Martin, who shepherded the book through the entire editorial and production process. Thanks for your steady hand and your quick responses to my numerous queries and suggestions.
- Tom Haushalter, Countryman's publicist, who grabbed onto the concept of the book immediately and who has geared up a regional and national blitz to get the word out about this book and the wonderful eateries it describes.
- Vicky Shea, my partner on many projects, who designed, laid out, and produced this lovely book. I've always admired your wonderful design skills, your amazing efficiency, and your unflappable optimism on all the books that you touch. Here's hoping we hook up on more projects soon.
- My wife, Ellen, and our four children: Nick, Natalie, Brian, and Max. You've all stood by me as I wandered the New England coast over the past couple of summers, working on shack books and learning more about this wonderful part of the world in which we live. To Ellen especially, for your patience and your support as I explore the wacky world of travel writing and all its ups and downs. You're the best!

—Mike Urban

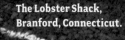

The Lobster Shack,
Branford, Connecticut.